Amelia Colby Luther

Amelia Colby Luther

*The Life and Times of a
Revolutionary Spiritualist Woman*

VICKI GROSE CORKELL

First published in 2023 by Vicki Grose Corkell,
in partnership with whitefox publishing

www.wearewhitefox.com

ISBN 978-1-915036-45-2
Also available as an eBook
ISBN 978-1-915036-46-9

Designed and typeset by Karen Lilje
Cover design by Karen Lilje
Project management by whitefox

For Amelia, and all those early Spiritualist women who
dedicated their lives to Spiritualism and social reform

CONTENTS

AUTHOR'S NOTE

I FOUND CAMP CHESTERFIELD in 1988, following the death of my youngest brother. A drunk driver hit him and his fiancée as they drove back to college following the Christmas holiday, and both died in the accident. He was a wonderfully caring and compassionate young man, and I grieved for months, searching for some meaning in his tragic death. Camp Chesterfield and the people who lived there were instrumental in helping me find, if not meaning, at least solace during that time.

Camp Chesterfield is a Spiritualist community of people who believe they can contact friends and family who have crossed into the spirit world. What is known as Modern Spiritualism dates to 1848, although stories of prophecy and supernatural activity fill history. On that first day, I found a measure of peace and tranquility, but I was also curious about the people who lived there. Over the following months, I attended seances, made appointments for clairvoyant readings, and took classes on how to open myself to the spirit world. I wanted more reassurance for my brother's well-being than orthodox ministers could provide. I was particularly comforted that the Spiritualists at Camp Chesterfield included all the major world religions as crucial to humanity. In other words, they were inclusive no matter a person's belief system.

Much of the time I spent walking the stately grounds filled with massive oak, maple, and evergreen trees. Flowers and shrubs provided a wild array of colors. There were spots where one could sit in silence and consider the beauty of nature. It was a peace that I had not been able to find in the outside world.

Camp Chesterfield is considered a community within a community. It covers approximately 34 acres just outside the town of Chesterfield, Indiana. It sports a bookstore, cafeteria, two hotels, a museum, an administration building, a gift shop, a guest house for visiting speakers, a chapel, and a cathedral that seats approximately 500 people. Statues on the grounds include the founders of all major religions. The residents live there throughout the year and offer various clairvoyant services, including trance and clairvoyant messages, astrology, tarot, and other metaphysical services. There are forty-six homes laid out in a U-shape covering approximately 20–30 acres. Most show their age, dating from the late 1800s to the early 1900s, and only a few show modernizations.

During my walks, one particular house held my attention. It was a two-story structure with an oversized wrap-around porch. It was in terrible shape, broken down, with holes in the massive roof, and paint chipped away from the ravages of Indiana's summer and winter seasons. It was clear no one had lived there for many years. Friends shared that the woman who had built it and lived there had been a feminist, using her home as a meeting place for other feminists and women's rights advocates. She had been a well-loved Spiritualist trance medium whose radical lectures had caused all manner of disruption and dissent nationally. Her name was Amelia Hunt Colby Luther, and while few remembered her, they recalled she promoted radical ideas about abolition, suffrage, Christianity, and women's rights. But these were only rumors and conjecture. No one had written her story. This is my attempt to do so.

Vicki Grose Corkell
Chesterfield, Indiana

INTRODUCTION

In MARCH 1848, KATE and Maggie Fox, two young girls from Hydesville, New York, began to communicate with a spirit they called "Mr. Splitfoot" via ghostly raps. Initially, the spirit would rap once for "yes" and twice for "no" in response to simple questions. This primitive form of spirit communication captured the interest of the girls' parents and neighbors. A system was ultimately created whereby the spirit would rap according to letters of the alphabet, so that one rap signified the letter A, two raps the letter B, three raps the letter C, and so on. The method was clumsy but effective. They learned that the spirit's name was Charles B. Rosna, and he had been a peddler, murdered in the house years earlier.

The Fox sisters' spirit demonstrated an intelligence that proved the human conscience existed after death. He provided astoundingly accurate messages to the adults who gathered and asked personal questions, and it didn't take long before daily visitors and curiosity seekers inundated the house. After months of disruption to the household, the girls' mother sent them to Rochester, New York, to live with their older sister, Leah. But the spirit raps followed them to their new home. They began to be overwhelmed with visitors again, and Leah reached out to her old friends Amy and Isaac Post for help.

The Posts were radical Quakers who advocated social reform, including abolition and women's rights. Originally Hicksite Quakers, they had been condemned by their sect and had broken away to form the Progressive Friends, or Congregational Friends, a group of like-minded individuals who supported the goals of abolition and other social reforms. The Posts involved themselves in the Western New York Anti-Slavery Society and often housed runaway slaves for Rochester's Underground Railroad.[1] They agreed to meet the Fox sisters and were fascinated by the demonstration of spirit communication. Ultimately taking the girls under their wing, they acted as mentors to them and were instrumental in introducing them to the larger outside world.

In 1849, Kate and Maggie Fox demonstrated spirit communication via raps at Corinthian Hall in Rochester, New York, at the Posts' suggestion. This demonstration moved them from the smaller venues of individual homes to a much larger public arena and solidified their celebrity status. As the popularity of spirit communication grew, others, primarily women, began communicating with spirits in small household settings. Some produced raps to communicate, while others gave clairvoyant messages via telepathy. Some women, such as Achsa Sprague, went on the road to lecture in a trance state. Sprague was considered Spiritualism's first known traveling trance medium, and people flocked to see her. An avowed abolitionist who advocated for women's rights, she was known as the "Preaching Woman."

Spiritualism continued to grow, and other women began traveling and lecturing in a trance to mixed audiences. At that time, a woman speaking to a diverse audience was considered promiscuous by Victorian standards. Following the dictates of Paul the Apostle, who said women should be silent, women were "not allowed" to speak in a public forum. Nevertheless, Spiritualist women broke those societal rules, and an enthralled public raced to see the spectacle of an unconscious woman standing on a platform, delivering spiritual truths. Spiritualist women upended Victorian ideas that a woman's place was in the home by their mere presence in front of an audience.

The Spiritualist movement reflected a rebellious spirit in America. Before 1848, women, specifically married women, had no legal rights. A husband could treat his wife with the same cruelty he might show his slaves. Marriage meant that a woman surrendered every right to property and person. If she worked outside the home, her husband confiscated her wages and used them as he pleased. He had unfettered access to her body, whether she consented or not. If she attempted a divorce, she lost full custody of her children to him and could be prevented from even seeing them. Women could not serve on a jury, leaving them without fair representation by their peers. Barred from universities, law, and medical schools, they were kept from educational and economic opportunities.[2]

By 1848, a new political party had formed called the Free Soil Party. Its slogan, "free soil, free speech, free labor, and free men," highlighted a growing discontent in America. Women advocated for the reform of prisons and insane asylums, and the New York Married Women's Property Act was passed in 1848, giving women, for the first time, the right to maintain and hold property in New York. It was a year of revolution, but the most significant revolution happened at Seneca Falls, New York.[3]

Four months after the initial spirit raps were heard, social reformers Elizabeth Cady Stanton and Susan B. Anthony called the first Women's Rights Convention in Seneca Falls. The women presented a list of resolutions denouncing laws that discriminated against their gender and demanded sexual equality. They called for "the abolition of the double standard of morality, and that women be given the same right as men to speak and take part in all public and religious affairs."[4]

Spiritualist women had already taken to the platform to speak, in trance, to diverse audiences on the social and religious issues of the day. The difference between Spiritualist women and women reformers was simple. Entranced women controlled by the spirit were only passive vessels of a higher authority, unlike women reformers, who blatantly gave their opinions with no authority other than their own. Therefore, Spiritualist women were more acceptable to Victorian society and certainly more unique. Still, Spiritualist women were instrumental in opening doors of opportunity for female public speakers in America and breaking down class barriers. They gave the general public a new view of religion and advocated social reforms for women in various spheres, most notably in the sphere of marriage.

While Spiritualism touched all classes, women from the poor and middle classes discovered more freedom than women with a higher social status. Poor and middle-class women were elevated in society by their mere presence on the lecture circuit or in the seance room. They enjoyed a professional and celebrity status that had not been possible before Spiritualism. Mediums gave seances for Mary Todd Lincoln in the White House, and a trance medium, Nettie Colburn Maynard, delivered advice to Abraham Lincoln. Susan B. Anthony was so enthralled with Spiritualist mediums that she made several trips to Lily Dale, a dedicated Spiritualist community in New York where Spiritualists and others gathered for several months during the summer. Finally, Victoria Woodhull and her sister Tennessee Claflin, who started as traveling carnival workers, were so successful as mediums that they ultimately advised Cornelius Vanderbilt on stock market picks. He was so impressed that he gave them money to create the first female brokerage firm on Wall Street.[5]

It was no surprise that women flocked to the new movement. Its messages of equality gave many women the courage to leave the church. They were no longer willing to sit passively and listen to a male preacher berate them for their inherent sinfulness and worthlessness. Further, Spiritualism brought far greater comfort to grief-stricken parents, husbands, wives, and other family members who wanted to hear a message from their deceased loved ones. Significantly, Spiritualist philosophy argued for universal salvation and dismantled the idea of hell. This premise was instrumental in defeating a Calvinistic religion that promoted fear and designated the "saved" from the damned. Men and women found spiritual relief and comfort in the idea that their loved ones had arrived safely in heaven. Spiritualists called it "Summerland." Every soul entered it when the physical body died, and because the soul did not die and remained connected to the physical world by an etheric force, communication was possible.

Historians disagree on the number of people involved in Spiritualism. Ann Braude writes that at its height of popularity, the estimate of Spiritualists "in thirty-nine states and territories" might reach "eleven million (out of a total population of twenty-five million)."[6] Early Spiritualists were anti-authoritarian and resisted national organizations. Consequently, it is impossible to give an entirely accurate account of the magnitude of the movement. Later, as their numbers began to decline due to accusations of fraud and repeated attacks from clergy and conservative news outlets, Spiritualists agreed to a national organization. At an 1893 Spiritualist convention, Spiritualism was identified as a "religion, philosophy, and science" to protect it from church and governmental harassment, and legal entanglements. The three-part definition remains an integral part of Spiritualism today.

When reviewing the entire history of women's struggle for social change, Spiritualist women and reformers such as Stanton and Anthony were making the same arguments on behalf of women. They were like two parallel streams that converged occasionally but remained apart for most of the time. After the Civil War ended in 1865, the women's rights movement declined due to internal bickering about what was important, what was proper, and what could be accomplished. Liberal women reformers wanted to advocate for, and grab, all the rights entitled to them, including suffrage, marriage, and property reforms. The more conservative reformers believed they should only address abolition and temperance and then make small steps toward everything else. Later, most liberal and conservative women decided that their focus should only be on the ballot.

Spiritualist women had no such conflicts in those early days. They spoke about every oppressive action against women, including the sanctity of marriage as defined by the church, the lack of suffrage, a woman's inability to control her own body, the lack of educational opportunities, medical hardships, quack doctors, and the loss of property rights. They were outspoken abolitionists and advocates of temperance, arguing that abusive men who drank and visited houses of prostitution did so to the detriment of their wives and children. Staunchly anti-authoritarian, they argued that church doctrine was oppressive to women and governmental laws kept women in an enslaved state. They also argued that medical and social restrictions placed on women were detrimental to their health and well-being.

Radical Spiritualist women called the church, the clergy, and the Bible enslavers of the human spirit, particularly the female spirit. While moderate women reformers based their policy platforms on Christian teachings, early Spiritualists rejected those ideas. They argued that the church and its ministers used scripture to support the ungodly institution of slavery, promote women's oppression, and line their pockets at the expense of the poor. Though Spiritualist women find themselves on the right side of history today, their stance did not endear them to the women reformers at that time.

Only recently have historians such as Ann Braude, Barbara Goldsmith, Joanne Passet, and many others recognized the contributions Spiritualists made to women's history. Spiritualist women who traveled and lectured on the platform kept all the reform issues before the public, whether accepted by others or not. Their philosophy relieved women from the restrictive Victorian standards regarding their "place" and offered them a freedom they had not previously enjoyed. Nevertheless, they were written out of women's history for several reasons, primarily due to their radical views on marriage, sex, Christianity, and social reform.

In essence, Spiritualist women argued for loosening marriage laws, asserting that if laws forced a woman to remain in an unhappy marriage, it constituted slavery. They further argued that women should be free to seek their "spiritual affinity" or "soulmate," and there should be no other reason for divorce than stating that their partner was not their soulmate. It was an outrageous argument for Victorian men and women, and critics interpreted it as a policy for promiscuity. Therefore, opponents argued that anyone who was a Spiritualist must necessarily be promiscuous or a "free lover."

The lectures of Victoria Woodhull did not help dissuade the argument. She was the most radical of Spiritualist women, and at first, reformers such as Stanton and Anthony embraced her for her progressive views. Unfortunately, she inspired public outrage when she demanded sexual equality both in and out of the marriage bed. Women reformers felt compelled to distance themselves from her for the sake of their suffrage platform. Woodhull influenced later Spiritualist women and some men who argued for birth control and denounced the idea that only procreation justified coition for women. Spiritualists attacked the church, the government, and societal norms, and people listened. Historically, people will never remain oppressed for long, and Spiritualism gave women the vehicle to break the bonds of oppression.

Spiritualists lost their public image as reformers, and much of their influence, for various reasons. Conservative women reformers had already distanced themselves from the Spiritualist movement and ministers throughout the nation denounced them from the pulpit. The general public may have secretly agreed with their reform measures, but many could not withstand the social pressure to condemn them. In addition, Spiritualists had begun to retreat from the lecture platform into the seance room by the late 1870s, and fraudulent activity began to surface at an alarming rate. They still lectured to the public, but for much smaller audiences. Consequently, it is probably no surprise that women's history omitted them. In 1881, Stanton, Anthony, and Matilda Joslyn Gage published the first three volumes of their groundbreaking work, *The History of Woman Suffrage.* They ultimately published six books in total. There was no mention of Spiritualist women or their contribution to women's rights in any of the volumes. The omission was unfair to Spiritualist women who fought just as hard, if not harder, for equal rights as women reformers.

Amelia Hunt Colby Luther was a female Spiritualist lecturer whose career spanned roughly forty years. Even though multiple Spiritualist newspapers documented her professional life as a trance lecturer, she is an enigma to history. Amelia was not as prominent as other well known Spiritualists, and her private life remains a mystery. However, as an itinerant Spiritualist lecturer, her speeches created a tidal wave of controversy in the many Spiritualist and freethinker societies she visited. Throughout her professional life, she was called the "female Ingersoll," a reference to the noted atheist and freethinker Robert G. Ingersoll. She was also called "a dynamic atheist," "infidel," and "the Mother of Indiana Spiritualism," titles that, while intended as compliments, did not do justice to the woman that she was.

By all accounts, she was large and loud. When she lectured to crowds, she made a statement with her words and presence. Reporters both reviled and loved her. She was "manly," forcible, and unseemly. An admirer, Theron C. Leland, secretary of the National Liberal League, wrote to *The Truth Seeker* in September 1878 that she was "250 pounds of well-proportioned woman in the Roman matron style, and all could hear her in a 40-acre grove over crying babies, 500 murmuring people, neighing horses, dogs barking and rustling leaves." Others described her as tall, not necessarily stately or elegant; and large-boned with her graying hair cut short and bushy. She spoke in stentorian tones with her head thrown back in a regal manner. At the peak of her career, she was a hurricane in a land where women were supposed to be gentle breezes, and hurricanes were not welcome.

Amelia started her career as a trance lecturer much later than others. The ethereal and ever-popular Cora Richmond began her career in childhood, as did many of the noted trance mediums. Richmond, known as "America's darling," was the most celebrated medium in America. She was the complete opposite of Amelia. Petite, blonde, and beautiful, she captivated audiences whenever she spoke. News outlets across the nation covered her lectures extensively, and more than one paid greater attention to her physical characteristics than the content of her speeches.

Amelia's career began when Spiritualism's popularity peaked. This did not diminish her presence in a large field of itinerant lecturers. In fact, she stood out as one of the more radical speakers on the circuit. Although she was born in the "burned-out district" of New York, where Spiritualism and the Women's Rights Convention coincided, her early life resembled that of nearly all women of the age—those with little education, few opportunities, and an expectation of marriage and babies.

Very little information documents Amelia's early years, and any account of her history must include some conjecture based on connecting a few dots in her family's history. A family tree constructed on Ancestry.com was the most significant help in this regard and brought previously unknown information to the forefront. She is lost in census records after 1870 due to her constant traveling. Like most Spiritualist lecturers, she was never in one place long enough to be included in these records. A review of all Spiritualist news publications and local news outlets helped track her movements in later years. Amelia wrote few pamphlets, unlike many of her colleagues, who were prolific writers and advertised themselves consistently in Spiritualist news periodicals and papers. The few pamphlets she did write are no longer in print or have not been preserved. The only known work, *The Colby Bombshell*, is archived at the Wisconsin Historical Society. No letters or diaries written in her hand appear to have been preserved.

Her letters may not have been retained, but newspapers captured her voice. Spiritualist newspapers reported her lectures in full on occasion. Generally, correspondents summarized her lectures to the Spiritualist newspapers, most routinely to the *Banner of Light*, the largest and most widely read of all the Spiritualist papers. Her lectures often lasted one to two hours and never with the benefit of notes. She spoke in "normal" and "abnormal" voices, and it is sometimes difficult to determine when she spoke in trance.

Spiritualist women often spoke in the abnormal, or trance, voice. It allowed them to maintain societal norms of passivity, which was more acceptable to mixed audiences. When Amelia spoke in her "normal voice," it meant the thoughts and ideas she offered were her own without the benefit of spirit. The general public often condemned these sessions since a woman's opinion was considered tasteless and inappropriate. She never gave seances or provided clairvoyant messages from deceased relatives—as Spiritualism moved from small gatherings to large organizations with settled speakers by the late 1880s, this made her constant popularity unique in the field.

When Spiritualist mediums retreated to the seance room, it created a gradual change in focus from philosophy to phenomena. People began to clamor for phenomena, and mediums who conducted seances gave it to them. The public wanted not just physical proof but astounding physical proof. Seance attendees were treated to materializations of flowers, food, music, and discarnate entities who touched and caressed the sitters' faces, arms, and hands. Sitting in a darkened seance room with men violated every norm known to Victorian women, and people relished it. It was exciting and naughty, and Spiritualism allowed it with no social consequence to the male or female sitter. Although Amelia participated in several seances as a secondary player, she never engaged in producing phenomena. This refusal to conduct seances should have reduced Amelia's lecture engagements, but it did not.

By the late 1880s, most Spiritualist societies clamored for workers who could lecture on Spiritualist philosophy and provide seances or clairvoyant messages to individuals during their engagement. It was a simple cost-saving measure for large and small societies that often found themselves in financial difficulty. Amelia was so popular that it did not affect her, and she was often booked up to a year in advance.

Amelia's lectures addressed Spiritualist philosophy, politics, economics, and the hypocrisy of orthodox Christianity. She repeatedly denounced the church and its ministers, upheld the Constitution, and advocated for complete freedom of conscience, freedom of speech, and a free press. Many of the Spiritualist societies who engaged her services admitted that they did so with some trepidation, but found that she packed their meeting places and provided a fiscal stimulus that other, more conservative speakers failed to deliver.

Amelia was legendary in her time, and this is her story.

ORDINARY TO EXTRAORDINARY

Amelia Hunt was born on November 23, 1827, in Holland, New York. She was the ninth child of ten and the youngest daughter in the family. Her father, Zaccheus, and mother, Hepzibah (née Challis), came from a long line of Quakers who had emigrated from Massachusetts to New York. Amelia's ancestors Edward and Ann (Weed) Hunt settled in Amesbury, Massachusetts, in the 1600s. Successive generations then migrated to Vermont, New Hampshire, and New York. Amelia's early years are sketchy, and it is impossible to describe her childhood concretely. Still, based on her later-life opinions, the family likely embraced the Hicksite faction of the Quakers once they settled in western New York.

Elias Hicks, a cousin to the noted abolitionist and women's rights activist Amy Post, had separated from the orthodox Quakers in 1827–28 due to his disagreement with strict limitations created by orthodox meetings. He preached freedom of conscience, which he felt was the original Quaker belief, instead of the strict dogmatic rules embraced by more conservative, orthodox Quakers. Those Quakers maintained strict rules about who one could marry, how they behaved in society, and who they engaged with socially. They did not believe in engaging with social or reform issues, and members could only marry within their own meeting.

Hicks felt this was wrong and supported the idea that freedom of conscience based on inner light was the number one priority for all members. In other words, the Quaker ideal of inner light, or "that of God in all people," took precedence over church authority. He said those who chose to engage in social reform, i.e., abolition, women's rights, etc., should have the freedom to do so without condemnation by the meeting house elders. He was also known as a rationalist and believed the Bible was not the actual word of God but instead used allegory to make its points, as, for example, in the case of the virgin birth. Hicks traveled to the rural areas of New York to preach this new doctrine, and many Friends agreed with him. Consequently, a division known as "the Great Separation" occurred among the Society of Friends.[7]

Several factors suggest the Hunt family, living in rural western New York, likely followed the Hicksite beliefs. The rural areas were too distanced from larger meetings in towns such as Rochester and Collins, and more susceptible to the preaching of Hicks. In addition, his arguments touched a nerve with those Quakers who set aside their peace doctrine and participated in the Revolutionary War. Those men could maintain their Quaker heritage and justify their participation in the war based on freedom of conscience. Such was true for the Hunt family. Amelia's grandfather, David, and his brother Zaccheus Hunt, Jr., had both served in the Revolutionary War and had been at Valley Forge.[8]

The most widely read document before the war was Thomas Paine's *Common Sense*. It spoke to all American citizens and had two main points: 1) Independence from Great Britain and 2) Creating a democratic republic. It was published anonymously on January 10, 1776, at the beginning of the American Revolution, and became an immediate sensation. Paine, an ex-Quaker himself, understood the meaning of liberty and freedom of conscience, and his words were the catalyst for the revolution in America. When the Pennsylvania and New Jersey Friends issued a "Testimony" in support of England's king during a general meeting in Philadelphia on January 20, 1776, and apparently in response to Paine's seminal call for freedom, Paine issued a scathing *Epistle to Quakers* included in the third edition of *Common Sense*. He chastised them for their stance against democracy, critiqued every policy point of their Testimony, and ended the *Epistle* by telling them to stop mixing politics and religion.

...as men and Christians, ye may always fully and uninterruptedly enjoy every civil and religious right, and be, in your turn, the means of securing it to others; but that the example which ye have unwisely set, of mingling religion with politics, may be disavowed and reprobated by every inhabitant of AMERICA.[9]

Amelia's paternal grandfather, David, and granduncle, Zaccheus, answered that call for freedom, and their Quaker meeting expelled them. Records show that Zaccheus returned to the Hampton Monthly Meeting (orthodox) in Massachusetts, but there is no evidence that David did so.[10] Thus, when Elias Hicks made his way to western New York, where the family had settled, the Hunt family may have found a way to return to the family's Quaker ideals with a new understanding and more freedom to engage in their own leadings or liberty of conscience.

Amelia's birthplace, Holland in western New York, was, in 1830, a small community with just over 1,000 people. It was populated mainly by prosperous farmers, who owned large tracts of land and were well situated, and a small but thriving business community. The farming community was close-knit and generally composed of Revolutionary War patriots, who understood the freedom they had fought for and who had passed that fierce desire for freedom on to their children and grandchildren. It also maintained a small cadre of Quaker families, mainly immigrants from Vermont. The Hunt and Colby families were friends, first in Vermont and then in Massachusetts, where they had migrated together. The Colby family relocated to western New York, and the Hunts followed soon after, in the early 1800s. Both Amelia's maternal grandfather, Enos Challis, and her paternal grandfather, David, fought in the New Hampshire regiment during the Revolutionary War. Remaining in the service, Challis served in the War of 1812, at the age of sixty. He died two years later, but it is unknown whether he died from injuries suffered in the war.

By 1827, the year of Amelia's birth, the "great separation" among Quakers was already underway. There were no meetings with leaders in the little town of Holland, but only a tiny home-church type where rural Friends sat in silence to wait for an inner leading of conscience. In this environment of patriots, Amelia received her first understanding of the importance of freedom. Influenced by her grandfathers' determination for freedom, including the Hicksite idea of freedom of conscience, she argued these concepts all her life.

Amelia was likely home-schooled. At the very least, she would have attended a small, local school just long enough to learn reading and writing, then returned to farm chores when her parents decided she did not need to learn anything further. She would have certainly read the Bible, as was common practice in rural areas, and her revolutionary grandfathers likely exposed her to all of Paine's major works, including *Common Sense, The American Crisis, The Rights of Man, The Age of Reason,* and *Agrarian Justice.*

The other popular works of the age, Mary Wollstonecraft's *A Vindication of the Rights of Women* and Margaret Fuller's *Woman in the Nineteenth Century*, informed her understanding of women's rights in the early to mid-1800s. In addition, her family experience made an impact on her. As the youngest daughter, she saw the devastating debility that multiple births inflicted on her mother, culminating in her youngest brother, Zaccheus—the tenth and final child—being born mentally deficient. Census records recorded him as "an idiot" and ineligible to vote later in life.[11]

The Spiritualist movement and the Women's Rights Convention likely influenced twenty-one-year-old Amelia. Despite her rural setting, she should have been aware of the hotbed of social, political, and religious activity in New York. As she explored both movements, they undoubtedly spoke to her understanding of liberty and freedom—an understanding that centered her perfectly within a growing movement of women's rights, Spiritualism, abolitionism, and Quaker liberalism.

Amelia married Hylon Colby on November 16, 1849, in Holland, New York. Friends for decades, their families lived on adjoining farms. Families often intermarried, particularly in rural areas where interaction with the opposite sex was limited. The two families had an ancestral history of intermarriage, dating back to well before their arrival in New York. Amelia's older brother Enos had already married Belinda Colby, sister to Hylon, earlier in 1842. Hylon and Amelia probably lived with one of the families during the first few years of marriage. She gave birth to their first child, Estella, in 1851. Not long after, Amelia and Hylon moved to Illinois, where Amelia's sister Dolly and her husband, Moses Fuller, had purchased land in Kankakee County.[12] They lived on the Fuller farm of 80 acres for five years, where Amelia gave birth to Augustus Tom (an apparent reference to her love for Tom Paine) in 1852, Lillian in 1855, and Emma in 1856. That same year, Hylon purchased 160 acres in Kankakee County to begin his own farming venture. Unfortunately, it appears that Emma died in infancy as she does not show up in the 1860 census, and there is no information other than her birth account.

Amelia's interest in Spiritualism increased following the death of baby Emma. Her liberal Quaker background and proximity to the early Spiritualist movement in Hydesville and Rochester suggest she had prior knowledge of Spiritualism, and baby Emma's death accentuated that interest. According to her own account, she began lecturing in trance around 1858 to local communities. Amelia's early Quaker beliefs of inner light and freedom of conscience gave her access to the political and social reforms of the day, chief among them abolition and temperance, while her Quaker background prepared her as a public speaker. Quaker women were allowed an equal speaking platform with Quaker men, whereas other religious denominations frowned upon and often denounced the idea of a woman speaking to the public.

By 1860, Hylon's farming venture in Illinois had apparently failed, and he and Amelia moved to Crown Point, Indiana, a short distance from Chicago. Hylon began farming again, and Amelia juggled children, farm chores, and, up until the start of the Civil War, short Sunday lecture trips. Her reputation as a speaker seemed to be growing, and in 1860 she spoke for Abraham Lincoln's presidential campaign at the invitation of the Republican National Convention. Lincoln ran on a platform stating he would not interfere with slavery where it already existed but would not allow further expansion. It was a painful compromise for abolitionists, but one that seemed better than nothing at all. Unfortunately, it did not stop the catastrophic war that followed.

Republicans were so impressed with Amelia that they asked her to speak again for Lincoln in 1864 when he ran for a second term.[13] She was a staunch supporter of Lincoln, if nothing other than for signing the Emancipation Act in 1863, so she was happy to speak on his behalf a second time. Few women received this honor outside of the Spiritualist community since a woman speaking to a mixed audience was still frowned upon by polite society. Amelia's Quaker background gave her the confidence she needed as a speaker since her liberal meeting afforded women equal, or nearly identical, rights in the meeting as their male counterparts. It is unknown whether she spoke in her normal voice or in trance during these speeches, but she was so impressive on the Republican stage that she became widely known among Spiritualists and national politicians, and her services began to be demanded across the nation.

The Civil War touched the lives of every American, and it touched Amelia in multiple ways. The number of people clamoring for news of loved ones fighting, dead, or missing seemed to triple, and those who could contact the dead were in high demand. Three of her brothers, Calvin, Obadiah, and Enos, enlisted in New York and fought on the side of the Union. All three returned to their family, unlike scores of others who did not. The Civil War, and its aftermath, only solidified Amelia's belief in Spiritualism, her support of Lincoln, and her ideas of freedom.

Spiritualism had grown into a national movement by the time of the Civil War. The first Spiritualist National Convention, held in Chicago, August 9–14, 1864, discussed the viability of organizing Spiritualists nationwide. After six days of arguing, the motion to organize was defeated, and it was recommended to allow local organizations free rein to do as they wished. The participants also haggled over policy issues, believing that some were more political than others. Ultimately, resolutions were formed that denounced slavery, supported Lincoln's second term, rejected a national organization, and advocated local organizing for free thought, free expression, and free platforms.[14] Local organizations met the demands of their specific communities, which were extensive during the war. There was simply no ignoring the liberating call for communication with the dead—particularly when the dead called to family members from the battlefield. Spiritualists had redefined Calvinistic ideas of death and offered more palpable comfort than current orthodox Christianity could provide. Family members and friends clamored for it at every opportunity.

Amelia continued lecturing, although travel during the Civil War limited engagements to local vicinities and northern principalities. Nevertheless, she was in great demand during this period, and it could not help but strain her marriage. Moses Hull would later tell the mourners at her funeral oration that during those early years, Amelia worked six days a week on the farm and, on Sundays, packed up her children and traveled by buckboard to her lecture engagement. She would then return home and complete her Sunday chores. There is no evidence that her husband, Hylon, traveled with her or took an interest in Spiritualism—a factor that would later play a part in ending the marriage.

By the late 1860s, daughter Lillian was a teenager, and Amelia was venturing farther from home. The *Religio-Philosophical Journal* reports her speaking for the First Society of Spiritualists in Crosby's Music Hall in Chicago on April 26, 1868. It identifies her as a new speaker who attracts a "full house on every occasion. She has many admirers, and those who are not attracted by her energetic, earnest, and forcible manner of speaking seem to find themselves drawn there by a peculiar and attractive psychological power that accompanies her in her manifestly inspired discourses."[15]

However, things changed in 1870 when Amelia listed her occupation on the 1870 Federal Census as "Lecturer," an astounding announcement for any female during that time. Every married woman on the same census page is listed as a "housewife" except Amelia. It was a very public statement of her move from the domestic sphere as a housewife into the professional sphere as a public speaker. It also indicates a possible division in her marriage, and she was unconcerned enough to label herself as something other than Hylon's wife.

By 1870, Amelia was more heavily engaged in Spiritualist work and attended annual sessions of the Indiana Spiritualist Association meetings locally. The September 1870 meeting, held in Richmond, Indiana, brought her into contact with some notable leaders in the field, such as Addie Ballou and Moses Hull of Indiana, Hannah F.M. Brown of Chicago, and Dr. Henry T. Childs of Philadelphia. It also gave her access to several editors of current Spiritualist newspapers, such as Nettie Pease of Michigan, the associate editor of *The Present Age;* Cephas B. Lynn of Boston, who acted as correspondent for the *Banner of Light;* and Hannah F.M. Brown, who owned, operated, and edited a newspaper entitled *The Agitator*, "devoted to reform," from 1858 to 1860 , when she sold her subscription list to the *Banner of Light*.[16]

The lecturers discussed various reforms at that meeting, including prison, marriage, and general social reform. The lecturers were liberal and outspoken, as the following report from *The Indiana Radical* illustrates:

> One of their speakers spoke very approvingly of "free love," and another lauded to the skies the inventor of easy divorces, Mr. Robert Dale Owen. Others were alarmed at the general prevalence of the Bible, which contains the basis of the only pure doctrines the Spiritualists teach. Others groaned over the tyranny of orthodoxy, the bigotry of the churches, and the uncharitableness of society.[17]

The reference to "free love" was primarily directed at Brown, a vocal proponent of free love and feminism. She often spoke of marriage in derogatory terms and called it "degradation and legalized slavery and prostitution."[18] A former disciple of the Universalist John Murray Spear, she was a well known ex-Universalist minister turned Spiritualist. Reporters considered Brown one of the most radical of all the speakers listed that day.[19]

Amelia was no stranger to the ideas presented by the liberal Spiritualists who were present. Still, it likely solidified her own thoughts and gave her a community of like-minded thinkers that she could not experience at home. She became increasingly active in the Indiana State Association of Spiritualists, and by 1871 she was elected one of the delegates to attend the National Convention of the American Association of Spiritualists.[20] The convention, held in Troy, New York, featured Victoria Woodhull lecturing on motherhood and children's rights. Other attendees included Moses Hull, H.F.M. Brown, Dr. Henry Childs, Ed Wheeler, and the venerable Lucretia Mott. Again, Amelia listened to the most radical speeches, including support of "free love" and a rousing debate on Mormonism.[21]

Woodhull's lecture on the rights of children particularly hit home for Amelia. It was a defiant diatribe of radical social reform that outlined the best way to raise children, including instructing them about their reproductive systems and sex. Woodhull even dared to use the word "abortion" and discuss its merits. She contended that men and women who were not prepared or willing to be parents would be better off not having children and included abortion as a viable option. Her clear statement that "cases of partial and total idiocy have been traced to the beastly inebriation of the parents at and previous to conception and ... mothers can trace the irritable and nervously disagreeable condition of the children to their own condition at this time" effectively placed all fault for disabled, mentally deficient, or criminal offspring squarely onto the shoulders of inept parents.[22]

It was a scandalous speech for that day and age, but convention attendees welcomed and accepted it. Indeed, Woodhull's speech likely hit home with Amelia, reminding her of her youngest brother, Zaccheus, who was mentally deficient and unable to care for himself. The burden of his care on the family was staggering. Multiple census records document that two of her older sisters, Ursula and Maria, never married but took turns taking care of their brother at different stages of his life.

At this convention, Victoria Woodhull was elected president of the American Association of Spiritualists, setting off a wave of controversy in Spiritualist papers across the land. Her reputation as an extremist overrode any benefits she may have given to Spiritualism, and conservative and liberal Spiritualists debated for months whether or not she was an asset to the movement. Nevertheless, a month later, when Woodhull delivered her infamous lecture "The Principles of Social Freedom," her Spiritualist opponents and proponents were further divided. A summation of her address, printed in multiple newspapers, created outrage nationwide. There is no record of Amelia's presence at the lecture. However, it is inevitable that she read it in news reports, and it is just as certain that she agreed with Woodhull's arguments. The speech advocated a woman's right to determine the use of her own body, opposed the idea of coercion in sexual relationships, and argued for equal footing in education. The policies, if initiated, would give women more economic opportunities and lessen their reliance on marriage, thus reducing marital slavery.[23] The audience only heard, and the public only read, her frustrating response to hecklers: "Yes, I am a free lover. I have an inalienable, constitutional, and natural right to love whom I may, to love as long or as short a period as I can; to change that love every day if I please."[24]

There is no indication that Amelia agreed with the concept of "free love" that opponents defined as promiscuity. However, her later lectures echoed Woodhull's arguments for sexual equality in and out of marriage. She may have favored Andrew Jackson Davis' concept of "spiritual affinities" regarding marriage and spousal relationships. Davis, the author of *The Harmonial Philosophy*, became Spiritualism's philosophical mouthpiece for social reform. His book included one of the foundations of the Spiritualist argument for women's rights: the idea that no one had to remain in a loveless, oppressive marriage. Davis' ideas were in direct opposition to current social norms, church ideology, and state laws that removed individual sovereignty from all married women, and Amelia certainly embraced these ideas.[25]

The broad swath of Spiritualists agreed with Davis' critique of marriage and advocacy for spiritual affinities. Still, opponents within and without Spiritualism argued that the concept of "spiritual affinities" opened the door to sexual promiscuity. It was enough to be labeled an outcast if one were brave enough to advocate for it, and many Spiritualists did.

This early identification with women's rights in a marriage affected the relationship between Amelia and Hylon as early as 1856, when Amelia's last child, Emma, was born and died in infancy. Apparently, Amelia decided she would have no more children, and with no contraception available other than abstinence, Amelia exerted her individual sovereignty by denying her husband access to her body. The effect on her marriage culminated many years later when she and Hylon divorced. However, both should be credited for remaining in the marriage until their children were raised and effectively independent adults.

Amelia returned home after the 1871 convention, and by all accounts, her lectures became more radical in substance. Concurrently, she became a popular speaker for Spiritualists and liberals alike. However, she remained a local phenomenon and participated in all the Indiana State Association of Spiritualists meetings within a short journey from her home. By October 1871, the *Religio-Philosophical Journal* records her living in Winchester, Indiana, thus easily making trips to Indiana Association meetings in Richmond, Indiana.

Increasingly involved in the Association's meetings, by November 1871 Amelia lectured and also participated in the Resolutions Committee, helping to construct the philosophy of the Indiana State Spiritualist Association for the coming year. The *Banner of Light* reported that she "electrified the large audience present with her logical and sledge-hammer blows at the Mrs. Grundys both in and out of the spiritual ranks to good effect." Mrs. Grundy was a figurative name for an extraordinarily conventional or prudish person.[26]

Amelia served on the Resolution Committee with Addie Ballou, Kersey Graves, Dr. J.L. Braffett, and J.H. Mendenhall. At least two of her colleagues, Ballou and Graves, were essential committee members and confirmed Amelia's already established philosophy of individual sovereignty and freedom of conscience. They also supported her belief in women's rights and her dissatisfaction with the church's hypocrisy.

Ballou was a suffragist, poet, author, and lecturer for social reform. She supported Victoria Woodhull's campaign for the presidency in 1872, promoted Spiritualism, and campaigned for prison reform and women's rights issues. Ballou shared the platform with Susan B. Anthony, Elizabeth Cady Stanton, and Woodhull in January 1872, when they met to present a list of 45,000 names of women to the House Judiciary Committee demanding their rights at the ballot box, as given by the 14th and 15th Amendments of the Constitution. She ultimately moved to California, where she made a more significant mark as an artist of note and a continued presence in the world of social reform.[27]

Graves was the most radical of the group. A Quaker abolitionist disowned by his Whitewater Monthly Meeting in Indiana, he was now a member of the Congregational Friends (later renamed Friends of Human Progress). It was one of the most radical of all Friends communities, advocating antislavery, women's rights, socialistic utopianism, health reform, temperance, and peace. Additionally, it felt bound to separate from anything that resembled papistry, Christianity, or belief in God at all. For Graves, belief in religion corrupted the truth. He was, by all accounts, both a Spiritualist and an atheist. By 1871, he had already written *The Biography of Satan.* However, his most important books, published at the end of the 1870s, were *The World's Sixteen Crucified Saviors* and *The Bible of Bibles or Twenty-seven Divine Revelations.* All the works were scathing critiques of Christianity.[28]

Amelia, Ballou, and Kersey, with the agreement of the rest of the committee, formulated one of the most radical sets of resolutions that would appear in Spiritualist print. The first amendment demanded equal rights, regardless of sex, as an inherent right of every American. The second amendment denounced a proposed amendment to the Constitution that required the recognition of "God or Jesus Christ as the chief ruler of nations and the Christian Bible as the fountain of all laws and the supreme ruler of our conduct." The third amendment argued for the taxation of all church property, and the fourth and fifth amendments addressed prison reform by claiming that prisoners should be considered invalids and treated with kindness and rehabilitation rather than punishment. These amendments also advocated for better prison conditions and educational opportunities for the poor to reduce crime. The last two amendments argued that Spiritualism embraced all social reform, and men and women were inconsistent in "accepting the Bible and Christianity and rejecting Spiritualism."[29]

The Indiana State Spiritualist Association members passed the resolutions without disagreement, reflecting the ideals of freethinkers and Spiritualists during that time. Only later would the division between liberal and conservative Spiritualists begin to fracture the movement.

There is no evidence that Hylon shared the radical views of his wife, nor is there any indication that Amelia took a safe route in the home. In other words, there is nothing to say that she was a radical, outspoken female in the meetings and later became passive and submissive at home. She was too strong and outspoken to suppress her views about marital rights and her expectations of the partnership between a husband and wife. It is no surprise that their marriage did not last, and their divorce is likely a product of her views about marriage, suffrage, abolition, women's rights, and religion.

Although records are sketchy, the couple must have separated and divorced sometime in late 1872. Their youngest living child, Lillian, was seventeen. Augustus Tom, now twenty, remained on the farm helping his father. The oldest daughter, Estella, had married and moved to Kansas, where she gave birth to a daughter in December 1873. It is not inconceivable that Amelia went to Kansas to be present at the birth of her first grandchild and simply never returned home. Although the *Banner of Light* records Amelia as living in Boston in January of 1874, a letter to the *Banner* a few weeks later reports that she is lecturing and traveling out west with Mrs. Olive K. Smith. The pair had become friends when they met at the National Convention of the American Association of Spiritualists in 1871. Olive complemented Amelia's trance sessions by singing and playing guitar before and after her lectures. She was also a decided contrast to Amelia's rough demeanor, as various reports called her sweet and pleasant. The letter writer says their address is Winona, Minnesota.[30] Letters to the *Banner of Light* often took two to four weeks to arrive, so she clearly was separated from Hylon by late 1872. It also marks the start of a dedicated and professional traveling lecture circuit with Olive as her constant companion.

There is little doubt that Hylon and Amelia's views on many subjects differed dramatically. Hylon, more conservative, would not, or could not, tolerate Amelia's radical views on everything, including marriage.

This is later borne out when records document his remarriage to a wealthy widow in May 1875. *A History of Delaware and Randolph Counties,* written in 1893, records the woman was Sarah Bundrant, a resident of Indiana with a farm of 80 acres. They remained married for eighteen years, working on the farm and maintaining a respectable presence in the community.[31] However, Amelia's post-marital life was anything but settled and starkly contrasted to Hylon's seemingly idyllic existence.

WEST TO FREEDOM

THE *BANNER OF LIGHT* maintained a weekly column titled "Movements of Lecturers and Mediums" and a "List of Lecturers," providing readers with scheduled appearances of their favorite trance speakers and mediums. It also provided information to family members on the location of their working loved ones. The *Banner* documents Amelia as living in Boston in January 1874, but it is clear from other newspaper accounts that she had been living and working in the western states, specifically Minnesota, for almost the entire year. Why she traveled that far west to begin a professional lecture career is a mystery.

On April 4, 1874, a correspondent for the *Banner of Light* reported that Amelia, together with her companion Olive Smith, had spent two months lecturing in Winona, Minnesota, for a newly organized Spiritualist society. The lecture, "The Cause and Cure of Intemperance," was widely applauded. The admission charge was $0.25 at the door, and she lectured to a packed Unitarian Church where the Spiritualist Society held its meetings. In May, Amelia possibly returned to Indiana to attend her daughter Lillian's wedding, but then immediately traveled west, this time to Wisconsin, to continue her trance lectures. The *Dunn County News* of Menomonie, Wisconsin, provided the first of many analyses of her speeches. The reporter called her a "somewhat noted apostle of Free Religion" and described her lectures as radical and materialistic. The series of lectures offered a unique view of immortality. Amelia also contrasted orthodox views of heaven and hell with Spiritualist ideals. The reporter stated, "She attacked the Christian idea of a personal devil; and reduced his satanic majesty to a nonentity in about fifteen minutes." Additional lectures addressed temperance and women's rights, and the reporter described Amelia in complimentary terms:

> Upon the platform, Mrs. Colby is at home and addresses her audience with the ease and self-possession of a practical speaker. She has a powerful voice, pitches it on a high key, and speaks with great rapidity. Her ideas of religion and morality of social and political reform are thoroughly radical and evidently based on the spiritualistic theory. But she asks no one to accept her statements unless satisfied with the proof and invites any person in the audience to step upon the platform and refute them. While perhaps very few are prepared to accept her doctrine and admit her conclusions, nevertheless, her honesty and sincerity in advocating her peculiar ideas will not be seriously questioned.[32]

The description of Amelia on the platform is a refrain that echoes throughout her speaking life. The article called her an "apostle of Free Religion," but she was likely an agnostic at this early stage in her career. It also identifies her constant arguments about the orthodox church, heaven, hell, God, and Satan. Whether in a trance or not, her comments address the freethinkers' idea of a materialistic universe. They also point to the Spiritualist idea of a co-existing spiritual universe. Ultimately, freethinkers and conventional Spiritualists would clash, but in 1874, most people identified freethinkers with Spiritualists.

Amelia remained in Wisconsin through September and continued lecturing. She also conducted a funeral for the infant child of a Spiritualist after the child's unexpected death. A local paper identified her as the presiding Spiritualist and mentioned her companion, Olive, who delivered "very sweet and appropriate singing with guitar accompaniment." The reporter noted that the funeral resembled orthodox funerals except that the ideas shared in Amelia's address "were utterly opposed to the orthodox belief of death and future existence." The report derided Amelia's belief in universal salvation and a beautiful hereafter open to all, calling it more imagination than fact.[33] Nevertheless, the sizeable Spiritualist crowd drew comfort from Amelia's words, and it was not the last time she delivered a funeral oration.

It was not unusual for Spiritualists to decline the services of an orthodox minister to conduct the funeral of a loved one. Instead, they acquired Spiritualist speakers, despite the disparagement of neighbors and the community. In this case, the local paper echoed the views of most orthodox articles and communities concerning Spiritualism—skeptical and unable to embrace the Spiritualist philosophy of the afterlife.

Most Spiritualists supported the idea that the spirit of the individual enters into one of several spheres in the hereafter and continues to grow and evolve. Comparatively, the notion of spheres was first promulgated by the Swedish theologian Emanuel Swedenborg in his 1758 work, *Heaven and Its Wonders and Hell: From Things Heard and Seen,* where he alleged that individuals in the spirit world have bodies, live in houses, and enjoy community life surrounded by an environment much like earth. Everything in the spirit world is enhanced, and their world reflects their inner life. It also reflects the type of life they lived on earth. If they were liars and cheats in this world, they went to a sphere designed for liars and cheats. However, they received no punishment, as orthodoxy claimed, but found opportunities to grow spiritually so they could move upward into higher spheres. The idea was wildly popular in Spiritualist circles and was the basis for Andrew Jackson Davis' work *The Harmonial Philosophy*, which many Spiritualists considered the gospel of Spiritualism.

During the winter of 1874–75, Amelia traveled to Chicago for a brief lecture tour at Grow's Opera Hall. In one of her lectures, she addressed the philosophy of spirit manifestation and the Katie King exposé, which was a hotly debated topic nationally in both Spiritualist and conventional publications. Katie King was purportedly a materialized spirit who first appeared between 1871 and 1874 in seances conducted by Florence Cook in London. The matter was investigated by noted scientist Sir William Crookes, who asserted the materializations were genuine. However, despite his claim, the London papers reported the exposure of Florence Cook as a fraud.

Between 1874 and 1875, Katie King began materializing in seances given by Nelson and Jennie Holmes in New York. Spiritualists believed that a spirit borrowed energy and matter from the medium, causing the materialized spirit to have substance and to even take on the appearance of the entranced medium. Sitters who were at first convinced by the Katie King materializations included notables Robert Dale Owen and Dr. Henry T. Childs, who both wrote confirmation letters to the *Banner of Light.* However, subsequent seances caused suspicion. Owen and Childs investigated the seances in more detail and retracted their support quite bluntly in December 1874. The ensuing controversy was widespread among Holmes' supporters and opponents. At issue was the confession of one Eliza White, who admitted that she had posed as Katie King during the seances. This did not deter supporters, though, who believed that it was White who was fraudulent.

No record of Amelia's lecture on materialization exists. However, based on later recorded lectures, she not only supported mediums and materialization at that time, but did so throughout her life. She verbalized the belief that spirits used the substance of the medium and argued that all materialization was natural law—and natural law was also spiritual law. She contended that the laws of Spirit manifested in physical form through the laws of nature; therefore, all materialization was possible and ultimately probable.

Years later, she would also argue that "if spirits can bring flowers and birds to a circle, cannot they also bring masks, rags, or anything they desire to have appear there? The visitors are as responsible as the medium for the results, for in their desire to detect fraud, they bring the spirits with them who overcome the medium and her control and produce conditions to which the mediums will never submit if true to themselves. They are as much under the control of spirits in as out of the form." In other words, Amelia believed that the success and truthfulness of the materializing seance was as much the responsibility of the sitters/visitors as of the medium. If strangers who came with the intent of exposing fraud were permitted to be seated, then it was no wonder that entranced mediums would be overwhelmed by negative spirits.[34]

Amelia's reputation for the support of Spiritualism, her radical, freethinking criticism of the church, and her advocacy of women's rights and political freedoms began to grow. She received accolades from some of the most respected members of the Spiritualist lecture circuit. Annie Lord Chamberlain (1842–1920) was a musical medium who began working with her father at the age of twelve. As she progressed, she became well known for her ability to manifest fresh flowers, raps, and the playing of musical instruments in broad daylight. Chamberlain once manifested thirty-seven written communications on new, unused paper, kept in a locked drawer, under daylight test conditions. One of the most respected mediums in Spiritualist circles, she hosted Amelia and Olive during their visits to Chicago in December 1874, and again in May 1875.

In a letter to the *Banner of Light*, Chamberlain praised Amelia's trance lectures as "radical, philosophical, and scientific," complimented Olive's singing and playing of the guitar and organ, and shared that they planned to remain in Chicago for the winter. She ended her praise with the words, "Friends, you need not fear to engage her."[35] Her reference is to the reluctance many societies had regarding Amelia's lectures, which were already noted as some of the most radical on the circuit. It was a fear that followed her throughout much of her career.

A second letter from Chamberlain appeared in *The Spiritualist at Work*, in June 1875. Again, she praised Amelia, reporting that Thomas Paine had been the spirit who instructed the audience at Grow's Hall in Chicago. Calling her "one of the most interesting speakers of the West," Chamberlain encouraged other societies to engage her so that she and Olive might extend their visit through June and July.[36]

Following her tour of Chicago, Amelia traveled to Omaha, Nebraska, in March 1875, where she was well received and praised by local papers. The *Omaha Daily Bee* reported that she delivered four lectures in Meyer's Hall, "which was so crowded that many of the audience were obliged to stand up." She was compared to Maggie Van Cott, who was the first woman to be licensed as a preacher by the Methodist Episcopal Church and was known nationally for her travels and evangelical work. The reporter wrote, "Mrs. Van Cott was nowhere as compared to her in eloquence, and as to her ability, she was chain lightning itself." The attendees were so pleased with Amelia that they took up a collection of $50 and engaged her for four more sessions. The sum raised for Amelia amounts to about $1,183 in today's market, which was a significant amount of money for an itinerant lecturer, whether male or female.[37]

Following this successful stint in Nebraska, Amelia and Olive began a whirlwind tour that took them to multiple states. In June 1875, Amelia lectured with E.V. Wilson, a male trance speaker, and Mrs. E. Parrey, a materializing medium, at the Northern Wisconsin Spiritual Quarterly Meeting in Omro, Wisconsin. The meeting opened with a song by Olive, and Amelia then electrified the audience with her lecture on "How to Educate Children," a speech that seemingly echoed the ideas of Victoria Woodhull. Nevertheless, most Spiritualists supported the revolutionary ideas for child-rearing, and applauded her address.

The reporter for the convention stated that Amelia provided many novel ideas. Asserting that "You cannot learn children only by evolution. They grow the same as trees. They are but photos of ante-natal conditions,"[38] she concluded that children were a direct product of parents' behavior while still in the womb. She repeated this idea in numerous lectures, arguing that alcoholism caused children's worst conditions, including mental infirmity and criminality. Amelia did not always lecture in trance, and here it is difficult to determine whether she did so or was in a "normal" state. However, on this occasion, she was not the attraction that generated the most discussion at the convention, as was usually the case.

Accusations of fraud were delivered against Mrs. Parrey and reported in multiple papers, both locally and outside Wisconsin, specifically the *Chicago Times*. Amelia and Olive attended her seances. A participant in the seance was a reporter for the *Ripon Free Press*, and he recorded the events as he witnessed them. Fifteen additional witnesses agreed with him, and *The Spiritualist at Work* reprinted his article on August 14, 1875. The reporter described the enclosure where Mrs. Parrey sat. It was a typical structure for materializing mediums.

...At ten, we adjourned to a room upstairs, the dimensions of which were about 10x12, across one corner of which a single thickness of boards had been roughly but securely nailed, making an apartment shaped like the letter V. Over the aperture, which was about breast-high, and two feet square, was hung heavy black cloth curtains to exclude the light. The windows to the room were curtained, and two lamps were burning on a chair, over and around which was thrown a shawl, to make the light mellow it was claimed. A person with good eyes could have seen to read in the room. The reporter inspected the cabinet and found it contained nothing but a chair, a small stool to rest the feet on (made of three pieces of board), and a pair of sheriff's handcuffs with the key in them. The cabinet was made by a carpenter there in Omro. There was no possible chance for deception in the simple construction of the compartment.

The reporter asked Olive her opinion on materialization, and she responded with honesty and somewhat cryptically: "The body is constantly throwing off portions of itself, and by some law of magnetism or electricity, the particles are attracted, and thus the spirit is clothed in material and made visible to mortal eye; this is the way we account for it, but this way may not be the truth of it; we are as ignorant of the actual cause of it as you are."

Mrs. Parrey was described by the reporter as a short, heavy-set woman who had been working as a materializing medium for approximately one year. He added that she was Irish, had been a washerwoman, and did not "appear shrewd enough to deceive the most credulous schoolboy." She was stripped of her clothing by two ladies in the audience and redressed with only slippers, stockings, a thin gown, and a shawl. He noted that "the shawl was sewn at the wrists and neck with white thread." The audience felt this would prevent any possibility of fraud.

Olive told the audience they could not guarantee a materialization from the cabinet, but "we shall claim the right to keep the money you have paid." She offered to refund anyone who wished to leave at that point. The reporter noted that Olive and Amelia had taken Mrs. Parrey under their wing, assisting with the seance and handling the money, since Parrey was illiterate and unable to transact business alone. The room had been darkened but not so dark that the reporter was unable to see forms and shapes in front of him. He described the materialization:

> ...a small white hand was seen to separate the curtain and reach out into the room. It disappeared, and a form appeared at the opening in fashionable attire, bedecked with costly jewelry, faultless in form, and of celestial beauty. The hand was well-shaped and very small (about one-half or two-thirds the size of the medium's), on the [spirit's] wrist was a massive gold bracelet, carbuncled, and from which a chain [hung] a pendant. The arm was bare nearly to the shoulders; the dress was of white lace and silk, tarlatan [sic] and other gossamer-like fabrics; the front of the dress was composed of heavy lace ruffles; the costume was nearly as elaborate and much prettier than the apparel of her less ephemeral sisters.

At this point, a latecomer asked for admission to the seance, and the door opened, allowing light to enter. Surprisingly, the form remained at the opening of the cabinet, and even when light came into the room, did not retreat quickly but "faded gradually away like the mists of morning." People in the room acknowledged that they had expected the form to retreat into the cabinet before the door opened if the medium was acting fraudulently.

After the door closed, the form reappeared. It seemed to be a young lady, and she pulled the curtain aside, so people sitting three feet from the opening could view her properly. A foot taller than the medium, with a fair complexion (the medium was dark-complexioned), she had long, curved lashes, a nose tilted upward, and eyes closed. The reporter asked if she would touch him, and the ghostly woman patted him on the head and shoulder. The spirit then took his wrist, and he recorded it "cold as death while the room was warm enough to induce perspiration."

The reporter noted that "seven or more different faces and bodies appeared," ranging from bearded men to little children, old ladies, and young men. He observed that the audience recognized each one as either a family member or a past citizen of Omro. A materialized spirit called Katie hugged Amelia when she went to the cabinet opening.

The evening seance did not proceed as smoothly as the morning one. When the spirit named Katie appeared, an attendee jumped up and grabbed at the lace ruffles of her dress. He shouted to the audience that it was "material." The spirit retreated to the cabinet with the attendee still holding her dress, but it dissolved in his grip, and he stared blankly at his empty hand, still muttering, "It's material."

Olive immediately replied, "Of course it's material. We don't claim it's anything else." She pulled the curtain away and prepared to show him the medium still sitting in the cabinet, her body still restricted. She then prepared to end the disrupted seance, but those who saw the materialized form dissipate in the man's hand requested that the medium continue, despite the late hour.

The reporter stated that if the form was indeed the medium, she could not have wriggled away from the man's grasp. He continued, "There was not a sound from the cabinet when he grabbed her, not a footstep or a voice." Mrs. Parrey was examined as soon as the face disappeared, and "the dress was found sewed up and fastened with a peculiar knot," known only to the women who had undressed and redressed her. At her next seance, Mrs. Parrey was handcuffed and her hands filled with flour. She was also placed in a sack made of mosquito bar netting, which was thrown under the cabinet and held by two men in the audience. The materializations continued in the same manner and appeared in white without any evidence of mosquito bar netting.[39]

The crowd's expectation of fraud dissipated almost immediately due to the test conditions implemented on Parrey during that seance and ensuing seances. However, it is worth mentioning that this was not the first time that Parrey had garnered accusations of fraud, nor was it the first time that Amelia and Olive were forced to vouch for her. The *Chicago Times* of March 15, 1875, contained an article titled "Rubber Ghosts" accusing Parrey of fraud. The report created a considerable stir in Spiritualist circles and resulted in the appointment of a committee—

three women and three men—to investigate the charges of dishonesty against the medium. For six nights running, before each seance started, the cabinet was moved away from the wall and every inch inspected. At each inspection, the committee found no fraudulent tools.

> ...the ladies accompanied Mrs. Parrey to a private room, removed all her clothing, examined her person critically, turned and examined every garment (shoes and stockings included), combed her hair, and escorted her to the cabinet, which had meantime been sedulously guarded by the gentlemen.[40]

The address given for Mrs. Parrey's seance work was the same address advertised for Amelia and Olive. Clearly, the three were traveling and working together for many months. Following what most participants believed to be a successful meeting in June, despite the accusations of fraud, Amelia, Olive, and Parrey traveled to New York and Michigan. In Michigan, Parrey was again accused of fraud, and Amelia and Olive continued to vouch for her. The medium demonstrated materialization only after a committee implemented strict test conditions, including using handcuffs. She was stripped naked by women who searched her clothing, tied to a chair, sealed in a sack, and had flour placed on her hands. Despite all this, some still believed she was a "humbug."

At the Grand Union Camp meeting in Saranac, Michigan, held over five days in September 1875, Amelia lectured with other trance speakers, including E.V. Wilson, the owner and editor of *The Spiritualist at Work*. His news periodical lasted two years before failing. Olive provided music while Parrey conducted materializing seances. Given his report on the convention, it is not surprising that his magazine failed. His printing of observers' comments regarding Amelia and Parrey was detailed and derogatory. He interviewed two attendees who complimented Amelia's ability but could not tolerate her physical appearance. "Lord, she is more like a man than a woman," said one, and she was condemned for her "harsh talk about God" and the church. Wilson wrote that he agreed concerning Amelia's "masculine" characteristics. The women complimented Olive's singing and playing but called Mrs. Parrey "a cheat" and "a humbug." Wilson refused to offer an opinion on Parrey but reported that Amelia and Olive once more testified that her materializations were genuine. He ultimately said that he believed in materialization and had "evidence that it is proof positive." In his article, he acknowledged that fraud existed but refused to accuse Parrey of it.[41]

There is no evidence that Parrey was ever fraudulent. However, some simply would not, or could not, believe her materializations, despite the restrictions placed on her physical body before her seances. Amelia and Olive continued to help with her finances until they left for a long trip west. Parrey decided to remain in Michigan and ultimately settled in Jackson. Welcomed by the Spiritualist community with open arms, she continued to give materializing seances.

"IT WAS NOT A SEEMLY ROLE FOR A WOMAN"

AMELIA AND OLIVE LEFT Chicago and took a train headed for Texas in late 1875. Typically, lecturers would arrange engagements on the way to their next destination, and Amelia was no different. She stopped in Cairo, Illinois, in late November to deliver lectures to the Liberal Religious Association. Cairo is in the southernmost part of Illinois, 340 miles from Chicago. With most trains traveling 20–30 miles per hour, the train trip would have taken approximately one to two days if the weather was good and required no layovers. The implementation of Pullman sleeping cars made a lengthy trip passable at the very least.

Despite the time it took to travel, railways were far and above preferable to horses and wagons. Civil engineer and author August Mencken described riding in a Pullman car:

> ...the cabin of a ship with a comfortable sofa above which a board was fixed at night, so as to form a second sleeping-berth. The beds are regularly made, boots put outside the door for cleaning, and hot water brought in the morning by an active black boy. Meals were served on a table carried into the cabin.[42]

The society at Cairo was thrilled to have Amelia and was effusive in its praise. Its secretary wrote to the *Banner of Light* that she was "the very highest talent in the country," and encouraged spiritual, liberal, and women's suffrage societies to engage her. Interestingly, the writer suggested that other organizations write to "her secretary, Mrs. Olive K. Smith," indicating that Olive was not just a singing partner and traveling companion, but a business partner as well.[43]

Amelia and Olive traveled from Cairo to their home in St. Louis, Missouri. It is unknown when Amelia purchased a home there, but it was presumably following her divorce from Hylon. After a short respite, they traveled to Texas via the Missouri-Kansas-Texas Railroad. The route took them through Missouri, to Parsons, Kansas, and Indian Territory (now Oklahoma), finally crossing the Red River into Texas. They had to change cars at Dennison for Houston through Dallas via the Houston & Texas Central Railroad. Even for the sturdiest of individuals, it was a challenging trip, and the journey from Chicago via St. Louis to Texas likely took one to two weeks.

By the time Amelia arrived in Texas, her reputation as a "free religionist" and freethinker had already preceded her. A letter to *The Spiritualist at Work* reported that the town's citizens were anxious to hear Amelia and "procured the only public building we have, which is used for meetings, schools, concerts, etc." A mixed audience of Spiritualists, liberals, orthodox ministers, and curious townspeople were present during Amelia's first lecture. Speaking for two hours, she "held her audience spellbound." The writer complimented her ideas and speaking ability but acknowledged that not everyone agreed with her premises. Nevertheless, her supporters voted for a continuation of the topic the following evening and attempted to secure the hall for another night. However, they were blocked by the conservative members and ministers of the town. The local Spiritualists were outraged by the apparent discrimination but could do nothing other than vow to build their own venue for future use. Amelia could do nothing more than support the Spiritualist Society by donating to its cause.[44]

Those who refused to allow Amelia to speak a second time disagreed with her views, but they may have also been influenced by an earlier medium who had conducted a seance in Houston that was so obviously fraudulent that the enraged audience demanded test conditions. When the medium refused to be handcuffed, the audience became unruly, and cries of "tar and feather" and "hanging from a lamp post" sounded through the hall. A sheriff protected him from the crowd. His money was confiscated, and the group voted to give it to the local orphanage. The man was then run out of town. Unfortunately, Amelia's reputation was significantly damaged by this medium, who had no connection to her. Despite the accolades of the liberal Spiritualists in Houston, it did not take long for multiple local papers to trash most of her appearances and speeches.

To minimize Amelia's influence in the area, ministers from a wide swath of local churches began to preach against Spiritualism. Amelia remained in Houston, and in February 1876 she challenged Rev. Dr. B.T. Kavanaugh of Houston to a debate on "When the doctrine of Spiritualism and the Bible differ, which should we follow?" Amelia argued for Spiritualism, while Kavanaugh argued against it. He was a D.D., M.D., and former editor, and was recognized in the southwest as one of the ablest thinkers among the Methodist clergy. Amelia's challenge to this educated minister was fearless. His friends tried to dissuade him from debating, believing it was beneath him to argue with a woman, but he accepted the challenge. No newspaper recorded the actual event, but *The Galveston Daily News* announced the debate:

Perkins Hall—The doors of this old theatrical place were thrown open last night, not as on former occasions for theater-goers, but to admit those curious to hear the discussion on Spiritualism between Rev. Dr. B. T. Kavanaugh of the Methodist Episcopal Church, South, and Mrs. Colby, claimed by the believers in the "New Science" to be a trance-speaking medium, under control of the spirit of the late Prof. Wood. Some of the members of Shearn Chapel, in a communication, asked Dr. Kavanaugh to decline a tilt with the Spiritualist, and it is understood, Mrs. Colby was the challenging party—the Doctor merely taking up the gauntlet thrown down to him by a woman.[45]

The paper's attitude is apparent—"thrown down to him by a woman" was perhaps the most demeaning statement the article could have made, so it is not surprising that Amelia was refused the opportunity to continue her lecture, as noted earlier. Indeed, some newspapers and clergy called for her to be ousted from the town.

The Tri-Weekly Herald of Marshall, Texas, reported the most devastating invectives against Amelia before the debate with Dr. Kavanaugh, and throughout her time in Texas. They accused her of blasphemy and claimed that "like most persons carried away by that delusion (Spiritualism), Mrs. C. is a non-believer and an assailant of Christianity. Many, if not most Christians in Houston, are astonished at the Dr. for entering into such a discussion with a woman."[46] A year later, the Secretary of the State Association of Spiritualists, Mrs. J.K. Painter, saw it from a different perspective from the local papers. In her letter to the *Banner of Light*, she wrote:

> She dealt such effective blows at theological ignorance and despotism that the press made an appeal to the citizens of Houston and surrounding country that she be driven from our midst! But her philosophical reasoning and arguments penetrated the mental faculties of our people until they demanded that Christianity defend itself. Thereupon our divines met in session, and the Rev. Dr. Kavanaugh, of this city, one of their strongest and most influential ministers, was chosen as champion and mouthpiece to meet Mrs. Colby in public discussion.[47]

Painter recalled that the debate lasted two evenings before "large and appreciative audiences." She wrote that Amelia provided proof of her philosophy with beautiful reasoning. Conversely, Dr. Kavanaugh preached "a hellfire sermon, fifty years behind the age, dotting it here and there with misrepresentations about the reformers of today, and not once referring to the subject under discussion." Painter concluded her letter by applauding the growth of the Spiritualist and liberal leagues since that initial visit by Amelia and welcomed them back to Texas. Amelia and Olive were traveling north in the spring, and Painter offered "heartfelt thanks, love, and esteem of the many friends in

Texas for their bold and fearless efforts in promulgating religious and political freedom over much of the State."[48]

During her time in Texas, Amelia refused to be intimidated by the local press. Multiple male Spiritualist lecturers had passed through the state before her, and none had received the treatment she experienced. Some might ask, why stay? Amelia's sense of righteous anger, her demand for equality and freedom of speech, and her sense of duty to her belief in Spiritualism drove her persistent efforts.

Sadly, it wasn't just the local press who condemned Amelia in Texas. A Spiritualist from the East wrote letters in advance of her arrival warning the local Spiritualists of her "social freedom" agenda. E.V. Wilson—who followed Amelia and Olive to Texas, and ultimately traveled with the two women—reported that Stephen S. Jones, editor of the conservative Spiritualist *Religio-Philosophical Journal*, sent a letter to the Texas Spiritualists warning them of Amelia's unsavory character. He accused the three travelers of being "free lovers" and advised the Texans to dismiss them from their midst.[49]

Victoria Woodhull originally promoted the "social freedom" question in her November 1871 speech in Steinway Hall, where she argued for the freedom of women to determine the use of their own bodies and the equality of women in sexual relationships. Opponents, such as Jones, claimed her ideas gave women and men the freedom to engage in purely promiscuous sexual relations and argued that this was not the foundational basis of Spiritualism. Proponents asserted that all social reform, including sexual equality, was pertinent to Spiritualism. Whether fair or not, Jones labeled both Wilson and Amelia as "free lovers" and attempted to warn Spiritualist societies against them. It did not work since the various associations welcomed both. However, Jones' letters to the Texas Spiritualists highlighted the growing division between liberal and more conservative Spiritualists, which continued well into the 1890s.

By June 1876, the repeated criticism of mediumship in the local press was enough to cause Wilson to leave Texas. He traveled to Minnesota, where people were more open to liberal ideas. His departure was also possibly influenced by one Prof. Baldwin and his wife. The Baldwins traveled across Texas, exhibiting an exposé of Spiritualism by reproducing the "tricks" of materializing mediums. The local papers praised them, and people came in their droves to see for themselves. It affected not only Wilson but also the attendance at Amelia's lectures.

Amelia never practiced clairvoyance nor held seances. Nevertheless, the Baldwin exposés had a negative impact on all Spiritualism, and the local press panned her lectures throughout the state. As she prepared to go to Waco in June, *The Austin American-Statesman* referred to her as a "spiritual honeyfuggler," in essence, someone who deceives by flattery, sweet talk, scams or cheating. She received the same treatment in nearly every community, and Baptist, Methodist, and Presbyterian ministers across the state preached the biblical warning, "Many false prophets shall arise, and deceive many" (Matt. 24:11) to refer to all Spiritualists and Spiritualism itself. As late as 1880, the Presbyterian Synod in Fort Worth still upheld Paul the Apostle's injunction that it was offensive for women to preach in public.

When the orthodox ministers could not relieve themselves of the Texas Spiritualists, the various city councils decided to intervene. In late 1876, Marshall and Austin were just two of the Texas cities that levied taxes on working mediums, clairvoyants, and mesmerists. City administrators in Marshall, perhaps the most vocal opponent of Spiritualism in Texas, passed a city law stating that all Spiritualists who plied their vocation for money were required to pay a $10 tax (approximately $250 today). The tax had to be paid before beginning their work. Violation of the city ordinance was a misdemeanor subject to a fine of up to $100 ($2,500 today). On the other hand, Austin levied taxes on *anyone* purporting to be a Spiritualist, whether working or not. Such was Texas.

In addition, Texas was no lover of "infidels," a title Amelia had already received due to her attacks on Christianity. In 1877, Ku Klux Klan members attacked a freethinking physician, Dr. J.A. Russell, for giving "infidel" lectures, stripped him naked, tied him to a tree, and gave him 100 lashes. When they finished, they left a placard on him stating that they would "burn out or hang any other lecturers who dared to utter blasphemies in the neighborhood."[50] Amelia was aware of this atrocity since it happened in Bell County, not too far west of her lecture circuit. Undeterred, she remained in Texas for one year, courageously lecturing to grateful members of liberal leagues and Spiritualist societies in various parts of the state. Her radical offerings included attacks on the hypocrisy of Christianity, the inequities and oppression of women, and the benefits of Spiritualism. Years later, Olive laughingly recalled one of Amelia's early meetings in Houston:

> Some years ago, while Mrs. Colby and myself were sojourning at Houston, Texas, where the Liberal societies were at that time composed entirely of male membership, we inquired the reason, and we were informed that no women were ever solicited to join, whereupon we conspired with them to form a "woman's radical club." They were delighted with the idea, and when Mrs. Colby gave notice, at the close of her lecture, that a meeting would be held in that hall the following Wednesday, for the express purpose above mentioned, one of that august body of men arose, and, with a dignified air, inquired "if he understood aright, that it was exclusively for women," to which she replied: "Yes, sir; you understood exactly what I meant. Tell your wife and daughter to be here." The meeting was held, an organization was effected, officers chosen, and it flourished like a green bay tree. They held festivals and sociables, had lectures, and the men actually attended, and within a year, they [the women's league] were urgently solicited to join, in a body, the [men's] Liberal League, to which a woman replied, "Ah hah! this means that we have a few dollars in our treasury that you'd like to handle."[51]

Long after Amelia left the area, local papers still remembered her, but in the most unflattering terms and language that betrayed their prejudice. Fort Worth recalled her as "...a woman of great ability and as for physique and voice, she would have made [William] Booth of Decatur ashamed of himself. But somehow, the impression, after listening to her, was decidedly unpleasant. It was not a seemly role for a woman. She seemed unsexed, standing on the lecture platform and proclaiming in a stentorian voice the virtues of skepticism and the defects of the Christian religion."[52]

Amelia left for Kansas City, Missouri, in April 1877 and continued to speak to large crowds of liberal religionists and Spiritualists. Her lectures against Christianity were the most popular in this group, and the local press was divided. Some applauded her reasoning and courage, while others both complimented and criticized her reasoning. Generally, they praised her for her earnestness and sincerity of thought and admitted that she was one of the ablest trance speakers on the rostrum. At the same time, they questioned the viability of Spiritualism as an alternative to Christianity. Some journalists argued that her accusations of the immorality of church patriarchs and the fallacy of the virgin birth and other biblical myths were no more valid than the assertion that life continues beyond death. They argued that the idea that the dead can communicate with the living also requires faith and belief without concrete evidence. One reporter expressed his admiration and provided the most detailed review of her lecture:

> It was my pleasure last Sunday morning to listen to a lecture from Mrs. Colby at the Unitarian Church. She is a bold, fearless, and emphatic speaker, with a well-developed physique, a full, deep chest tone bordering on the masculine. Mrs. Colby, unlike her predecessor, Mrs. Fox [Nettie Pease Fox], does not bring a great lumber of a husband with her to read the Scripture and give out the hymn, but she launches at once into her subject *sans ceremonie,* which was, last Sunday morning, "Influences and Their Effects."[53]

Amelia told the audience that she did not believe that God created a man, or that from one man sprang humanity. She added that the biblical explanation of the different races was incorrect and that each race of people was the effect of the minerals, vegetables, gases, and climate of the country they inhabited. She then went on to say:

> Men often pay fabulous sums of money and take all the pains in the world to get the best breed. A man will pay $500 for a hog, and why? Because it brings money into his pocket. If the state would offer one million dollars for the best-developed girl, do you suppose we would find so many dwarfs and pigmies, so many wasp-waisted women, so many whose parents put small shoes on their feet and then small gloves on their hands to keep their fingers and toes from growing? No; we should have girls finely and fully developed with waists as large as their busts, and with good healthy

bodies, fit to become mothers and beget healthy children, and why, because it would be money in their parents' pockets.[54]

Amelia blamed parents and society by arguing that cities that erect saloons on every corner "and houses of ill-fame" are complicit in men's negligence to their families. She referenced the scandals of Victoria Woodhull and Henry Ward Beecher as prime examples of parents' moral failings in influencing their children's characteristics. Woodhull's first husband was an alcoholic, and their first child was so mentally deficient that he could never live alone. Her statement about Beecher likely referenced his public affair with his friend's wife, Elizabeth Tilton.[55]

Amelia went further, placing blame for future criminal behavior on the upbringing provided by parents. Not only did she address parents' behavior after birth, but she looked at their behavior before birth. Her general policy on antenatal and postnatal parenting was undoubtedly ahead of her time. Finally, she blamed society for providing the establishments that lead to male vice and, ultimately, parental neglect. Her sarcastic reference to men paying vast sums of money for a pig but nothing for their child's health—unless they profited from it—made scores of men in the audience squirm in their seats and their wives sit up just a bit straighter. Looking closely at the news report, it appears Amelia was offering her own opinions, and this too was astounding for an audience used to women speaking in trance, or not at all.

Even when critical of her reasoning, Kansas papers, unlike those in Texas, respected her presence on the platform while disagreeing with her policy statements:

> In listening dispassionately to Mrs. Colby, one must acknowledge that she is imbued with earnest and sincere motives ... Though she may claim that science has driven God from heaven, and hell from the center of the earth, that there is no longer a need for the Christian religion, we think Mrs. Colby and all other progressive lecturers do wrong in not first seeking to establish the tenableness of their own position before endeavoring to demolish the groundwork whereupon rests the basis of the principles they seek to root out from the human mind.[56]

Amelia continued lecturing in various parts of Kansas throughout 1877. Olive remained at her side, performing musical solos before and after each lecture. The press either complimented Amelia, criticized her, or ignored her. While she generally remained above the fray, she was not wholly immune to criticism and could strike back in the sharpest terms possible. One paper, *The Pleasanton Observer-Enterprise,* was the recipient of her sarcastic wit following a critique of her performance. The editor noted that Amelia attracted a large audience and complimented her speaking ability. He referred to her caustic remarks about "the wickedness" of men and arguments for "the rights of downtrodden women." Amelia claimed that "all the woes of America will be mitigated immediately when women get their rights, and it is time we lords of creation should remove the yoke of oppression from the neck of the weaker sex." The editor continued his appraisal of Amelia:

> By request, Mrs. Colby again occupied the platform Sunday evening and had a crowded hall for an audience. Her subject on this second occasion was "Food for the Starving Million," a political theme which she handled with no little ability. Mrs. C. claims to be inspired, but by what or whom, she does not state. The idea of inspiration is repugnant to us, as the only "inspiration" we have seen undeniable examples of is that drawn from a whiskey bottle, albeit they do tell us Moses and Mark and St. Paul and other saints and fathers were inspired. But while we cannot swallow Mrs. Colby's "inspiration" claim, we are perfectly willing to give her due credit for being a good speaker. Her grammar is far from faultless, but she is nevertheless to be commended as a lady of more than average power, ability, and eloquence.[57]

The article has the tone of an abusive husband—beat her up, praise her, comfort her, and then beat her up again. Apparently, Amelia felt the same way, and in one of her very few letters to an editor, she responded:

> Ed. Observer: Having read your article in which you express your opinion of my lectures given here last week, let me, as a friend, say I am sorry

that the plain, good and inteligent [sic] people of the little village [sic] of Pleasanton are compelled to receive their newspaper communications from an editor who knows little else but "slang," particularly when speaking of woman [sic]. You say, "you cannot swallow Mrs. Colby's inspiration." Let me say, neither can you swallow Mrs. Colby.[58]

The editor printed her letter and castigated her for responding to the original news article as if an editor could criticize, but she was not allowed a voice. He also attacked her intelligence and poor spelling and called her "silly" for writing the letter. Describing her lecture as "a cheap sideshow" with "some of the worst grammar" he had ever had the misfortune to hear, he argued that male lecturers were often criticized but didn't find it necessary to respond to the criticism. He added that his younger colleague had written the article, and if he had written it, "we should say that it was the trashiest harangue we ever heard." Claiming that her inspiration was "an arrant humbug," he then ended the piece with an offensive reference to the final statement in her letter:

Mrs. Colby relieves us upon one point in regard to which we might otherwise feel some anxiety. She says we "cannot swallow her!" We really hope that is a fact, for there is no certainty as to what possibilities one may in a moment of "inspiration" or something, undertake, and the result of such a feat as that would be something horrible to contemplate. We advise Mrs. Colby to trade off her old spirit for one that knows how to spell and will not inspire any more foolish notes to editors.[59]

There is no documented response to this rant against Amelia, but there was outrage within the Spiritualist and liberal societies in the community. Relishing in this, the editor, Dr. Henry Plumb—who had only been an editor for two years—took comfort in hiding behind his editorial status without giving his name. He was a surgeon by trade, and it is not surprising that the good doctor was outraged by the audacity of a woman who questioned the authority of the paper and vicariously himself. His arrogant, authoritarian tone was typical not only of his profession but of those with the same social standing within the community.

One of the founding members of Pleasanton, Dr. Plumb served on the city council. His assertion that male lecturers took criticism without comment is untrue since both men and women maintained lively debate via newspapers that often went on for weeks or even months. It is quite possible that the paper began losing subscribers following his attack on Amelia. By April 1, Dr. Plumb had sold his share of the paper to the younger and more circumspect original editor, Joseph Bacon.

The doctor's words highlight the very point Amelia was trying to make in her letter. The editor "could not swallow" or abide a female who dared to lecture in public, whether inspired or not, and draw huge crowds who supported and praised her. Amelia's grammar and spelling errors may have highlighted her lack of education or simply reflected her anger such that she wrote the letter quickly and sent it without further thought or review. These attacks were the typical reception and response that female Spiritualist lecturers received from those outside the community of believers.

Amelia continued to lecture to crowded houses in Kansas and made one final lecture trip to Texas in March of 1878. In April, she started for home with the *Banner of Light* reporting that she and Olive would spend June and July in Indiana, and were willing to lecture in Indiana and Illinois during those months. It would also be a personal trip so Amelia could visit her three adult children and her grandchildren, all living in the Muncie, Indiana, area.

Amelia gave lectures to Spiritualists in Indianapolis and Colfax, Indiana, on her way from the West. A small town northwest of Indianapolis, Colfax was significant as a midway point for all rail traffic. Trains intersected from north, south, east, and west, so it was a natural jumping-off point for lecturers heading in every direction. The response to Amelia's lectures in Colfax is in stark contrast to Pleasanton. A correspondent to the *Banner of Light* heaped praise on Amelia and Olive. They identified Amelia as being from Chicago and Olive as "a musical medium" from California.

Amelia delivered two lectures on what the reporter called "the bigotry of a strongly orthodox community," stating that Amelia's eloquence electrified the audience. Held in a Christian church, the first lecture was so astounding that it was "the principal topic under discussion upon our streets all the next day." On Sunday evening, Amelia delivered the second lecture to a standing-room-only crowd. She discussed the beauty of Spiritualism and shared the Spiritualist view of immortality. The audience was both thrilled and utterly enchanted by her performance. People likely heard the concept of universal salvation for the first time and reveled in the idea that individual conscience existed beyond the grave. It was an eye-opening experience, so much so that "a good Methodist (of an intelligent and liberal type) becoming enthusiastic, arose and announced another lecture for Monday evening, declaring that he would defray all expenses himself." The good Methodist and others donated funds, and Amelia spoke on Monday night for nearly two hours upon the "Comparison of Bible and Modern Spiritualism." Comparing their similarities, Amelia concluded that the divinity of the Bible proved the divinity of Spiritualism. The reporter called it a "grand success" and stated that Spiritualism would be the death knell of "bigotry, superstition, ignorance, and priestly intolerance."[60]

Amelia's lectures highlighted the benefit that itinerant speakers gave to a curious public and helped spread the philosophy of Spiritualism in ways that small parlor seances could not. Despite the growing discontent with Spiritualism due to fraudulent mediums, the philosophy was a breath of fresh air to those indoctrinated with fears of Calvinist and Catholic ideas of heaven and hell. She also confirmed the legitimacy of Spiritualism by linking it with the manifestations in the Bible. If the accounts in the Bible are valid according to orthodoxy, then the manifestations of Spiritualism must also be true. The difference was that the phenomenon of spirit communication was "scientifically" proved now, and believers did not have to rely on clergy to "interpret" for them as they interpreted scripture for others who remained ignorant.

Amelia's lecture itinerary during June and July was limited in Indiana, and by August 1878, she and Olive had left for New York. The East, and particularly New York, was the hub of Spiritualism. Despite plans to return to Kansas after their New York engagement, they stayed in the East for years as Amelia's reputation for political and spiritual agitation became legendary.

THE FEMALE INGERSOLL

BACK IN NEW YORK, after years of marriage and travel as an itinerant lecturer, Amelia felt as if she had returned to her childhood home. The old "burned-out district" of New York now fueled a new fire of freethinkers, atheists, agnostics, Spiritualists, and women suffragists. In truth, the fire had been lit in the late 1850s when Spiritualism raced across the nation. New York and Massachusetts were hotbeds of freethinkers who pushed the societal envelope as far as possible. In addition, Seneca Falls—where the first women's rights convention was held in 1848—nurtured women who would not be silent, and religious organizations such as the Quakers were changing their approach to the world.

Amelia's assaults on Christianity were not new, and she may have initially been inspired by women reformers at Seneca Falls, just before her marriage. Elizabeth Cady Stanton and Lucretia Mott were some of the first women to identify Christianity as the source of women's oppression. Both made their attacks on Christianity well known, and Amelia, as a young woman in western New York, found them impossible to ignore. In addition, her revolutionary war patriot grandfather shared with her Thomas Paine's book *The Age of Reason*, which includes an attack on Christianity. This suggests that Amelia was revolutionized long before her marriage to Hylon. By the time she returned to New York in August 1878, she was in league with some of the most radical thinkers in the nation, and she reveled in it. However, she continued to speak almost exclusively to Spiritualist organizations, and her lectures included information about the afterlife as well as social reform issues. Her more radical political lectures were generally reserved for freethinker conventions and liberal Spiritualist societies.

Despite the lack of modern-day, super-speed communications, word traveled in nineteenth-century America. By the time Amelia reached New York, her reputation as an outstanding trance lecturer had preceded her, and she was in great demand. While attending a Spiritualist camp meeting in Freeville, New York, she met with Theron C. Leland, who told her about the Freethinkers Convention at Watkins Glen, New York, that had just ended. The events that occurred there outraged Amelia's sense of freedom of speech, freedom of the press, and individual sovereignty, so much so that she took the Watkins Glen issue as the subject of her lecture that afternoon.

Watkins Glen was a small orthodox community whose citizens had no idea what they were about to witness. The speakers at the Freethinkers Convention held there in August 1878 comprised a Who's Who of the country's freethinkers. They included Matilda Joslyn Gage; Elder Evans, a freethinker from the Shaker community; Andrew Jackson Davis; Frederick Douglass; and Julia Ward Howe. Additionally, there was Mary Tillotson, a dress reformer who wore her *pants* to the convention; Ella E. Gibson, author of *The Godly Women of the Bible by an Ungodly Woman of the Nineteenth Century*; and Laura Cuppy Smith Kendrick, a Spiritualist and free love advocate. Lucy Colman, an abolitionist and radical freethinker, and Amy Kirby Post were also attendees, while Robert Ingersoll and Elizabeth Cady Stanton were scheduled to speak but had to send regrets at the last minute. Finally, De Robigne Mortimer Bennett, better known as simply D.M. Bennett—who was the editor of *The Truth Seeker*, the nation's largest freethinking newspaper in America—completed the honorable mentions. He recalled the effects of the freethinkers on the citizens of Watkins Glen:

> The Watkins people are excessively pious, and they hate freethinkers with an intense hatred. Several of them made the humane remark that we ought all to be hung [sic]. As we walked their streets, we

more than once heard uncomplimentary and uncalled-for remarks made about us as we passed.[61]

After three days, the convention became ugly as orthodox preachers from town asked for and received a voice on the platform. At that point, they immediately denounced the freethinkers in no uncertain terms. Rumors flew that attorneys and clergy from the town planned to arrest and jail some of the participants at the convention, and by Saturday the mood had turned hostile. The convention became chaotic when law enforcement descended upon the grounds and arrested D.M. Bennett, Josephine Tilton, and W. S. Bell, a freethinker and Boston publisher, for selling obscene literature, specifically *Cupid's Yokes* by Ezra Heywood. The pamphlet offered a severe critique against marriage, arguing that it was no more than a contract to keep women in legal prostitution for life, and proposed free love as the remedy.

The pamphlet also discussed contraception and issued a scathing critique of Anthony Comstock and the "Comstock laws." Anthony Comstock was a religious zealot who in 1873 lobbied Congress to pass an anti-obscenity law making it illegal to send obscene literature through the mail. Comstock became a special agent for the U.S. postal service and was secretary for the New York Society for the Suppression of Vice. The law was so vague that it gave unlimited freedom to postal employees to determine what was obscene. In Comstock's eyes, obscenity included any book or pamphlet that addressed birth, contraception, or abortion. He also included gambling and prostitution in his efforts to bring morality to the people of New York. Outraged by the contents of *Cupid's Yokes*, Comstock had the author, Heywood, arrested and jailed in the summer of 1877. Heywood ultimately received a pardon from President Rutherford B. Hayes, in large part due to the efforts of Lucy Colman. Although the contents of the pamphlet remained illegal under the law, he continued to sell it after receiving the presidential pardon.

D.M. Bennett was arrested for selling *Cupid's Yokes* at Watkins, even though he neither wrote nor necessarily agreed with it. He had been selling the pamphlet for some time through orders via *The Truth Seeker*. Josephine Tilton, the sister-in-law of Ezra Heywood, had brought the pamphlets to sell at the convention in hopes of giving financial aid to Heywood's wife and children while he remained in jail. She left her booth for a short time, and Bennett and Bell watched over it for her. One of them sold the book to the wrong person—the brother of the Schuyler County grand jury judge, who immediately gave it to the judge. The minute the orthodox judge read the booklet, he dispatched the local police and arrested all three. Amy Post provided bail for Bennett and Bell, and another offered to pay bail money for Tilton so that none would have to go to jail. All three returned to the convention that same day.[62]

Amelia, along with nearly all freethinkers in the nation, was appalled and outraged at this miscarriage of justice. When she spoke about the Watkins fiasco, she did not hold back—every Freeville Convention attendee knew what had happened and how she felt. Theron Leland wrote to Bennett:

> The morning session was addressed by Amelia H. Colby—and I am glad I didn't sell a "Cupid's Yokes" and get shut up at Watkins, and so have failed to hear this grand, brave woman. She is a magnificent structure on the most approved mental and physical model—about two hundred and fifty pounds of well-proportioned woman of the Roman matron style. I wish all the world could have heard her, and, with a trifle of addition to her voice, they might. I never heard so powerful, so sonorous a voice in a woman. It is especially adapted to grove-meetings, of which she has addressed many hundreds. She can compete successfully with rattling leaves, loud talkers, crying children, and neighing horses; and, in church, no snorer could be heard enough to disturb the meeting. And yet it is a voice which the fair owner—for she is fair—knows how to manage with artistic and thrilling effect.
>
> ...So she took for the subject of her discourse, "The Watkins Convention," and she came to its support bravely and well, and denounced the pious conspirators against intellectual and social freedom with all the force and fervor which a brave, talented, untrammeled woman can bring to bear on such a subject.[63]

Bennett's *Truth Seeker* reported the entire convention proceedings later that year, including the facts of the arrests. Bennett made it his mission in life to share every sordid detail he knew about Anthony Comstock and his scurrilous operations on behalf of the government. It was well known that Anthony Comstock had been after Bennett for years. His primary goal was to end the publication of *The Truth Seeker,* which Comstock saw as one of the country's most diabolical and obscene newsletters. Comstock determined he could do this by getting rid of Bennett outright.

D.M. Bennett had published his first issue of *The Truth Seeker,* a news journal dedicated to liberal thought, in 1873. The journal advocated not just the separation of church and state, but the complete disintegration of Christianity. It included articles about free love, abolition, free speech, birth control, and other liberal ideologies that spanned a wide variety of thought. Comstock first arrested Bennett in 1877 for writing and selling his *Open Letter to Jesus Christ* pamphlet and for publishing a scientific tract titled *How Do Marsupials Propagate Their Kind?,* written by a former minister turned amateur zoologist.

The *Open Letter* was an incendiary document that offended orthodox Christians far and wide. Often referring to Christianity as the "youngest mythology," Bennett directed a series of rhetorical questions to Jesus. Had Jesus participated in the Crusades and did he approve of the Holy Inquisition? Then he asked, "Has not the religion called after your name caused more bloodshed, more persecution, and more suffering than all the other religions in the world?" Bennett also, and more frivolously, tweaked the noses of all Christians with a series of questions that were sure to enrage them. He asked Jesus whether he had been "begotten by the Creator" and was it the same process as for every other living being? He then wondered whether love had anything to do with it, "and if so, was it an example of free love?"[64]

Comstock condemned both works as obscene but seemed particularly offended by the sex habits of both humans and animals in the *Marsupials* pamphlet. The 1877 charges were dropped only after Robert Ingersoll, an eminent attorney nicknamed "The Great Agnostic," intervened on his behalf.[65] Bennett escaped the second arrest at Watkins, but Comstock tricked him into mailing a copy of

Cupid's Yokes a year later. He promptly arrested Bennett for violating the mail laws, a federal offense.

Comstock's methods were well known. He set up publishers, sellers, and writers of allegedly obscene literature by ordering a book under a false name. When the unsuspecting seller mailed the book to him, Comstock would swoop in and arrest the seller. Bennett was well aware of Comstock's persecution and trickery. He spent months after his arrest castigating Comstock and criticizing his methods and fanatical bent toward what he considered to be obscene—whether it met the federal definition or not. Nevertheless, Comstock had the federal government behind him and most judges in his pocket. It was not particularly helpful for his trial when Bennett used *The Truth Seeker* to denounce Comstock in print. He knew that Comstock read every issue:

> ...He is a mercenary, false-hearted, unprincipled, persecuting bigot. He got up his society, called "The Society for the Suppression of Vice," he procured himself to be appointed its Secretary and Chief Mogul at a salary of $4,000 a year, besides traveling expenses, hotel bills, etc., amounting to some $2,500 more. Whether he pockets the usual share of the plunder which goes to informers one-half the fines obtained, there can be but little doubt that his income from blackmail is by no means inconsiderable...[66]

In the same issue, Bennett reviewed the beating of Dr. J.A. Russell by the Ku Klux Klan, which had occurred while Amelia was lecturing in Texas. He compared the Klan to Comstock—a comparison that was sure to infuriate him:

> They performed this Christian deed not because the Doctor was guilty of any impropriety or had done aught that was wrong, for they declared to him that his life among them had been without fault, but they beat him within an inch of his life because he doubted the truth of the Christian religion and believed in nature rather than supernaturalism. Comstock is just such a Northern Christian Ku Klux ... He is vindictive and cruel and delights in making his power felt and in inciting terror in his victims. The Christian Ku Klux of Belton County [Texas] ought

to elect Anthony Comstock an honorary member of their pious order. He is worthy of them. If they apply the lash and the thong, he applies odium, fines, and imprisonment. If they deprive of life, he deprives of liberty. There is a natural affinity between them. Comstock is virtually a Ku Klux, and his Christian clique is a Ku Klux Klan.[67]

Bennett used *The Truth Seeker* as his voice. It also reflected the voices of all freethinkers who battled for freedom of speech and a free press. He argued that the United States postal laws violated the Constitution's mandate for freedom of speech and a free press and observed that men had been indicted for owning or selling Thomas Paine's books.[68] He also pointed out that others had violated the laws far worse than he. However, Comstock ignored them, either on purpose or as a social favor, and Bennett argued that he focused solely and unfairly on freethinkers. By the time Bennett went to trial, his condemnation of Comstock in the press had sealed his fate, as a furious and revenge-driven Comstock collaborated with the judge to convict him.

The trial was a travesty. It lasted four days, and the newspapers reported it in the most sensational terms. Bennett was not allowed to introduce any significant evidence, and the judge overruled nearly every objection by the defense. Ultimately, the sham trial was not about obscenity but about Bennett's blasphemous views on Christianity, marriage, and social reform. Sentenced to hard labor for thirteen months, Bennett went to the Albany Penitentiary in July 1879. He was sixty years old.

The horror and abuses of the prison were widely known, and Bennett reflected on his possible death more than once. Amelia and Olive, as well as multiple other friends, began a year-long correspondence with him. Bennett originally professed skepticism about Spiritualism and argued for the philosophy of Materialism. However, in one of his letters, he confessed to Amelia that he believed in spirits and the afterlife.

Amelia shared this information with Jay Chaapel, a fellow ex-Quaker, Spiritualist, and freethinker. Chaapel not only confirmed her report with his own experience of discussing the matter with Bennett, but also chose to share it with the world long after Bennett had died. Such a revelation likely elicited disbelief, disappointment, or celebration, depending on where one stood on the matter. In a speech to the newly formed Bennett Liberal League on December 23, 1883, Chaapel revealed that Bennett had professed his belief in phenomena in multiple conversations between 1877 and 1882—and having reviewed his letter to Amelia and Olive, he concluded that Bennett was a Spiritualist rather than a materialist.[69]

The National Liberal League descended into chaos following Bennett's incarceration. Half of its members called for a full repeal of the Comstock laws, and the other half called for a simple modification. The National League ultimately split into two factions after months of arguing. Amelia was entirely in favor of the complete repeal of the laws she saw as an abject suppression of free speech and a free press. Angered by what she regarded as a threat to freedom, she began a series of radical lectures directed against the orthodox church, current political issues, and the government in general, emphasizing Comstock's outrageous behavior. In addition, she and Olive made an all-out effort to sell subscriptions to *The Truth Seeker,* whose operation had been turned over to Eugene MacDonald. Amelia saw their efforts to sell subscriptions as twofold: one, that it helped Bennett's wife with financial concerns, and two, that the journal's continued national voice and presence infuriated Comstock.

In late August 1879, friends Thomas and Marion Skidmore invited Amelia and Olive to Laona, New York, where they attended an initial convention of Spiritualists at Cassadaga Lake. The Skidmores asked Amelia to name their new association, augmenting the beginning of a new camp meeting on the lake. Unsurprisingly, Amelia reported that her spirit guides offered the name "Cassadaga Lake Free Association," a hopeful reference to the importance of free thought and freedom of individual conscience. The Skidmores and other association members embraced the ideas of free thought and happily adopted the new name. Following a year of hard work, and by the time the 1880 camp season arrived, a correspondent predicted that the Cassadaga association would become the "Lake Pleasant of the West"—a reference to the largest, most active, and most popular camp located in Massachusetts. The words were prophetic. Many years after those initial beginnings, and long after Amelia and the Skidmores were gone, the name was changed to Lily Dale Assembly. It is the largest and most popular Spiritualist camp in the nation today.

Amelia and Olive remained in New York to continue their work. In early September, Amelia lectured to the Friends of Human Progress, and a few weeks later, spoke at the National Freethinkers Convention held at Chautauqua Lake, New York. It was a five-day convention filled with a wide array of liberal speakers—according to *The Brooklyn Daily Eagle*, the convention's final day brought 5,000 people to the lake. Amelia shared the platform with Robert G. Ingersoll, Elizur Wright, Frederick Douglass, Elizabeth Cady Stanton, Susan B. Anthony, and Parker Pillsbury. Sadly, there is no extant report of the lectures, but most speakers likely lashed out against Anthony Comstock and his obscenity laws in no uncertain terms.[70]

Amelia traveled to Springville, New York, to speak at a political meeting scheduled by the Greenback Party of the town of Concord. But when Amelia arrived at the hall and approached the speaker's podium, the organizer advised her that she was not the speaker for the evening. Apparently, her admirers and supporters in the organization had invited her to speak without the organizer's knowledge. The *Buffalo Sunday Morning News* recorded the events that followed:

> ...the woman arose and said she had been invited to speak, and as she weighed one hundred and fifty pounds and her hair was short, proposed to hold the floor herself. Although Mr. Briggs is a bachelor and is said to have the kindest regards for the gentler sex, he informed the lady that such was not the arrangements and that he had himself paid for the house in irredeemable paper money, and would insist in presenting the "next Senator," whom he had invited. The lady took the remarks in high-dudgeon, and donning her top-coat and umbrella, rushed down the stairs and—struck Briggs under the left ear! No! No! But walked to the door saying, she was invited to speak upon finance, and if not permitted to speak, she would demand her pay, showing conclusively that finance was her strong hold.[71]

One person in the assembly proposed that the people choose the speaker, who "clamorously called for the female orator." Consequently, the scheduled male speaker stepped aside (taking his water pitcher with him), and Amelia talked for nearly two hours about the financial crisis of the day. When she had finished, she left the hall, and almost the entire body of people left with her, leaving a small cadre to hear the speaker initially scheduled. It is doubtful that Amelia ever knew that she had not truly been invited to speak. However, when confronted by the "no, you can't" command, her anger was evident at the attempt to suppress her voice. Did she strike Briggs on purpose? It is quite possible. Notably, the newspaper focused on her appearance rather than her reputation or her ability as an orator. This seemed to be the case with many of the national newspapers covering her lectures. Buffalo seemed particularly enthralled with Amelia's looks. As she continued to lecture in the city as late as January 1880, the paper described her again:

> ...a large, heavy woman, very dark-complexioned, with masculine features, heavy eyebrows, black eyes, and wears her hair cut short and parted in the middle. Mrs. Colby spoke in a coarse deep-toned voice, and ... she failed to use them [words] in their right meaning if Noah Webster is any authority.[72]

Later in the article, the author almost grudgingly agreed with her policy platform, arguing for the taxation of churches and the idea that millions of dollars were wasted on a failed church when money should be helping the people. Amelia's lectures on both church and state bordered at times on socialism. Her ideas concerning democracy, equality, and freedom gave birth to her belief that wealth was created by the working classes and wrongfully appropriated by the church and wealthy nobility. In other words, the upper class benefited disproportionately from the underpaid labor of working-class citizens. Later lectures were directed explicitly at the nobility in England and compared their ideas of entitlement with the rich in America, who, she argued, were trying to emulate the noble classes of England.

In mid-September, the camp meetings drew to a close. However, Amelia and Olive continued to receive requests to give lectures in the New York area, so much so that they delayed a planned trip back to St. Louis. They kept their mailing address with the Skidmores in Laona and used that as their resting spot. However, it does not appear that they rested much. The *Banner of Light* reported that they were to dedicate a spiritual hall in Springville in December and travel to Buffalo for the Liberal League a few weeks later. They planned to travel to Gasport for lectures in January and return to Buffalo for an additional engagement. Finally, they ended at Lockport, where Amelia was engaged for several weeks.[73]

The amount of travel undertaken by Amelia and other itinerant speakers was staggering. She and Olive likely took a packet boat along the Erie Canal, thus avoiding the more demanding and bumpier stagecoach ride. Packet boats were popular for travel in the New York area and could accommodate up to 120 passengers. They were colorful and often decorated with flags or bunting. Three horses towed the boats along the canal, but it was still much faster and cheaper than the stagecoach. A trip from Buffalo to Lockport cost $0.38, and at 4–5 miles per hour, it took approximately six to seven hours. Consequently, lecturers could travel reasonably long distances inexpensively and in a relatively short time, making New York a profitable venture.[74]

The Spiritualist Society at Lockport planned a two-day convention in March 1880. Amelia's lectures and Olive's singing were so popular that the society asked them to remain for their Anniversary of Modern Spiritualism celebration at the end of March. Amelia spoke to capacity crowds at Lockport—her lecture titled "The Age of Progress in Which We Live" pointed to many similarities between modern Spiritualism and the Bible. She referred to John of Patmos, who heard the "voice of God," and included Saul and the woman of Endor as examples of manifestation. She concluded that manifestations in biblical times were also present in the modern day, and the church could not refute them.[75]

Amelia and Olive returned to Buffalo for a one-day engagement before traveling to Rochester, where they spent the remainder of April. Rochester, the home of Amy Kirby Post and other freethinkers, was much more amenable to Amelia's ideas than Buffalo had been, and not nearly so concerned with her appearance. On April 5, her lecture titled "The Demands of the Hour" elaborated on the previous address given in Lockport by contrasting scientific progress with the "moral and religious degradation of society." She argued that "60,000 ministers, 64,000 churches, and their $700,000,000 of property" showed no effort to assist the poor. Denouncing the churches for "taxing" the people to support ministers and "maintain so many thousands of costly and elegant edifices of worship," she claimed this injustice "was one of the great demands of the hour." She opposed the union of church and state—and putting God in the Constitution—and finished her speech by calling intemperance a curse and reviewing its harmful effects on the family.[76]

The *Democrat and Chronicle* objectively shared Amelia's views with their readers. Her lecture on "Spiritualism from a Bible Standpoint," presented in the Odd Fellows Temple in April 1880, was one such report. Addressing her eager audience for an hour and a half, Amelia argued on behalf of Spiritualism by stating that the "same laws, the same forces that exist now had always existed" and that scripture proved spirit manifestations from Genesis to Revelations. Her examples of manifestation included the visit of the three angels to Abraham (Genesis 18:2) and the appearance of Moses and Elijah to Jesus (Matt. 17:3). She included the hand that appeared and wrote on the wall of Belshazzar's palace (Daniel 5:24–28) as an example of the hands that manifested in seance rooms across the country. She also alleged persecution against modern-day mediums just as Saul persecuted those with a "familiar spirit" in the past. The news article praised Olive's singing and suggested that she was a "most efficient Sankey" to the distinguished speaker.[77]

These rational lectures, drawing on real examples, made Amelia one of the most popular lecturers on the circuit. She and Olive had been in the western part of New York since late 1878—they now canceled their plans to return to St. Louis after receiving an overwhelming number of requests to lecture in New York, specifically from liberal leagues and Spiritualist organizations. Amelia had become wildly popular, and people were clamoring for her services.

All Spiritualist and liberal lecturers found rich ground in New York, Massachusetts, and other New England states. The call for speakers was not as great in Midwestern and Western states, so it is no wonder that Amelia and Olive delayed their return to St. Louis. This is not to say there were no organizations in the Midwest and West—many of them flourished and begged for speakers to help sustain and grow their organizations. However, the concentration of activity in the East made for a more efficient and prosperous lecture circuit. Even so, travel could be brutal. Lecturers such as Amelia traveled a wide circuit, and popular speakers who commanded hefty fees were kept busy throughout the year. Generally, they traveled from city to city, giving lectures, clairvoyant messages, and seances. Speakers noted for their lecturing proficiency and ability to simultaneously offer clairvoyant messages to individuals in the audience, such as J. Frank Baxter and J. William Fletcher, were in high demand since audiences received the benefit of a general lecture from a spirit being who addressed the entire audience, while many individuals also received personalized clairvoyant messages from loved ones. This made Amelia's immense popularity even more astounding, since she gave general lectures in trance only, without addressing individuals in the audience.

The late 1870s through the early 1890s was a period when many Spiritualists focused on phenomena, and the public demand for new and different phenomena created an environment for increased fraud. Spiritualist papers like the *Banner of Light* dutifully reported accusations of fraud but just as quickly reported the exoneration of those involved. Even when mediums admitted fraud, many Spiritualist newspapers found ways to excuse them. For example, they alleged that negative spirits had materialized masks and cheesecloth unknown to the medium to give the appearance of fraud. Mediums generally argued for increased protection as well as increased pay. They stated that if the payment was better, mediums would not fall into poverty or, in desperation, resort to trickery. Amelia agreed that mediums should receive greater protection, but she would not endorse fraud or deceit, no matter the reason. She also understood that mediumship was the foundation by which Spiritualism lived, and she was determined to ensure its safety.

Amelia and Olive were so popular that the Spiritualists of Rochester encouraged them to remain with the organization through June 1880. This is not unsurprising. Rochester had a robust Spiritualist community, and leaders and freethinkers such as Amy Post were instrumental in giving it life. The *Banner of Light* records Amelia's popularity by reporting that the "large and commodious hall [in Rochester] is filled to overflowing."[78] Most Spiritualist societies survived on donations and the income they received on the door receipts when speakers visited. At first, speakers were given donations from the door receipts. However, for speakers such as Amelia and other popular lecturers, more prosperous societies could offer them a fee of $40–50 outright (equivalent to $1,000–$1,300 in today's purchasing power). A speaker who spent the month in one city, and lectured on four Sundays, could earn a splendid amount, allowing them to continue traveling. However, only a handful of itinerant speakers could command substantial fees, and other lecturers struggled to make ends meet. Consequently, some lecturers would travel with a materializing medium to share expenses and attract a larger audience.

Although all newspapers advertised Amelia as a "trance lecturer," she did not always speak in trance. Several lecture titles are repeated throughout her career, indicating that she spoke in her "normal voice" just as often as her trance voice. It pointed to the growing freedom of women to speak on their own authority rather than being controlled by a spirit. It also sets them outside the typical role for women of the age. Her topics generally addressed the church's hypocrisy, the beauty of Spiritualism and the afterlife, and the day's political issues. She was savvy enough to shape her lectures according to the audience's needs.

Her engagement in Rochester was interrupted by one important event—the "welcome back" meeting held for D.M. Bennett, newly released from prison. The National Liberal League sponsored the event. The NLL was composed of a president, Hon. Elizur Wright, a secretary, Theron C. Leland, and multiple vice presidents who lived across the nation. Amelia was one of the vice presidents serving New York. The celebration was held in Chickering Hall, New York, with a capacity crowd in the 1,500-seat auditorium. However, approximately 3,000 people crowded the standing-room-only hall and outside chambers. Amelia shared the platform with some of the most influential freethinkers of the age, including Stephen Pearl Andrews, Lucy N. Colman, Moses Hull, Ezra Heywood (author of *Cupid's Yokes*), Amy Post, and Thaddeus B. Wakeman. Missing from this exemplary line-up was Robert Ingersoll, who had other speaking engagements.

Amelia's lecture was printed in full in the May 8 edition of *The Truth Seeker*. She electrified the audience with bold statements on liberty and freedom of speech. More importantly, she argued hotly against putting God in the Constitution—a reference to the National Reform Association's multiple attempts to alter the Constitution's preamble. When the Constitution was presented to the states for ratification, outrage and controversy ensued. Attempts to put God in the Constitution and acknowledge that America was a Christian nation began almost immediately. Many were furious at the omission of God and Jesus, who they believed to be the governing power of the country. Still, the founding fathers avoided the reformer attempts to add God to their newly written Constitution, and understood that it posed not "an obstacle to government interference in religion, but to religious interference in government," thus maintaining the separation of church and state.[79]

The original association, the National Association to Secure the Religious Amendment to the Constitution, was formed in January 1864, and its name changed to the National Reform Association in 1875. The bulk of the members were Presbyterian, Methodist, Baptist, and Episcopalian, and its objects were:

> ...the preservation of the Christian Institutions of this country; such as our civil Sabbath; the Bible in the public schools; the securing of a uniform marriage and divorce law conformed to the law of Christ; the retention of the oath in our courts; chaplains in our army and navy, etc. Also, to secure an amendment to the Federal Constitution that would in suitable terms recognize the authority of Jesus Christ as the Governor of the Nation, thus placing the Nation in right relation with God and at the same time affording a legal basis for the Christian Institutions of our country.[80]

The amendment of the preamble, proposed in February 1863 before the Association's formal organization, remains on its website today (2022):

> WE, THE PEOPLE OF THE UNITED STATES, recognizing the being and attributes of Almighty God, the Divine Authority of the Holy Scriptures, the law of God as the paramount rule, and Jesus Christ, the Messiah, the Savior and Lord of all, in order to form a more perfect union, establish justice, insure domestic tranquility, provide for the common defense, promote the general welfare, and secure the blessing of liberty to ourselves and to our posterity, do ordain and establish this Constitution for the United States of America.[81]

At the time of Amelia's 1880 lecture, the battle to put God in the Constitution still raged across the nation. The idea was first presented to President Lincoln, and the National Liberal League argued strongly against the National Reform League's proposals. When Amelia spoke, liberals across the country understood that if religion were allowed to influence government, men such as Anthony Comstock would be unfettered in their attacks on a free press.

Amelia spoke in trance and in her normal voice during her delivery. She warned the crowd that the demand to put God in the Constitution was an outrage, and "you are standing upon the brink of a political abyss, of a national revolution, that nothing can save you from unless you educate yourselves, or unless you use the sword and bullet as in days gone by." She then argued that it was not God in the Constitution that lifted the foot of slavery off slaves and gave enslaved men their citizens status, but rather a reasonable and discerning population. She asked why young and old men died in the Civil war: "Was it so that a priestly power sixty thousand strong should say to the American people what they should send through the United States mail and what they should not? I answer, No!" She ended with the most emphatic statement of liberty that anyone could make:

America's freedom should be protected; that every child belonging to her soil; that every person who came and supped with us beneath our sunshine, that every human being who came to our shores, whether begotten in America or upon the shores of the Old World, should have equal rights, privileges, and liberties throughout every condition belonging to the government of the United States and the statutes of your states. Are these of a necessity? Are these things facts? Is it a fact that a man has been imprisoned unjustly? Is it a fact that two men, hundreds of men, have been defrauded of their property? Their good name has been destroyed under these rules of tyranny that the power of the church has been wielding ever since you and I have had any history of her existence. Whenever you put God into your Constitution, you put every American citizen out.[82]

At this ending, "Whenever you put God into your Constitution, you put every American citizen out," the reporter stated that the vast crowd applauded for five minutes. Amelia's statement was not original. It was a paraphrase of a statement made by Robert Ingersoll in an 1873 lecture titled "Individuality," which said, "They knew that to put God in the Constitution was to put man out."[83] Amelia's use of the words "every American citizen" in place of "man" pointedly ensured women's place in the Constitution, and her meaning was evident to the massive crowd of liberals and women's rights activists.

HEAVEN, HELL, AND A RAG BABY

AFTER A SUCCESSFUL WELCOME-BACK celebration for D.M. Bennett, Amelia returned to Rochester for a lengthy engagement. Her popularity and lectures drew huge crowds that filled the Odd Fellows Temple and allowed the Spiritualist Society to profit by adding monies and people to their organization. Her lecture on May 9, 1880—"The Effect of Influences"—had been given on previous occasions in other parts of the country. This was proof that she spoke in the normal voice as often as in trance. A lecture delivered at the Odd Fellows Temple two weeks later was reported in nearly full text in the *Democrat and Chronicle* the following day.

The lecture—"What is Hell, the Existence of Which is Denied by the Progressive Clergymen of Today"—began as a rant against Calvinism. Amelia claimed that early church fathers presented hell to the populace at the "dawn of the Christian religion." Since then, ministers had pounded people with a fear of hell and the idea that only the church could save them. She quoted Mark 16:16 to accentuate her point: "He that believeth and is baptized shall be saved, and he that believeth not shall be damned." Accusing the church of murdering nonbelievers, she said that the death of 400 Scottish Covenanters was just one example.[84]

Amelia acknowledged Calvin as the author of "eternal damnation," which linked him to the concept and theology of hell. His eternal concept of predestination says "All are not created on equal terms, but some are preordained to eternal life, others to eternal damnation..."[85]

Calvin's ideas and the Protestant Reformation traveled to Scotland via John Knox (Calvin's disciple). Amelia may have been referring to the battle between Scottish Covenanters and the English king, who refused to give them freedom of religion. That period, from 1684 to 1688, was known as the "Killing Times," when thousands of Covenanters or Protestants were tortured or killed for refusing the Catholic church and, thereby, King Charles II—at least in the king's eyes.[86] Amelia continued her attack on Calvin by referring to his denouncement of Michael Servetus, who was burned at the stake for heresy.

Michael Servetus was a Spanish theologian, physician, cartographer, and Renaissance humanist. He rejected Calvin's concept of the Trinity and stated it was not based on the Bible but on the Greeks who originally formulated it. Advocating a return to the simplicity of the Gospels and the teachings of early church fathers before the Nicene Council, Servetus wrote *Christianismi Restitutio* ("The Restoration of Christianity"). This was a response to Calvin's *Institutions of Christian Religion*, where Calvin declared the theology of predestination. It was an act of courage, and this alone endeared him to every living freethinker—but more so was his refusal to recant his "heresy." Amelia's "horrible death" reference was well known. Servetus was led to the stake, "surrounded by green and leafy oak. On his head was placed a crown of straw, or leaves, besprinkled with sulfur. His body was bound to the stake by an iron chain, his neck held by a strong rope ... and to his thigh was strapped a copy of the fatal book *Christianismi Restitutio*."[87] The fire was slow-burning, lasting for hours until some compassionate soul added fuel, and Servetus' life ended thirty minutes later. Amelia referred to Servetus in multiple lectures to exemplify her disdain and disgust for the brutalities of the orthodox church.

She continued her attack on the church by referring to the St. Bartholomew's Day Massacre of 1572 in Paris. She stated that "60,000 Frenchmen were put to death because they could not believe fully in the doctrines of the church, and the pope thanked God that he had been so successful in getting rid of that number of heretics." The massacre that followed was perpetrated by Catholics who attacked any Protestants they could, including women and children. The number of Protestants butchered that day and in the ensuing three months remains unclear and may never be known.[88]

Amelia continued her analysis of hell, pointing out that there were many clergy members who no longer believed in it. She even named some of them—including the most popular minister in the country, Henry Ward Beecher—and told the audience that even those who did preach a hellfire and brimstone sermon did not believe in hell, they just wanted the congregation to believe it. It was easier to use fear as a tool to receive funds and maintain control of the populace. Amelia appealed to the audience's reason:

> How can the loving wife be happy in heaven, while her kind and loving husband, yet dying unbaptized and out of the church, is to suffer eternally the torments of hell? Can the father, the mother, enjoy the beatitudes of heaven while the child of their love is doomed to the eternal consuming fires of hell? Yet such is the force of early education and the teachings of theology ... According to this same theology, the fires of hell must be immense ... I do not recall any instance where the fires came up from that region and destroyed towns, cities, and human lives. But we read of repeated instances when fire came down from heaven and destroyed cities and many lives. Fires came down upon Sodom and Gomorrah, and fires came down from heaven and destroyed a captain and fifty men on two occasions.[89]

Amelia's sarcasm was not lost on the audience. The reporter summarized the remainder of her speech by stating that she closed with an earnest appeal to all to work for the elevation of humanity, and stressed the importance of extending love and sympathy to the sinful instead of threatening them with eternal damnation. Loud applause from the large audience signaled their approval of her talk.

Amelia and Olive spent May and June in Rochester, providing lectures and music to a grateful Spiritualist Society. Her talk "The Necessity for the Advancement of Spiritualism as a Science" emphasized that Spiritualism had existed throughout the ages, but the populace had not recognized it. She argued that "spiritual science would demonstrate this truth." She also gave lectures on "Death—Its Necessities and Philosophies," "The Opposition to Modern Spiritualism and the Inconsistencies of its Opponents," and "Who Are Christians and What is Christianity."[90] Unfortunately, no reports of the actual lectures are recorded, but several of the titles are seen in later speeches to other societies. At the end of her tenure, the Spiritual Society of Rochester thanked Amelia and Olive with a series of resolutions, which was not uncommon for that time. The resolutions were elaborate and effusive, heaping praise and gratitude on the women. They called Amelia a gifted speaker, who presented the truth of Spiritualism and her views on history, philosophy, and other belief systems, even when those views "were at variance with general public thought." They praised Olive, calling her "the sweet singer of our Israel." Their final resolution was to provide a copy of the resolutions to Amelia and Olive, and to the *Banner of Light* and the *Religio-Philosophical Journal* for publication.[91]

The wordy and very formal "thank you" did several things. First, formal "thank you" resolutions were standard for most Spiritualists, who appreciated good lecturers, while publishing them in Spiritualist newspapers gave an added gold star to the speaker. Other societies took notice, and it wasn't long before the speakers' talents were requested elsewhere. It was an effective marketing tool, but it was not done in every case, making it more rewarding. The second resolution acknowledged that Amelia's lectures weren't "cookie-cutter" and that while not everyone accepted her views, they provided "food for thought"—which was the whole point of learning. Finally, they gave a lengthy statement, telling others that the society was closing for the summer, a common practice for nearly all Spiritualist societies. Organizations stopped all meetings so their members could attend the numerous grove meetings throughout the nation. Grove or camp meetings were usually held near a lake or, at the very least, in a wooded area, where the cool breezes off the waters or the shade of mammoth trees gave people relief from the summer heat in the city.

After agreeing to return to Rochester for a month-long engagement in October, Amelia and Olive began an extensive tour that lasted through the summer. They traveled throughout New York in July and presided over the dedication of Champlin's Opera House in Little

Valley, New York; lectured and sang at grove meetings in Byron in early August; and traveled to the Cassadaga Lake camp meeting for the remainder of August. They included a Freethinkers Convention in Hornellsville during September after their engagement at Cassadaga. Amelia and Olive identified their permanent address as Laona, New York, and suggested that anyone who wished their services along these routes should contact them there.[92]

The Laona address suggests Amelia and Olive remained in contact with their old friends the Skidmores, and likely planned to stay with them by the time they reached the Cassadaga campgrounds. Their route and mode of travel are unclear, but the assumption is that they used boats, trains, and coaches throughout the journey. Their New York trip during July and August covered an astounding 625 miles, and their return to Rochester in October added another 70 miles to their schedule. Whether Spiritualist, liberal, or freethinker, lecturers were grateful for engagements that lasted a month or more in the same locality.

Amelia and Olive spent several weeks at Cassadaga, which held its dedicatory services on June 15, 1880. The camp meeting did not open until August 8 and continued to the end of the month. In addition to Amelia, Spiritualist powerhouses W.J. Colville, Elizabeth Watson, A.B. Spinney, and O.B. Kellogg were scheduled to speak. Mrs. Elizabeth L. Watson was the principal speaker, dedicating her speech to "Free Thought, Free Speech, and Free Investigation."[93]

On August 31, Amelia and Olive attended a five-day Freethinkers Convention where Amelia spoke to a crowd of approximately 1,000 people. The list of speakers was impressive: Robert G. Ingersoll, Lucy N. Colman, Elizur Wright, George Chainey, Thaddeus B. Wakeman, C. Fannie Allyn, Parker Pillsbury, and Charles Bradlaugh, a Member of Parliament in England, to name but a few. The convention was reported in multiple papers nationwide, including in North Carolina, Pennsylvania, and New York. *The Charlotte Observer* titled its column "Howling Infidels." The heading is misleading as the column provided a relatively fair and objective review of the general convention, and noted that the freethinkers were confident enough to allow a Christian evangelist to address the crowd. In truth, the "evangelist" was a Catholic who spent his lecture time criticizing Protestants rather than freethinkers. Parker Pillsbury answered him, and "he dissected the Catholicism and Protestantism ideas ... there was more food for thought in Pillsbury's lecture than in all the sermons that have preached in town for the last ten years." The paper acknowledged Amelia and pronounced her "to be the ablest female speaker on the continent."[94]

The objective tone of the southern paper is uncommon. Generally, freethinkers and Spiritualists were not welcome in most southern states, which upheld the Bible as the ultimate authority. It is also curious that this paper provided more detail than its northern counterparts, such as *The New York Times,* which only printed a very brief paragraph on the event. Sadly, no newspaper sent a journalist to record the speeches.

George Chainey, an ex-minister and recent convert from Christianity, reported the convention in more glowing terms for the readers of *The Truth Seeker.* His description of Amelia contrasts with conventional papers, whose journalists described her appearance in less than savory tones.

> ...Her presence is majestic and commanding. The poise of her head with every feature revealed a majestic and imperial mind. Whatever may be the source of her power, I cannot but admire and be thankful for the presence among us of such a storm and tempest of thought. Her audacity takes away the breath almost of ordinary people. In one of her addresses to the political situation she trod so hard upon the toes of some of the partisans in the audience they forgot themselves and hissed, but she thanked them for acknowledging that they were hit and passed on to hit somebody else. Her logic sometimes limps, and occasionally she begs the question with an assumption. Still, these are only as a few dead limbs upon the great, all-powerful stream of passion, sarcasm, and eloquence with which she bears the freighted vessels of thought to every mind. I care not whether she speaks from her own splendid intellectual and moral power or by the help of the spirits. I am only too thankful to know that wherever she goes, she cannot help but do much to purify the dead calm of ignorance and faith.[95]

Amelia and Olive returned to Rochester, where they spent October, November, and December. During their stay, Amelia gave a political speech, unlike most Spiritualist lecturers of the day, titled "Cause and Political Remedy for the Present Condition of the Country." She shared the platform with Olive, as well as Lucy N. Colman and Amy Kirby Post, both well known abolitionists and women's rights advocates. There were no male speakers on the platform that evening, and Lucy Colman pointed out that "we must be progressing when an audience like that, on such a night, came to listen to a political lecture by a woman."[96]

The journalist for the *Democrat and Chronicle* commented first on Amelia's appearance before getting to the gist of her speech. He described her as medium height with a "somewhat peculiar face," adding that she was dressed in black and wore her hair short. He continued:

> Mrs. Colby's voice is very powerful, and she spoke for nearly two hours without showing any signs of exhaustion. To hear without seeing her, one might easily imagine himself listening to a man. But undoubtedly, the lady will consider this a backhanded compliment. She very distinctly expressed the opinion last evening that men are only "poor critters..."[97]

Before Amelia's speech, the reporter observed Olive singing "Only Three Grains of Corn, Mother" while accompanying herself on the guitar. Amelia then compared the song with the current state of hunger in America where people were "dying for want of food." Disagreeing with this assertion, the reporter stated that America was currently enjoying "good times." Whether Amelia was referencing the immediate past or the very near future cannot be known. However, the country had just come out of the "Long Depression," which lasted from 1873 to 1879. By 1880, there was more prosperity in urban areas, but not necessarily in rural locations. In 1882, America would enter a recession that lasted through 1885. In that period, poor speculation and outright corporate fraud created conditions for bank suspensions and a few failures, but more harshly, a cash suspension that restricted access to funds and further exacerbated the burden on the working class and the poor, as well as on businesses. Amelia's statements may have been pure prophecy from a savvy woman who vociferously read political and liberal news.[98]

Amelia continued to discuss the current candidates for the upcoming 1880 presidential election. Describing America's financial situation before the Civil War, she reminded the audience that "the country had become bankrupt." The reporter observed that she made "some very cutting remarks relative to the Democratic party, considering it dead and buried." She added that envoys tried to borrow foreign money but were unsuccessful:

> The cry for gold filled the land. There was no gold in circulation, it was either locked up in the vaults of the wealthy, or it had been shipped to other lands. Something must be done, and $250,000,000 of treasury notes were issued. Subsequently at different times there were issued $150,000,000, $100,000,000, $400,000,000, and $900,000,000. The people did not expect this money was a debt which had to be paid, but that it should be the money of the people put in circulation to do the nation's business. The speaker saw ruin staring this country in the face from the fact that it makes use of two classes of money, one kind for the poor and another for the rich.[99]

Amelia was racing through history in this lecture. Her reference to a lack of money and war refers to the Civil War, when—under President Lincoln—America found itself short of gold, and issued paper money, known as "greenbacks." This currency was backed by federal bonds rather than gold, the standard currency before the war. Fearing a gold shortage, the American people tried to exchange their paper for gold, creating a run on private banks. This caused banks to suspend the payment of paper money for gold, and further panic ensued. By 1863, Congress created the National Bank, which issued a third form of paper currency. At the war's end, Congress began withdrawing paper money from circulation, attempting to re-establish the gold standard. Banks and wealthy industrialists supported the move, but farmers and working men found it easier to repay debts with paper currency. By the late 1860s and early 1870s, the country was pushing westward, and the government helped construct railroads via loans and land grants to private companies. By 1873, an economic surge effectively burst, and the nation was thrown into depression with bank failures across the country. The "Long Depression" lasted through 1879 with no movement on the part of either Republicans or Democrats, both advocating a return to the gold standard but differing on tariff issues. This governmental fiasco resulted in the formation of a third party, the Greenback Party, named for its support of moving to a paper-based currency for the entire country.[100]

The Greenback Party condemned the National Banking System created by the National Banking Act of 1863. It also condemned the Coinage Act of 1873 for its demonetization of silver, and the Resumption Act of 1875, which mandated that the United States Treasury issue specie (coinage or "hard" currency) in exchange for greenback currency upon its presentation for redemption, beginning on January 1, 1879. These acts effectively returned the nation to the gold standard, and the measures created an inflexible currency controlled by banks rather than the federal government. Greenbackers contended that such a system favored creditors and industry to the detriment of farmers, miners, and other working-class laborers.[101]

By 1880, the Greenback Party was the most liberal of all parties. They promoted an eight-hour workday, a graduated income tax, and women's rights, including women's suffrage. It is no wonder that Amelia, Olive, Lucy, and Amy were conducting the meeting to support the Greenbackers and their presidential candidate.

The journalist disagreed with Amelia's statement of "two classes of money," writing that gold, paper, and silver are paid indiscriminately to the rich and the poor. The poor working class and farmers could not repay debts without a standard value for paper money commensurate with gold and a free-flowing currency. However, it was well known that paper money was redeemed at a lower rate than gold, and wealthy speculators could purchase greenbacks at a lower rate and then redeem them for gold. Amelia pointed out they would hoard or redeem them overseas for an even greater amount. She argued that "money is to the body politic what blood is to the human body, and when the circulation is impeded, disastrous results follow." According to the journalist, Amelia supported the "rag baby," arguing for establishing a national greenback currency. She asserted that national banks were unconstitutional "and founded upon the indebtedness of the nation," and maintained that national banks were not needed without national debt.[102]

The "rag baby" was a derogatory term used by Republicans and "hard-money" Democrats to refer to greenbacks or soft money. Denouncing the term, Amelia argued for establishing a national greenback currency that did not have to be redeemed. To do so meant that the working class would have the same buying power as the wealthy. The reporter noted that Amelia had been billed as the "Female Ingersoll" on advertising bills and considered it a worthy title. He also observed that most of the massive crowd in attendance were women—and he didn't have to tell his readers that they had no voting power. It may be that Amelia, Amy, Lucy, and Olive were hopeful these women could influence their husbands to vote for a Greenback candidate for president. If so, they envisioned moving women's rights, workers' rights, and other free thought agendas forward to fruition.

Amelia and Olive continued to serve the Spiritualist societies and the liberal leagues in Rochester through December. They were so popular and successful that the societies retained them until March 1. They stayed with Amy Post throughout their engagement. This was not unusual since many freethinkers, Spiritualists, and other radicals often stayed with Amy for weeks, months, and sometimes years. Notably, Jay Chaapel stayed with her for four years, from approximately 1879 until 1883.[103] In addition, Amy and Amelia were close friends based on their shared liberal beliefs and Hicksite backgrounds. They even traveled together to several freethinker conventions, where both participated by giving lectures to a grateful audience.

At the end of her Rochester engagement, Amy hosted a reception in Amelia and Olive's honor, with many friends gathering at her home to share food and well wishes. After the reception on March 1, 1881, Amelia and Olive left for Ridgeway, New York, for three lectures, and then went on to Gasport for another series of lectures. After these brief stops, they made a long journey to Cleveland, Ohio, to participate in the Anniversary of Modern Spiritualism exercises, a two-day "Jubilee meeting" at the end of March.

The March 5, 1881 issue of the *Banner of Light* noted that Hudson and Emma Tuttle, Parker Pillsbury, Amelia, and Olive were scheduled to speak. A follow-up letter from a correspondent, Thomas Lees, in the April 23 edition of the *Banner* reported that a raging two-day snowstorm kept the audience small, but the celebration carried on as scheduled. Pillsbury was taken ill, and Moses Hull, who happened to stop by, served in his place. Only a brief mention in the *Banner* recorded Amelia lecturing on the second day; however, Grace Parkhurst summarized Amelia's lecture for *The Truth Seeker*.

In Parkhurst's account, Amelia claimed "the church pays a reward for vice, as witnessed in its dealings with Prof. [David] Swing, Dr. [H.W.] Thomas, and H.W. Beecher." Amelia noted that of these three clergymen, the first two were accused of heresy while Henry Ward Beecher had been unfaithful to his marriage vows. Amelia told the audience that Beecher's "punishment" for infidelity was to receive a $10,000 increase in salary. She reminded them of the cruelties surrounding the death of Joan of Arc and denounced the church for its dark and bloody deeds throughout history. By comparison, Amelia claimed that "Spiritualism had shaken theology, shipped off gods and demons, closed the gates of hell, and set humanity free."[104]

Once again, Amelia pointed to church persecution. Prof. Rev. David Swing was accused of heresy by the Chicago Presbytery in 1881 and brought to trial in one of the most sensational acts delivered by the church. Accused of not strictly adhering to the church's "articles of faith" by a Calvinistic fellow minister, it became clear during his trial that he veered only gently from some of the articles of faith and was considered a conservative Presbyterian who preached their accepted doctrines. After a three-day trial, he was acquitted with the public loudly on his side.[105]

Dr. H.W. Thomas, a Methodist Episcopal minister in Chicago, was accused of preaching heterodox sermons by casting doubt on the inspiration of scripture and on the atonement doctrine. Although the Methodists did not race to trial as quickly as the Presbyterians, he was ultimately brought up on charges of heresy. His trial ended in October 1881, after which church leaders expelled him from the Methodist Episcopal Church.[106] Amelia made her point by comparing these two men with the adultery scandal of Henry Ward Beecher, who appeared to have been rewarded by the church despite his behavior. Amelia's continued attacks on the hypocrisy of the Christian church and its outrages against humanity may have offended some members present. However, the liberal Spiritualists who were present wholeheartedly expressed their admiration.

Amelia's pointed attacks were legendary, but this one, delivered on a celebratory Anniversary of Modern Spiritualism, may have been misplaced. The entire lecture is not recorded in any newspaper. Still, Parkhurst's summation in *The Truth Seeker* was enough to reveal that Amelia's first order of business was to discredit the church and its hypocrisy. Her attacks were not unlike those of other women reformers, such as Elizabeth Cady Stanton, Matilda Joslyn Gage, and fellow Spiritualist C. Fannie Allyn. All believed the core root of women's oppression directly resulted from church policy and its sacred scriptures. Amelia was fearless in her lectures and did not care whose toes she might step on. Parker Pillsbury identified this trait, saying that she and Allyn were no longer welcome in some Spiritualist societies. These societies only wanted lectures on "trance, table-tippings, materializations and other mere Spiritual phenomena."[107]

Pillsbury referred to the work Amelia and C. Fannie Allyn had done for the Rochester meeting from October through February. Her lectures often pointed to the good that needed accomplishing on this earth—suffrage and other women's rights, abolition, and freedom of conscience, among others. She tended to the political and material rather than addressing the afterlife, and she often echoed Tom Paine's mantra, "The world is my church, to do good, my religion." Pillsbury's reference to "mere Spiritual phenomena" highlighted a controversy in Spiritualist circles that phenomena had overridden the original intent of Spiritualism and that "faith plus works" was a concern for the living and the dead. He also argued that for all their good works, the Spiritualists in Rochester, the "Bethlehem" of Spiritualism, had still not erected a temple or meeting hall. Although he felt this was a tragedy, he recognized that historically Spiritualists were resistant to creeds, rules and organization. Early Spiritualists felt that permanent structures and organization would constrict the philosophy and free-wheeling intent of Spiritualism.

Nevertheless, Pillsbury's observations regarding Amelia's relationship with some Spiritualist organizations gave voice to a subject not often mentioned out loud. Leaders of some Spiritualist societies feared engaging her due to her attacks on Christianity and the church. However, people showed up in droves to hear her, and those same leaders realized the financial gain she brought to their society. She was more often than not invited back to speak again. More conservative Spiritualists made a case for "Christian Spiritualism" and found examples of mediumship in the Bible that proved their beliefs. Amelia agreed with the idea that mediumship, spiritual healing, and other prophecy examples documented in the Bible verified Spiritualism's legitimacy. However, she maintained that many stories were merely myths, and the church used them to abuse and oppress people. She argued that the greatest tragedy was the hypocrisy of the ministers and priests who oppressed free, rational, and thinking people, specifically women.

Conservative Spiritualists simply did not hold the same view. Spiritualist newspapers such as the *Religio-Philosophical Journal* argued that the "social freedom" question had no place or platform at Spiritualist conventions. The editor and other individuals felt that the "social freedom" question was more about "free love" and that only "pure Spiritualism" should be presented at convention and grove meetings. "Pure Spiritualism" can only be defined by the activities of mediumship, spiritual healing, materialization, and trance work. Thus, Pillsbury correctly identified the issues related to Amelia's work. While she spoke in trance at many sessions, she also spoke in the "normal" voice, meaning that her thoughts alone were the inspiration for some of her speeches. Not everyone wanted to hear her radical views.

"SHE IS A HURRICANE"

FOLLOWING THE CLEVELAND JUBILEE, Amelia and Olive returned to New York. On May 12, 1881, they attended an "indignation meeting" held by the Liberal League of Buffalo to protest against the latest outrage concerning the United States Mail. It seemed the entire state of New York was in uproar over Anthony Comstock's latest attempt to further infringe on the freedom of the public, although the majority of protests came from liberal freethinkers.

Comstock had introduced a bill to the New York legislature that would allow him to enter a person's home without a warrant to look for evidence of obscenity. He asked to have free rein, whether there was evidence or not. Nor would he have to summon local law enforcement, but would be able to arrest and jail alleged offenders without due process. Thaddeus. B. Wakeman, a member of the National Liberal League, appeared before the New York Assembly and argued for the bill's defeat in a lengthy address. The New York legislature agreed with him and voted the bill down. *The Truth Seeker* printed his address over four issues, from April 9 to May 7, 1881.

Comstock, in anger, focused his attention on the alternative health field. He started confiscating health journals at the post office, on the grounds they were obscene. Postmasters were instructed to open packages and read postcards. Anything that remotely pertained to the human body, advertised medical appliances to help relieve pain in certain parts of the body, or was designed to prevent pregnancy, was tossed into the trash. Comstock then arrested and jailed the editors of alternative health magazines for sending obscenity through the United States Mail.

At that meeting, Amelia, Olive, Parker Pillsbury, a delegate from the Rochester Liberal League, and George Whitcome were appointed to the Business Committee and worked on a series of resolutions. Amy Post, president of the Rochester Liberal League, also attended with Pillsbury. Amelia was a member of several liberal leagues in different cities, and her work on behalf of the National Liberal League was well known. The resolutions passed at this meeting were in keeping with indignation meetings held in Boston, Syracuse, and other parts of the country. Still, they were more defined and certainly more explicit in their condemnation of Anthony Comstock and the New York Society for the Suppression of Vice.

The first resolution expressed the Committee's anger that the United States Mail refused to send health journals such as *Physiologist*, published by Dr. Sara B. Chase, *Health Monthly*, by Dr. E.B. Foote, and the *Agent's Advocate* to their subscribers. The United States Post Office refused to forward them "under the most grossly false and absurd pretense that they contain matter indelicate, obscene, and unfit for public perusal." The second resolution stated that problems of increasing abortion, infanticide, and child murder were the direct result of ignorance regarding health and well-being. These journals assisted in educating the public. The third resolution acknowledged the committee's abhorrence of truly "obscene and lascivious" literature. The fourth resolution denounced Anthony Comstock and his New York Society for the Suppression of Vice for "unconstitutional as well as unrighteous attacks upon the freedom of the mails and the press." The fifth resolution thanked T.B. Wakeman for his appearance and efforts in destroying the bill that would increase the jurisdiction and powers of the New York Society for the Suppression of Vice. Finally, the members ordered all resolutions to be forwarded to New York's city editors for publication in their columns—*The Truth Seeker* and the *Daily Truth* in New York; the *Investigator* and *Banner of Light* in Boston; *Mind and Matter* in Philadelphia; and *Western Light* in St. Louis.[108]

The liberals were outraged because it was clear that Comstock persecuted some journals but left others alone. Comstock's friend Samuel Colgate, a prominent New Yorker who supported him and who was president of the New York Society for the Suppression of Vice, had advertised Vaseline as a birth control measure in a pamphlet that was mailed to the general public—a clear violation of federal law. Comstock refused to charge him with any crime.[109]

After the Buffalo meeting, Amelia, Olive, Parker, and Amy returned to Rochester to hold another indignation meeting with the Friends of Progress. At first driven by anti-slavery sentiment, the Friends' focus broadened in later years. Specifically, their main principles were the liberty of conscience; absolute individual freedom of speech and action; freedom of action in each meeting (worship); annual meetings with advisory powers only; meetings open to all; no recording of ministers; whole-hearted support of the anti-slavery cause and support of abolitionists; absolute equality of the sexes, including suffrage; and the reformation of penal laws and the abolition of the death penalty.[110] It should be no surprise that early leaders of the dissident faction included Rhoda DeGarmo, Lucretia Mott, and Isaac and Amy Kirby Post. Quaker Progressives continued to advocate for social reform, continuing the work of the six women who initially met at Seneca Falls. [111]

The Rochester Friends of Human Progress included a non-Spiritualist and abolitionist, Lucy N. Colman, and Spiritualists Amy Post, Parker Pillsbury, Amelia, Olive, and other stalwart liberals. Their resolutions echoed those compiled at Buffalo but made one crucial addition. They acknowledged that current political parties failed to address the liberty and freedom needs of the people, and they called for the creation of a Liberty Party to counteract the failed Republican and Democratic Parties.[112]

Sadly, the resolutions of the various New York societies seemed to have little effect, and Comstock continued his abuses despite growing and widespread outrage. His persistent efforts to restrict all information relating to birth control, the procurement of abortion, or the prevention of venereal disease—which the health journals had contained—continued for years.

Returning to the road, Amelia and Olive traveled to various grove meetings, including Michigan and Pennsylvania. Amelia's reception in Pennsylvania was so great that she was engaged in Philadelphia and Pittsburgh for three months. While in Philadelphia, Amelia and Olive attended a birthday celebration for John Murray Spear, an eccentric but notable Spiritualist. Several mediums brought forth spirits to greet and congratulate Spear, and Amelia gave a trance address from Thomas Paine. A correspondent called it "a grand and most forcible address of congratulation and commendation from the spirit of that great apostle of Liberty ... which was worthy in every respect of that mighty spirit intelligence, and the true, faithful, patient and benevolent man to whom it was addressed."[113]

Spear, an ex-Universalist minister, had come to Spiritualism as a natural result of his early reform work, including his Garrisonian abolitionist activity and efforts toward penal reform in the 1850s. After the Civil War, Spear, as a trance medium, and his wife, Caroline (Hinckley), gave lectures and conducted seances and spiritual healings. They also devoted a large part of their time to reform issues, including organizing a chapter of the International Workingmen's Association in San Francisco, helping to organize Victoria Woodhull's Equal Rights Party, and advocating for women's rights, free love, and suffrage. At one time, Caroline served as secretary of the National Women's Suffrage Association.[114]

Amelia's association with Spear may have placed her in the category of free love advocates, although there is no indication that she spoke either for or against it. She also counted among her many friends Moses Hull, Lois Waisbrooker, and Dr. Juliet Severance, all outspoken advocates of marriage reform and free love equality. Amelia's fierce dedication to liberty, freedom of conscience, and free speech compelled her to see the hypocrisy of Spiritualists who spoke about freedom of religion on the one hand while denouncing the free lovers who argued for removing marriage laws from the state level and allowing people to find their own relational happiness, in whatever way they saw fit.

The success of Amelia and Olive in Philadelphia caused the First Association of Spiritualists to invite her back for a November engagement (to follow a series of lectures in Pittsburgh, in October). Although her speeches were not recorded, they were typically critical of orthodox religion. A correspondent reported to the October 22 edition of the *Banner of Light:* "Rarely have a people been so thoroughly shaken from the ruts of old tradition-land superstition as by the powerful and unique control of Mrs. Colby, which hold her large audiences spellbound throughout the whole series. She is certainly a speaker of great power..."

She received the same accolades in Pittsburgh for her lecture "Who was Jesus Christ?" A correspondent for *The Truth Seeker* reported her speech was "grand, startling, thrilling, and no doubt shocking to the meek-looking, smooth-faced Clergymen present. To them, it came like a clap of thunder from a clear sky. Ten minutes apiece were given them to reply, but they cut a sorry figure attempting to do so."[115]

On her return to Philadelphia, Amelia spoke in trance to an audience of 500 in Lincoln Hall. The *Democrat and Chronicle*, and *The Bucks County Gazette*, reported the lecture. Unsurprisingly, her control was Thomas Paine. Through Amelia, Paine said that a stern, liberal-minded Quaker father had raised him, and his parents had instilled a love for individual liberty in him. He shared his pain when his young wife, Mary Lambert, went into early labor, and died with their child in childbirth. Describing the composition of *The Age of Reason,* he told the audience that every light in the jail was extinguished by 9 p.m. However, he says he wrote his book between 10 p.m. and 2 a.m. as his jail cell "was lighted by an unseen power that enabled me to write as by daylight. I was also endowed with a sensitive faculty that enabled me to tell the location of any verse in the Bible, although I had none." When he reached the spirit world, he found that it was his wife "who had made the light of my cell with the aid of two ancient philosophers and that she had saved me from the guillotine once when my earthly life hung by a thread." Tom described a congress he attended in the spirit world, presided over by an ancient Chinese philosopher who blessed him, and who consented to labor with him "to free the world from the festering chains of theology."

After the revolution, Paine traveled to Europe, where he divided his time between Britain and France. During that period, he wrote another revolutionary tract, *The Rights of Man,* arguing for equality for all people, denouncing hereditary government, and promoting a genuinely democratic republic. The work was acclaimed in France, America, and among the poverty-stricken of Britain. The English monarchy would have none of it, and Paine fled to France before the courts in England could imprison him. Three months later, a London court found him guilty of seditious libel *in absentia.*[116]

Paine's agitation for democracy offended Robespierre, and he was incarcerated in Luxembourg Prison in Paris, where he penned *The Age of Reason.* Whether he accomplished it as told by Amelia is unknown. He did not have a Bible while writing the first part but received a Bible when he wrote the second part.[117] Paine's dissection of the Bible and his criticisms of the church and all monarchies made him a pariah in nearly every country. *The Age of Reason* was effectively a deist manifesto to its core. Paine declared that nature was the only form of divine revelation, for God had established a uniform, immutable, and eternal order throughout creation. The work rejected Christianity, denied the Bible as God's revealed word, condemned many Old Testament stories as immoral, and claimed that discrepancies marred the Gospels. This argument is found in Amelia's later recorded lectures, whether in trance or in her normal voice. In a now-classic observation, Paine states:

> I believe in one God, and no more; and I hope for happiness beyond this life. I believe in the equality of man; and I believe that religious duties consist in doing justice, loving mercy, and endeavoring to make our fellow-creatures happy ... I do not believe in the creed professed by the Jewish Church, by the Roman Church, by the Greek Church, by the Turkish Church, by the Protestant Church, nor by any church that I know of. My own mind is my own church.[118]

After the publication of *The Age of Reason,* Paine was almost universally condemned by the church, upper echelons of government, and upper-class society. However, the "common man" in America and

France never forgot the revolutionary *Common Sense* that led them into a free democracy. They rightly understood that *The Age of Reason* was, as Paine admitted, an "organized religion set up to terrify and enslave mankind, and monopolize power and profit."[119] The poor, the laborer, and the lower classes understood this—even if they did not understand theology, they understood oppression and helplessness. Freethinkers, Spiritualists, and working-class people revered Thomas Paine and celebrated his birthday every year, on January 29, with lectures, music, and food.

Amelia's trance control of Thomas Paine in Philadelphia was the first recorded use of his thoughts, and it would not be the last. When Amelia and Olive's engagement in Philadelphia ended in November, friends hosted a reception in their honor for services to the Philadelphia Spiritualists. The reception included Mrs. Thayer, a flower medium, and John Murray Spear, who "recounted some of the labors of Mrs. Colby, and her very marked success as a lecturer in this city, saying that after her first engagement to speak for the Society, she addressed the Neshaminy Camp Meeting, and many then, he thought, regretted her engagement, fearing that so outspoken a thinker might be dangerous to the welfare of the Society ... and no one has gained a more tender respect by her faithful sincerity."[120]

Spear wrote what many societies thought—that Amelia was too radical in thought, stepped on too many toes, and her political speeches, as well as her repeated attacks on Christianity, would keep many people from attending her lectures. Societies that depended on income generated by speakers and mediums were reluctant to "rock the boat" too hard with someone as reportedly radical as Amelia. Spear's reassurance and "packed house" reference ensured that Amelia would receive continued engagements. Another correspondent from Philadelphia echoed his sentiment:

> She is supposed to be very radical, but she has not harmed us; on the contrary, she has filled our large hall to overflowing with very intelligent and appreciative audiences, whose interest in the lectures has been of the increasing rather than of the waning order. When a speaker can not only draw but hold an audience composed largely

of some of the most intelligent and thoughtful people in our city, it is evidence that the speaking is of a high order. These lectures have not only been an intellectual treat but a financial success, inasmuch as they have interested a class of people who cheerfully aid in defraying the expenses of the Association. Mrs. Colby also gave a benefit lecture on a week-day evening, which netted a handsome profit to the Association ... I will only add that our hall has been insufficient to contain the people who have desired to hear Mrs. Colby, especially on Sunday evenings, when the aisles and vestibule have been densely packed, and many have been obliged to turn regretfully away, unable to gain admittance.[121]

Amelia was so successful that the society engaged her for another month in April 1882. They brought her back again and again for the next ten years. To say that she found a home in Philadelphia, or at the very least, friends of like mind, would be an understatement.

However, it is doubtful that Amelia, while she was in Philadelphia, avoided controversial topics related to orthodox religion or politics. Her speeches may have been somewhat softened compared to those at freethinker conventions, but given her propensity for freedom of speech, she likely spoke as she had always done—and the citizens of Philadelphia were far more radical than their leaders realized. Her success brought many requests for appearances in either case, and she and Olive left for Vineland, New Jersey, for the better part of December. She returned to New York City and appeared at the Harvard Rooms on New Year's Day, in 1882. Her lecture must have taken the same anti-orthodox approach that thrilled the liberal Spiritualists and distressed the orthodox ministers. An anonymous correspondent shared a tribute with the *Banner of Light* editor in a private letter.

She is a hurricane. I like her very much. Last Sunday, her lecture was on "Spiritualism as Warfare," and I regretted exceedingly that there was no stenographer there to report it. I really think it was the grandest lecture I ever heard—so full of telling points and arguments unanswerable that it had a visible effect on one hundred or more orthodoxites who formed a part of the audience. One man, evidently a minister, went out of the hall in a precipitous manner and coming in contact with him in the entry, we had some words together; the result of which was that he went home with some food for thought.[122]

Amelia and Olive remained in New York City through February, then traveled to Boston for the thirty-fourth Anniversary of Modern Spiritualism. The list of speakers was impressive. In addition to Amelia, Mrs. Helen J. "Nellie" Temple Brigham of New York, an inspirational and trance speaker well known by 1882, was also present. As the "settled speaker" for the First Society of Spiritualists in New York City, Brigham routinely worked as a trance lecturer. She often asked the audience for a topic, then composed a poem on the spot. Following travels to England and Australia, she later became internationally known.[123] Also engaged were Mrs. F.O. Hyzer, a well known trance speaker from Baltimore; Edward S. Wheeler, an abolitionist, freethinker, and Spiritualist from Philadelphia; W.J. Colville, a medium, lecturer, and author of numerous books on Spiritualism, new thought, and other esoteric subjects, from England; and several other speakers.

The event was held in the Boston Music Hall, one of the largest venues in the nation. The hall was 130 feet long, 78 feet wide, and 65 feet high, and was capable of seating 2,585 people at maximum capacity. There were two tiers of balconies on either side, with two more on the north end to provide additional seating. An orchestra stage platform girded the southern end of the building. The ceiling, which soared 40 feet above the upper balcony, connected with the walls by a large cove, in which seventeen semicircular windows lit the hall by day. A row of hundreds of gas jets illuminated the hall by night. It was one of the most ornate venues in the country.[124]

Amelia's lecture, "Truth is Immortal, and Cannot Die; Error is Mortal, and Cannot Live," was given in trance to a packed house on March 31 and recorded in its entirety in the *Banner of Light* on May 6, 1882. She began by acknowledging that the lecture's title reflected a statement made by Andrew Jackson Davis years before, and elaborated on the statement's truth. Her comparison between

Christianity and Spiritualism permeated the speech, highlighted with pointed questions:

> If Spiritualism is true, why did it wait all these years and all these ages before it came to the children of earth to give an expression? I might answer it by asking the question, If Christianity be true, why did it wait four thousand and four years before the advent of the supposed Jesus Christ, who was expected to atone for the sins of the world? Why did not Jehovah have Jesus born the first child in the universe? Why did he wait until the souls and spirits of human beings went down into the vortex of hell for four thousand and four years, like the waters of the Niagara which descend over the falls tonight?

Amelia argued that Spiritualism was not a new development but had existed for centuries and was evident in every branch of science, philosophy, art, and spiritual thought. She reported that it, and it alone, was the basis for human growth and progress. Spiritualism "comes to human life"—to the lowly as well as the rich, to America and the people of other continents, to all people, whether good or bad, slave or free, just or unjust, pure or impure. It comes alike to Jew, Gentile, Christian, or heretic; to "all classes of individuals, to everybody that lives in the life of immortal understanding." She asserted that Spiritualism was hidden for years only because the tyranny of the church had been the ruling power in every age. "Tyrants, like demons, are hard to destroy." Thus, she argued, the world had to wait until men and women became wise enough, knowledgeable enough, and refined enough to understand the freedom that arises from a rational mind and a spiritual awareness. Consequently, she said the Declaration of Independence gave Americans their rights. She continued more specifically:

> It declared that every man, woman, and child had the right to life, liberty, and the pursuit of happiness. It declared that they were governed by these inalienable rights and conditions. It also declared that you had the right to worship God according to the dictates of your own conscience or not worship God at all. Hence these liberties and these privileges meet you as you cross the line of life; they shake hands

with you; they unite their forces, and with the liberty and the purity of principles that your forefathers in the days of the Revolution gave you, they come in contact with you today...

Amelia told the crowd that Christians had been crying out for years and demanding an expression of the spirit. She said they always called on the Holy Spirit and asked God to appear amid their revival meetings: "Oh, Lord, come *now! Now* is the day! *Now* is the accepted time; *now* is the day of salvation. But when the Spirit came, what did the churches do? They closed every door of the church; they said, 'It is untrue.'" She reminded the audience that the spirit raps continued and did not stop despite the investigation of ministers and other men. At this point, Amelia, noted for her sarcastic wit, couldn't help herself. She asked the audience what would have happened if the spirit of Jesus, the Holy Ghost, or God had actually appeared to Christians following their prayers? "I will tell you what I think would have been the result—I think they would, 19 out of every 20, have fled and declared it was the devil." The crowd roared with laughter and applauded loudly.

Amelia reminded the crowd about accusations of fraud against the Fox sisters in the early years. Critics accused the children of cracking their knee and toe joints to produce raps. At that time, an investigative committee led by Rev. Henry Ward Beecher reported that the little girls could not crack knee and toe joints to produce raps. Rev. Mr. Beecher summed up his investigation by alleging that the raps were from the devil:

What made the Rev. Mr. Beecher think it was the devil? Why, for the simple reason that all of God's attorneys suppose they know all of God's business [applause], and as Mr. Beecher did not know that God had anything to do in this matter ... hence he, knowing of only two persons, or personages in the universe; one God and the other the devil, he supposed that if God had anything to do with it, he would have informed Mr. Beecher, of course [applause] and as God had not informed him, he felt bound to say it was the devil.

After this observation, Amelia verbalized what most people thought of her by then: she was an infidel or, rather, an atheist by telling the crowd that it did not matter whether God or devil; she had no use for either. Amelia added that she could hardly take care of herself and had no time to care for gods or demons. "Hence, I stand independent and alone, without either." And then she thumbed her nose at God and Christians. In this instance, Amelia had undoubtedly returned from the trance state and spoke in her normal voice:

> I have often been told, "you will surely be damned." Well, now, I won't—I shan't be damned. God can't damn me. Why? Because I won't be damned. That is the reason. You cannot damn a person when he or she won't be damned; no power in the universe can. Oh, you may shut me up, you may chain me with the chains that burden and destroy my conditions, but you cannot damn a spirit that won't be damned. [Applause]

Her criticisms did not stop with Christianity. She next critiqued her freethinker friends, who ascribed to the materialistic view. They argued that since Spiritualism is not concretely proven, it is therefore not legitimate—and claimed it is no different from Christians who worship an absent God and Christ. Turning that argument back on them, Amelia took issue with them for the first time. First complimenting their intelligence and wisdom, she followed that by saying, "And if they will demonstrate to me those facts, that an individual does not live after he has passed through the ordeal called death, I will give a million of dollars. That is, demonstrate it." She echoed their constant refrain: "I cannot believe a thing that is not proved; I have got to have proof." In other words, materialist freethinkers hold only to the five senses. It is invalid if they cannot experience it with their five senses. Amelia concluded, "If man does not live after he leaves the physical body, who knows it? *Not anybody.*"

She discussed the investigations related to Spiritualism and compared it to Christianity, arguing that no matter what charges had been leveled against Spiritualism, whether called humbuggery or diabolism, Spiritualism had never closed its doors to an investigation.

She further asserted that if Christianity were held up to the same investigative standards as Spiritualism, and reasoning applied, within "26 hours, he would be an infidel." She criticized the church and its ministers by stating that "the church wants to be in complete control of everything. The result is they now have 65,000 ministers, 55,000 of whom are salaried ministers. Yet, they dare not meet the investigations of one simple, uneducated, unlettered, untutored medium that you have now." Here there was wild applause from the crowd. Amelia continued to argue the difference and the benefit of Spiritualism by pointing to the large amount of money that churches required to maintain their structures and ministers. At the same time, Spiritualism, with simple raps, "rocked every church from its base to its steeple." It shook the beliefs of a populace who believed in a personal God and served to rescue humanity. She noted that the church was "1,900 years old," and while Spiritualism was only thirty-four years old, Spiritualism "has opened the door to set humanity free."

Amelia claimed that Christianity only served to make God a tyrant; thus, man becomes a coward and a slave. Arguing that God was not as good as she was, because she would not enslave anyone, Amelia said she would set everyone free by making them "conscience and conscientious." She would have them use their intelligence to investigate every natural law of life. Her sarcastic wit bubbled to the surface to the delight of every female in the audience:

Where is woman now? You scarcely ever hear a lecture or a speech on your rostrums, or in your meetings at any time, or under any circumstances, but that the slavery of woman is talked about. Why is she a slave? You say, by the power of the priesthood; you say, by the powers of the church. Why? They tell you and me that she is not quite as good as the man. Why? Because the man was made first. What was he made out of? Dirt? Yes. [Applause.] Holds his own well! [Laughter and applause.] We don't know what it was mixed up with, but [we] should think from this age that it was tobacco and whiskey. [Applause and laughter.]

How much of him was dirt? All but the breath of life; all the rest of him was dirt. God, after he got him fixed up, breathed into him the breath of life, and he became a living soul. Why didn't God make woman that way? He couldn't do it. [Laughter.]

...Why? Got to have something finer; got to have something better; got to have something purer. What did he do? Why, he took this mud-man that he made, breathed into him the breath of life, and he became a living soul; he took from his side one of his ribs, and out of that rib, he made a woman. I don't know, but that is a fact; I don't think it is, and I will tell you why. I have several reasons for not thinking so, but one of my prominent ones is, that there are not brains enough and tongue enough about the rib of a man to make a woman. [Laughter and applause.]

Amelia continued by claiming priests wanted women to be slaves because they feared their intuition. When "you allow women her rights, when you allow woman's intuition to be appealed to, supplemented by love, her offspring will be a superior class." She believed that if children were of a superior class and allowed to reason and think, they would see that Christian stories were myths, and priests would have no power. Nevertheless, she conceded that she had no objections to Calvinists, Baptists, Catholics, or Presbyterians. She allowed them and everyone else their beliefs. But she stated firmly:

I have objections to their making any controlling law to compel me to believe what they believe. Nature has spread her garments of life out before me; she has given me certain necessities and wants and endowed me with the faculties of reason to enable me to make an effort to supply those wants and those necessities, and I am wholly unwilling that anyone should take the cross, if you will allow me to use the term, that is necessary for me to carry; to take this life of mine, that belongs to me, not to somebody else. My life is mine, not yours; my life is mine, not the gods. I live today—I will live tomorrow, I think, because I live now.

Amelia finished by stating that as the world progresses, the beauty of Spiritualism will continue to blossom and benefit all humankind. She urged her listeners to remember that the "greatest and grandest gift ever given to a human being is the liberty to think, the liberty to act, the liberty to speak, the liberty to investigate, the liberty to apply his own knowledge to all the things that surround him." She ended her lengthy speech with a prayer—not to God, but to her audience:

> ...It shall be my prayer, silently, unexpressed, that the loved ones may gather the flowers that have fallen, in the depths of innocence, and purity, and justice, that they may weave them into garlands, and crown your heads with an immortal crown, they may imprint an immortal kiss upon your brow, and they may baptize you in the immortal fountain of life: that you may listen to the watchword which Spiritualism has ever voiced to the children of men: "Come Up Higher!"

LOSING A FRIEND

AMELIA RETURNED TO PHILADELPHIA for a delayed anniversary celebration with the First Association of Spiritualists. Ed Wheeler, her friend and fellow freethinker, gave the anniversary address. Their combined presence highlighted the Association's freethinking nature, and they reveled in the lectures of both speakers. The corresponding secretary, James Shumway, praised Amelia's speech and reported, "Every inch of seating and standing room was occupied, and if our hall had been twice as large, it would have been filled."[125] Another correspondent described Olive and Amelia's work and stated that people should get to know both to understand their efforts for Spiritualism:

> They have been together nine years. Mrs. Smith is a most excellent soloist; and Mrs. C. an old-fashioned trance speaker whose lectures are replete with practical facts, combining reason, logic, and philosophy, till one is astonished at her power and almost lost at times in the strains of eloquence and beauty given through her mediumship...[126]

Following a successful engagement in Philadelphia, Amelia made a short trip to Chicago for the Second Society of Spiritualists, then returned to Buffalo for a brief stint. Finally, she returned to Rochester in June 1882 to deliver two lectures for her old friends Amy Post, Lucy Colman, and Jay Chaapel. Although the lectures were not recorded, their titles—"The Descent of Man or Rather the Ascent of Man" and "Labor and Capital"—highlight Amelia's efforts to address spiritual and political issues to the same audience. Jay Chaapel observed that "the collections for the day were the largest ever taken here at a spiritual meeting, showing conclusively that Spiritualists and Liberalists in this city not only appreciate radical thoughts but are willing and anxious to pay for them."[127] Chaapel provided her travel schedule, stating she was going to Yorkshire, New York, 83 miles southeast of Rochester, then to Holley, and traveling to the Neshaminy Falls grove meeting in Pennsylvania for a lecture—an astounding 366 miles south of Holley.

Amelia returned to Rochester for a "welcome back" reception on July 27 for D.M. Bennett, who had returned from a trip around the world. Bennett had written essays about his travels, which filled *The Truth Seeker* for nearly a year. He was welcomed at receptions from California to New York, showing the depth of love for him and the esteem in which he was held by freethinkers nationally. At the Rochester event, hosted by Amy Post, Jay Chaapel, Lucy Colman, and others, Amelia praised Bennett and condemned Comstock. She told the audience that Bennett had been "a servant of the American people" and held the "foremost rank among the liberals of the world." His name, she insisted, would live long, and his reputation "will be taught to the infant in the cradle ages after Anthony Comstock shall have passed away."

Amelia then urged the audience to subscribe to *The Truth Seeker* to enlighten their minds. She argued that the church has been "master long enough," and people who have been slaves must now become the country's rulers. Only then will the churches be held accountable and rightly taxed, and she added that the "Christian church has done more to restrict and break down the liberties of the American people than any other agency." Amelia closed by paying a beautiful tribute to Mrs. Bennett for her devotion and self-sacrifice during her husband's imprisonment at Albany.[128]

Bennett closed the dinner by thanking Amy Post for posting bail for him following the Watkins Glen arrest and expressed gratitude to Amelia and Olive for their efforts in obtaining subscriptions to *The Truth Seeker* while he was imprisoned at Albany. The next day, a hundred friends entertained Bennett at the Sea Breeze resort, where they enjoyed dinner, dancing, and a steamboat ride. Olive Smith and another friend supplied beautiful music for the affair, indicating that Amelia and Olive interrupted their travel schedule to welcome their friend home. A much larger reception was held during the Freethinkers Convention at the infamous Watkins Glen in late August, which Amelia and Olive could not attend. Olive had become ill and could not travel with Amelia, whose schedule included a New York journey from Clarendon to Johnson's Creek, Lockport, and ended at Cassadaga for the camp grove meeting at the end of August 1882. She spent the month of September in Pittsburgh and returned to Boston for October. Olive next appeared with Amelia in Boston.

Thomas Lees, a correspondent for the *Banner of Light,* was effusive in his praise for Amelia and her lecture at Cassadaga, making a unique comparison between her and other trance lecturers of the day: "Of all the speakers on the platform, she is probably the most forcible, certainly the most fearless." He called her a champion for free thought, insisting that even those who could not agree with her surely admired her fearless advocacy of the truth. Listening to the more poetic mediums was lovely, but "it needs the giant oaks and hemlocks to stand the hurricane." Lees concluded that the world needed more people like Amelia, "strong enough and brave enough to speak the stern truth at all times."[129]

The Boston Spiritual Temple was unique as a society compared to other organizations. It was much larger and employed a stenographer for all its trance speakers. Consequently, we have a much better idea of Amelia's lectures to Spiritualist societies. She was only scheduled to speak on the first two Sundays of October, but following the success of her initial lecture, she was asked to remain for the rest of the month. She fearlessly addressed the issue of "True and False Mediumship," and a summary of the speech appeared in the *Banner of Light.* Amelia reviewed the history of Spiritualism, from its inception to its spread throughout the world. She informed her audience that mediumship was a gift found in young and old, rich and poor. "Mediumship is not dependent on character," any more than moral character affected the ability of scientists, astronomers, or geologists. She said she was unaware of anyone who was perfectly moral, but mediumship visits an individual despite their flaws. Amelia believed that the recipient of spirit messages was just as responsible for receiving accurate messages, and that no matter how gifted a medium was, the negativity of a recipient would affect that message—it prevented "a full and free expression of the spirit." Finally, she told the audience that if they wished to help mediums deliver accurate spirit messages, they must "be true to themselves" and work on perfecting their own nature.[130]

Amelia offered a unique observation often overlooked in Spiritualist communities. The success of mediumship was not reliant on the morality of the medium alone but included the recipient's character as well. A review of the Bible shows that Abraham, Isaac, and Jacob were liars and cheats, David committed adultery with Bathsheba, and Moses committed murder before the burning bush episode. The presence of Spirit had nothing to do whatsoever with the morality of either medium or recipient—Spirit exists despite who we are.

However, Amelia emphasized that the individual choices and behavior of both parties affected the success and accuracy of the message, and that morals resulted in each individual being true to their own beliefs. It was a clear statement about relationships, but included the introduction of Spirit into the relationship. This relationship of the two participants—medium and sitter—with Spirit was an idea far ahead of the time. It is comparable to the modern practice of spiritual direction today—a method initiated by the Catholic church, which postulates that a spiritual director can assist another's spiritual growth by helping them to understand their relationship with God. Spiritualists viewed the medium as the "director" for Spirit and assisted with the recipient's relationship with Spirit.

Amelia lectured in the morning and evening each Sunday. However, the crowds at her evening lectures were generally much larger once word of the morning lecture had circulated. The report of her evening lecture in the October 28, 1882 issue of the *Banner*—"What Must I Do to be Saved?"—may have raised some eyebrows among her liberal friends, but the attendance remained solid and large. Her unique take on what constituted a savior was thought-provoking if nothing else.

Amelia acknowledged that God had the power to save, but it was not our task to interpret what constituted saving—God "will do his own work." Telling her audience that it was up to all of them to investigate claims made by religion and determine how to apply them to ordinary life, she alleged that "sin resulted from ignorance" and urged them to learn the true laws that govern the world—natural law. She continued by saying, "Ignorance of any natural law does not relieve the transgressor." As examples of the various saviors of the world, she claimed that Muhammad advocated giving mathematics, currently held by the privileged class, to the common people. Consequently, mathematics elevated their intelligence, which would act as a savior to them. Indeed, she regarded mathematics as the savior of the people more so than Muhammad, and recited the scientific "saviors" throughout the centuries:

> The fourteenth century gave birth to a savior—the compass; who can do without this in commerce? The fifteenth century gave birth to a savior—printing—a power that sways the world; the sixteenth century, the signs of astronomy; the seventeenth century, trial by jury; the eighteenth century, geology and mesmerism; the nineteenth century, steam and electricity, and that growing savior, Spiritualism, and man will so far advance as to need and have another savior in the twentieth.[131]

Amelia argued that these and others were saviors because they assisted the advancement of humanity to such an extent that it was elevated and made better by them. Her unspoken words questioned the benefit that Christianity offered to humankind with its one savior, Jesus. As a man, he was commendable, but his words had been twisted and misinterpreted by the church. She reminded her audience of the church's oppression rather than its advancement of humanity.

Amelia tackled the man Jesus in her lecture the following week, "Who was Jesus Christ?" According to the four Gospel accounts, Jesus was a "remarkable man—a wonderful man." But she then asked, "What does history say?" Arguing that someone as remarkable as Jesus should have been acknowledged in the annals of secular history, she concluded that after looking at every historian's work, "his name only appears in Josephus once, and that is acknowledged to be an interpolation." Asserting that there is no documentation of Jesus before the fifteenth century (other than church history), she pointed out that the Gospels did not agree on the activity of Jesus. However, if he outlined the rules for his disciples, we should apply those same rules to Christian ministers today. She asked, "Does he [the minister] lay his hands on the sick that they may recover? Not to say aught regarding the drinking of poison or the handling of serpents." The correspondent reported that Amelia's controlling influence was Thomas Paine, who gave a radical analysis of the record regarding the characteristics and doings of Jesus while on earth.

Thomas Paine acknowledged that the historical Jesus lived and was crucified for sedition against the Roman government but argued that every other aspect of his life was a pure myth. He connected Jesus to the fable of Jupiter, who defeated a race of giants and placed its leader under Mount Etna. Paine asserted that the Jewish faith created Satan after the story of the giant, and instead of putting Satan under a mountain, they put him in a pit and called it hell. Although Christians acknowledged the story of Satan in hell, the Christian *story* does not work unless "they bring him out again," so he became a snake in the Garden of Eden.[132]

Paine (through Amelia) argued that the immaculate conception was a myth—not only a myth, but an obscene story about a "young woman, engaged to be married, and while under this engagement she is, to speak plain language, being debauched by a ghost, under the impious pretense (Luke 1:35), that the Holy Ghost shall come upon thee, and the power of the Highest shall overshadow thee."[133] Paine continued to destroy the New Testament based on the conflicting reports of the life and death of Jesus. Amelia, an avid supporter of Thomas Paine, must have based most of her lecture on *The Age of Reason*. Indeed, so well read was she on Paine's works that most believed it was Paine himself speaking through her. And perhaps it was, since there were times when she quoted from his works almost verbatim.

Amelia returned to Philadelphia in November and planned to travel to New York City to visit friends. However, her family called her home to Holland in the western part of the state due to her sister's severe health. Consequently, she was in Holland when she received the devastating news of D.M. Bennett's death on December 6, 1882. His funeral was held four days later at the German Masonic Temple. Amelia could not return in time to attend the funeral, but she and Olive wrote to Bennett's wife, Mary, to express their condolences. A second letter to Mary Bennett from Amelia appeared in the January 13, 1883 edition of *The Truth Seeker*—uncharacteristically, Amelia had allowed it to be published. After expressing her sorrow and offering consolation, she acknowledged that words fail when losing a loved one and pointed to Bennett's deep love for Mary. She reminded her that the separation from Bennett would last only a short while, and that they would reunite soon—death could not touch their great love.

Amelia went on to tell Mary that Bennett "will live as a defender of human rights and be placed alongside of those of the noble heroes who have passed on before him," and that she was so glad she knew him as brave, faithful, and noble. Apologizing for not attending Bennett's funeral, she explained that her sister had been "near death," and she could not leave her family home in time. She prayed that Mary would not grieve "too much," for she would see Bennett again when she left this material world behind —and then made a rare statement with the following words:

Some two weeks after his funeral, I had a vision. This occurred in the morning, just as it was merging into sunlight. I promised to give it to you and will do so. I felt I was in the presence of Mr. Bennett. He looked, as usual; only a slight shadow seemed to come over his countenance. He spoke of you and asked me to write you these words: "Tell her not to mourn thus. The ages for love are as countless as the rays of sunlight through the eternity of past time, but the days for mourning are numbered." A smile was around him, and he passed from my vision.

That he lives and loves you still I know, and your great distress is felt by him, and he fain would tear it asunder if possible. We [Olive and Amelia] shall both see you at our very earliest opportunity ... Now please try and be cheerful, and your spirit will be better prepared to feel his influence as he is near you.

Amelia was in Boston when she wrote her letter to Mary Bennett. It is one of the rare times she gave "a clairvoyant reading," based on her vision of Bennett and his message to his wife. Amelia, who had corresponded with him during his stay in prison, had acted as an agent for *The Truth Seeker,* gaining subscriptions to keep the paper afloat and his wife financially comfortable. They were close friends, and she was devastated by his death. So perhaps it was her grief that caused her to respond to a request from the editor of the *Banner of Light,* two days later. Amelia's letter to him appeared in the *Banner*'s January 27 issue with a side note from the editor, Luther Colby.

BOSTON—Mrs. Amelia H. Colby writes, Jan. 15th: I have not forgotten your very generous offer, to allow me an amount of space in your weekly columns to present something of a synopsis of my lectures given each Sunday in Paine Memorial Hall of this city. But in reading the Banner of Light, I discover that there are several of our speakers who feel the necessity of keeping before your readers not only much of their Sunday work but that in more private circles during the week; so that I think the remaining space can be used to better advantage for destroying the power of the tyrant over the slave, by stepping between the priest and the people, than by my trying to give your readers an idea of what was spoken through my voice in yesterday's lecture.

During the past twenty-two years, I have been before the public as a medium, the most positive manifestations having been on the public rostrum as a trance speaker. During this time, I have traveled over many states, become acquainted with thousands of people, all of whom know that wherever I am, I am constantly fighting for liberty of speech, liberty of press, liberty of mails, not only for the people of this vast country but of the populated globe. I have ever been in the front ranks of radicals, never fearing to have the truth given through my mediumship anywhere, regarding any subject pertaining to the progress of human life; and if there is any one thing connected with these twenty-two years that I am prouder of than another, it is that my most radical lectures have been a decided success: not only in calling together the thinking people of all beliefs but in their remunerating the same in dollars and cents.

My life alone has not filled this great mediumistic wave, for each year, I, like every other medium, have been compelled to use much of the physical life of others. During the past ten years, Mrs. Olive K. Smith has been my constant companion and business partner—being ever ready to step between the people and my sensitive mediumistic nature. I have been kept in motion and lived upon the responses, congratulations, friendships, and loves of the public. She has worn out for the want of the same: her life used in a work where she is little known, though always present until worn in spirit as well as body, she sinks beneath the load. When we learn that necessitated associations of mediums need the expressed appreciation for the value of worn and wasted lives, we shall be able to place Spiritualism in its real worth before the world by better protecting its mediumship. Our lectures thus far in this city have been listened to with deep interest. We shall continue to occupy the rostrum in Paine Hall the remaining Sunday afternoons of this month. On Sundays, in February, we shall speak in Springfield, Mass. During that time can be addressed care J. G. Hart, 15 West Street.

This is perhaps the most intimate letter Amelia had ever publicly written, and her love and respect for Olive are present. She rightly, and somewhat tartly, points to the prominence of other speakers who felt the need to advertise their every move, and perhaps this was just the humble Quaker in her. In other words, her work lifting the church's oppression was more important than advertising it in the paper. More curious is her tribute to Olive and her use of the word "we." She includes Olive in the importance of her work—they have been companions for ten years, but she feels Olive is not appreciated by people other than herself. It is a simple statement of loyalty if nothing else. However, the attempted explanation of their relationship is curious, and the *Banner* editor's commentary may shed light on possible gossip about the two:

In another column will be found an interesting statement from the energetic spiritualist worker, Mrs. A. H. Colby, now speaking to the people from the rostrum in Parker Memorial Hall, Sunday afternoons. She has been a laborer in the vineyard for the space of twenty-two years and says she is proud of the position she holds in the estimation of the people, notwithstanding the malicious thrusts several professed Spiritualists—by stabs in the dark—have made to injure her reputation.

It is impossible to understand the meaning of Luther Colby's remarks or Amelia's uncharacteristically public tribute to Olive since there is no other reference to their relationship, no gossip or hint of scandal attributed to them in writing. If their relationship was in question, it was done quietly behind closed doors. Whatever was being said, it was apparent enough for the editor to comment on the "malicious thrusts from several professed Spiritualists." It is possible that some lecturers, jealous of Amelia's popularity, attempted to smear her reputation. She was not wrong in stating that lecturers and other workers' advertisements were often over the top. Their financial well-being depended on their ability to obtain engagements. Those lecturers who performed in trance only, without giving clairvoyant messages from the platform, were less engaged than those who offered both lecture and clairvoyant messages. Amelia and Olive came as a pair—Amelia lectured and Olive sang. They continued to receive substantial donations from the societies they served, enough to travel comfortably and extensively.

On the other hand, one must wonder about the relationship between Amelia and Olive. The timeline for their relationship is unclear. They had known each other since the American Association of Spiritualists convention, where they heard Victoria Woodhull speak in 1871. They may have maintained a written correspondence until they reconnected in 1872 and started traveling together. Of course, women can love each other in ways that men do not. They are nurturing and supportive, and Amelia expressed her love for Olive by acknowledging her loyalty and care during their time together. But it's possible that Amelia's unwavering belief in liberty of conscience and individual freedom gave the impetus for entering a relationship customarily frowned upon by conventional society—and her repetitive digs at men might be another clue. However, there is no concrete evidence of an intimate relationship between the pair.

After this mysterious exchange in the *Banner,* Amelia completed her engagement in Boston and traveled 90 miles for a month-long meeting in Springfield, Massachusetts. The dialogue between Amelia and Luther Colby was not lost on the Spiritualist societies, and many came to her defense. W.J. Colville presided over her last engagement in Boston, and he "introduced the ladies very happily." The corresponding secretary to the *Banner of Light* reported that Amelia spoke on "The True Basis and Most Effectual Methods of Reform." Emphasizing the individual's morality and abhorring all unhealthy practices, she made an earnest plea for a "truthful, individual life" and stressed that "to be true to ourselves" was the essential groundwork of radical reform. The correspondent also made it a point to thank Olive for her songs and reminded the readers that she had been the "companion of Mrs. Colby ten years and is indispensable to Mrs. Colby's success on the rostrum."[134]

Amelia and Olive received the same praise and accolades in Springfield, with Amelia lecturing to packed houses throughout their stay. She gave old lectures from previous engagements, including "What Shall I Do to be Saved?" and "Who are Christians?" She and Olive were labeled a success during their time with the society. Mr. J.S. Lewis reported, "So many persons are being attracted by her eloquence and the radical truths she utters that scarce a seat can be obtained."[135]

Amelia joined Ed Wheeler in Philadelphia for the thirty-first Celebration of the Advent of Modern Spiritualism. The correspondent reported the hall was packed all day, and in the evening, when Amelia spoke, "hundreds went away, as they could not even find standing room."[136] After her Philadelphia engagement, Amelia must have returned home to Indiana, where two of her three children lived in the Muncie area. She did not address the visit, but the June 9, 1883 edition of the *Banner* reports that she is "much improved in health." The amount of travel she undertook, coupled with the continued grief for her friend Bennett, must have played heavily on her health, and Amelia began to make return trips home more often to refresh herself.

She returned to western New York, spoke at Clarendon at the end of May, and then traveled to Cassadaga, 105 miles south, to provide the main lecture for the annual June 1883 picnic, just before the opening of the Cassadaga camp meeting. The honors were shared with O.P.

Kellogg, a trance lecturer from Ohio who had been in the field as long as Amelia. She remained at Cassadaga, with the *Banner of Light* reporting that she and Olive had been "rusticating at the Skidmore mansion for a few weeks."[137] After a cheerful time with the Skidmores, she returned to Clarendon for a few lectures, then traveled south to Neshaminy Falls in Pennsylvania, 367 miles away, to give several talks. She returned to Cassadaga for the opening ceremonies of their summer season.

After a pleasant time at Cassadaga, Amelia and Olive traveled 447 miles to her next engagement at Lake Pleasant, Massachusetts. The trip would have taken over eleven hours by train at 40 miles per hour. Traveling between camp grove meetings was typical for all itinerant lecturers during the summer months. Smaller Spiritualist societies stopped all activities so members could leave the hot cities, enjoy the cooling breezes of a lakeside resort, and continue enjoying Spiritualist lectures and clairvoyant messages. It was not unusual for the larger camps to host up to 5,000 or more people on any one weekend, so it also provided more significant income for both medium and camp organizers. Lake Pleasant was the largest and most popular camp meeting in all the eastern states, but it would also become the most notorious by the end of the 1883 season.

CAMP UNPLEASANT

W HEN AMELIA AND OLIVE arrived at Lake Pleasant for their scheduled engagement, the organization's president, Dr. Joseph Beals, informed her that she would not be allowed to speak. Amelia did not know what had caused Beals' decision, and a heated exchange lasted for several days until Amelia was finally permitted to give her lecture to the camp meeting attendees. Amelia only learned afterward the reasons for Beals' attempt to silence her.

A controversy occurred before Amelia's arrival, resulting in a public split between conservative and liberal Spiritualists. The difference between the two factions was not new, but the division became public warfare as the two sides took to the newspapers. The blow-up centered on Dr. Juliet Severance, a radical proponent of free love; Ed Wheeler, a liberal abolitionist and freethinker, who stepped in to support Amelia's right to free speech; and Beals, a conservative Spiritualist.

The Lake Pleasant camp meeting at Montague, Massachusetts, was managed by the New England Spiritualist Association. It was not the oldest camp meeting but certainly one of the most popular, with attendance ranging between 5,000 and 10,000 on any one day from July to August. The Association had leased the grounds from the Fitchburg Railroad Company every year since 1874, and the train supplied multiple excursions to the grounds daily.[138] In addition, ferry boat excursions for people who came by the lake made it easy to amass many people in the resort-like setting. The formal New England Spiritualist Association was formed in 1879, and in August 1880, the first annual camp meeting took place. The Association had leased 50 acres by that time, with 90 permanent cottages built on the site.[139] There were large temporary tents for those who simply wanted to rent, as well as a hotel, a dance pavilion, and multiple other buildings for the comfort of guests. Dr. Joseph Beals presided over the Association board from its inception until 1892.[140]

On August 22, 1883, Dr. Juliet Severance was honored by several supporters at a reception. It was held in a large tent owned by one of the members. This was not unusual as many campers and homeowners hosted receptions for their favorite speakers. During the event, Severance began a talk on "social freedom," a topic she had lectured on before. She was known as "the Woodhull of Wisconsin," a reference to radical feminist Victoria Woodhull. Severance earned the title due to her fierce advocacy of women's rights, denunciation of marriage laws, and promotion of free love and free speech. Her "Lecture on Religious, Political, and Social Freedom" was initially composed in 1881. However, a woman in the audience—claiming that the lecture on social freedom equaled advocacy of free love—took offense and complained to Beals.[141]

The lecture did address free love, but not in the unsavory manner suggested to Beals. He stopped the reception and forbade any other receptions to take place on the grounds. Severance was not surprised— six years earlier, she had been forced from the platform for denouncing marriage as a form of slavery and advocating labor reform issues.[142]

This time, however, her enforced silence set off a firestorm in the camp that lasted for months and elicited a heated debate in print between Severance and David Jones, the editor of *The Olive Branch*. Beals, Col. John Bundy (the editor of the *Religio-Philosophical Journal*), and Jones were all known for their conservative views and dislike of social reform. Bundy was known for his exposés and attacks on mediums and was not well liked in most circles. Beals attempted to shift the blame away from himself, Bundy, and Jones by claiming that the Fitchburg Railroad was at fault for restricting speeches on "social freedom." Most felt this was not entirely true.

The three-day controversy was recounted by multiple letters to the editor of *Mind and Matter,* while the *Religio-Philosophical Journal* and *The Olive Branch* set out their views in editorials. As usual, the *Banner of Light* refused to enter the fray. The truth was a matter of perspective, but the recorded details of the event appeared similar. When Beals silenced Juliet Severance, many people in the camp were outraged at his seeming autocratic behavior and restriction of free speech. Ed Wheeler was scheduled to speak on Sunday, August 26. At the start of his lecture, he expressed righteous anger at the perceived tyranny of the leaders at the camp.

A journalist for the *Springfield Republican* wrote a summary of the episode, which was picked up by *The Kansas City Daily Times* of Missouri (August 27, 1883) and the *Quad-City Times* in Davenport, Iowa (August 24, 1883). The following report is taken from the latter two papers as the *Springfield Republican* archives only go back to 1886. The headlines screamed, "Trouble in the Camp. An Attempt to Introduce Free Love Doctrine in a Spiritualists' Meeting." According to the reporter, Wheeler "launched into free love doctrines." Wheeler, believing Beals' lies in attempting to deflect blame onto the Fitchburg Railroad, then said, "If the Fitchburg railroad company forbids our saying anything at the peril of a revocation of our lease, by my God in Heaven, I will come here at midnight, at the peril of my life, and say what I please, and bid the Fitchburg railroad company do its damnedest!"

Wheeler finished his planned lecture, and while he was still on the platform, Dr. Beals rose to speak. He gave a history of the Lake Pleasant camp, relating how free love doctrines had resulted in libel suits in the past year. Accusing Wheeler of making a political speech designed to influence the election of officers to be held later in the day, he further accused him of being in a conspiracy with free lovers—and finished by denouncing him in front of the 10,000 people present. Wheeler attempted to refute Beals' accusations, but Beals shouted at him to sit down; he had "said enough." Wheeler then moved past Beals and stated that he *would* say something, and the crowd began to chant, "Wheeler! Wheeler!"

As Wheeler denied the conspiracy charges, Col. Bundy, standing near the platform, shouted, "It's a lie, and you know it!" A distraught

Wheeler left the platform, and Bundy rushed to take his place. He tried to speak, but the crowd refused to listen and kept shouting, "Wheeler!" When Bundy claimed "there was a conspiracy" and that Wheeler was part of it, a man in the audience rose and shouted, 'It's a ---- lie, and I hurl it at you as you gave it to the audience!" The massive crowd booed and hissed at Bundy until he left the platform.[143]

Ed Wheeler, a long-time abolitionist, Spiritualist, reformer, women's rights activist, and freethinker, did not practice or endorse free love in its loosest term. He did, however, endorse free speech, free press, free religion, and freedom of conscience. J. William Fletcher's letter to the September 29, 1883 issue of *Mind and Matter* gives a more accurate report of Wheeler's comments.

> [Wheeler said] This platform is the platform of universal truth. We must see and know all before we can decide that which is best. You have admitted a discussion of fish, the Mound Builders, etc., [referencing previous lectures given at the camp] and it is well; and when any other branch of thought is advanced, you bring up the lease and say a stop must be put to it. Which is of the most importance, the hotel, the brass band, the Fitchburg Railroad, or the truth? If I felt I had a truth to speak, I would come down here, if at midnight alone, and *speak it,* and the Fitchburg Railroad might do its d----dest. Yet Spiritualism is the theme of the hour, etc.

Fletcher added, "And a lecture on that general theme followed. Now, is there anything about free love in all this?" Fletcher's letter continued by describing the people's anger at Beal and Bundy's suppression of free speech. He remarked that when Mrs. Colby arrived, "she was told she could not speak, and someone else was put in her place. Mrs. Colby, an unconscious trance speaker, must not be allowed to speak because her guides in telling the truth might say something to hurt the feelings of the fellow from Chicago [Bundy]. She spoke, however, for the people would hear her." Fletcher related how the episode so affected the camp that mental mediums could not provide clairvoyant messages, and the crowd became even more unruly. The anger at the outrage perpetrated against Wheeler and the inability of mediums to perform grew to unsettling proportions, so Beals ended the day.

The interaction between Amelia and Dr. Beals was disclosed at the end of November when Amelia published an account of the conversation in her pamphlet *The Colby Bombshell*.[144] She described how Beals told her he had sent a telegram to Cassadaga, her last engagement before Lake Pleasant—which she did not receive. Beals stated she was not required as a speaker and offered her $10. Amelia refused to accept the money unless she earned it by speaking, as scheduled. Beals declined to give his reasons for not allowing her to lecture, finally refusing to speak with her at all. Amelia asked to talk to a member of the Committee on Speakers, and Mrs. A.T. Pierce rose and offered to host a meeting with Dr. Beals and Judge A.H. Dailey. Amelia stated that she did not want to attend the meeting alone and felt it necessary to bring witnesses.

Amelia asked multiple people to attend the meeting with her, including David Jones of *The Olive Branch*; J. Frank Baxter, a mental medium; Cephas B. Lynn, a correspondent for the *Banner of Light*; and Mr. J.S. Hart of Springfield, who introduced her to a reporter for *The Boston Globe*. Lynn, Baxter, and Jones refused to attend the meeting, but her constant friend, Olive, as well as Hart and another gentleman accompanied her. Amelia reported that a stranger approached her on the street and asked if she could "be hired not to speak." Amelia replied, "Yes, I can." When the stranger asked what the charge would be, Amelia—in her typical sarcastic fashion—responded, "Not a penny less than one thousand dollars! I shall commence suit against the Association as soon as I can go to Boston if I am not allowed to speak."[145]

The committee continued to deny Amelia an explanation for its decision until Beals finally admitted that there had been some "trouble with E.S. Wheeler," and someone had told him, "Wait till Mrs. Colby comes; she will throw a bombshell into the camp." Thus, Beals felt it easier to refuse Amelia the platform. Later, Amelia heard that Beals and the committee had heard she was a free lover, and she believed they "were mortified" when they realized their mistake. Amelia had never spoken in defense of free love but, like Ed Wheeler, she was avidly in favor of free speech. She also believed in freedom of conscience, and if another person believed in free love—no matter how it was defined—she honored those beliefs, so long as she was not forced to hold the same views until she determined them to be truthful.

Amelia was finally allowed to address the crowd on Friday afternoon. She reported that Dr. Beals was the first to congratulate her after the lecture by saying, "You have delivered the lecture of the camp meeting. It was pretty radical, but your radicalism is in time and place."[146] Her lecture is not recorded, but it is suspected that the "radicalism that was appropriate" had to do with the church's suppression of women and the advocacy of women's rights. It did not address free love, and Beals was obviously relieved. Amelia later found out that J. Frank Baxter, who had initially refused to get involved, had gone to Col. Bundy to plead Amelia's case. Bundy agreed that Beals had gone too far, and there was no need for another explosion in the camp. He then spoke to Beals, who relented.

To say the mood at the camp was becoming ugly would be an understatement. Amelia reported that a gentleman approached her after the lecture to say he was happy she gave her speech. He continued, "Had you not been allowed to give it, there was a committee of 50 men ready with axes to split up the platform and seats, and make a bonfire of them on the border of the lake, to show the officers of the Camp Meeting Association that the people had rights which must be respected."[147] Amelia had likely been made aware of the suppression of free speech against Juliet Severance and the horrible treatment of Ed Wheeler. She had too many friends and admirers at the camp not to have been told of the treatment of her old friends. She and Olive left Lake Pleasant and traveled back to Rochester for a Freethinkers Convention, where she believed she would receive a more favorable welcome than she had at Lake Pleasant.

Freedom of speech was paramount to Amelia, and she expected no problems when she arrived at Rochester. They were freethinkers, after all. However, once again she was slighted, sadly by friends of like mind. She was scheduled to speak twice at this convention. Unfortunately, the scheduled slot for her first speech was taken by another speaker, who went over his allotted time. When the convention leader decided to take up a collection for the hall, which encroached further on her expected time slot, she decided enough was enough. The September 1, 1883 edition of *Democrat and Chronicle* reported the slight and her lecture in its entirety.

At noon, Amelia came forward with "burning indignation" and stated she had been kept on the platform for hours while her time had been given to others. She was supposed to have lectured at 11 a.m. and had still not uttered a word. Her reaction was not surprising since she had just had to fight to speak at Lake Pleasant. After a quick meeting with the convention organizers, they announced that she would lecture after lunch.

Amelia spoke that afternoon on "The Hatred of a God That Sent All to Hell Who Were Not Disciples of Christ." This lecture is significant as it was the first public announcement of her atheism. Wondering if God had any use other than supporting "65,000 ministers and $175,000,000 worth of untaxed property," she said that despite Christianity's claim that God burns errant individuals for all eternity, she belonged to the universe, and God did not. "Do you ask me if I believe in a God? I answer most emphatically that I do not and hope I never shall."

The ensuing speech was a full rant against God and Christianity. She described God as being outside natural law as the Bible recorded it and argued that this was impossible. She failed to see the connection between the biblical God and the natural law of the universe. She continued by saying that if God is the author of all things, "if he had in himself all that is in nature, if everything came from God, if he is supernatural, then everything is supernatural." She concluded that if all things are supernatural or infinite as God, she could not be a finite being and must be infinite. In this, she was poking a bit at the materialists in the audience.

Amelia didn't limit her criticism to God but tackled Jesus and his teachings too. She asked, "What did Jesus want a hell for? If you follow his teachings, you must hate your friends and love your enemies. If you were to follow his practical life, you would all be bachelors and then think, in such an event, what a fine world this would be to live in." Her sarcasm was not lost on the audience, who laughed in appreciation. Still not finished with Jesus, she denied the virgin birth, stating that the immaculate conception violated natural law, and challenged "65,000 ministers to prove it." Recalling the Christian idea of a fixed universe, where heaven is above and hell below, and the Calvinist notion that everything was preordained, she then argued, "What good does it do to pray to an omnipotent God if he has got everything all fixed? Would he make any changes for my whim? No." In other words, she concluded, there is no point in prayer.

Finally, and almost as if she couldn't resist it, she addressed the issue of women in today's world, as well as the biblical world, and included a mild affront to the leaders of the convention:

> Woman is the great soul of life, for from her life is ebbing and flowing. Woman, therefore, demands a hearing today. The Free Thinkers of the state of New York should see that women should have the same rights as men, and you, Mr. Green; you, Mr. President, are here, but where are your wives? [Mr. Green—my wife is in the audience.] More of you would let your wives come if they had taken in washing to pay their expenses. Mary was forced to give birth to a child in a manger. There is hardly a man in this state, the most wicked one in the Union, who would not take into his house a woman who is about to give birth to a child. But still, the Infinite One, the merciful one, allowed Mary to give birth to Christ in a manger.[148]

She added that people should find their sanctuary in the home rather than the church, and no one should "rely upon what was written 10,000 years ago." She finished by urging her listeners to "protect women and children, pay no mind to what tomorrow might bring, but take care of today."[149] This was not the first time Amelia appeared to contradict herself. She likely understood her reference to Matthew 6:34 and paraphrased it accordingly. But it is odd that she would end with a statement from the same book she had spent the past hour trashing.

On the convention's final day, Amelia spoke on "The Necessity for a Union of the Radical Liberalists of the Present as a Voice to Mankind." To an audience filled with materialists, she argued for the existence of an afterlife, claiming that cause and effect are of little use if it has taken the natural laws of the universe eons to perfect humanity and have it all end in death. In other words, we work to live and grow in wisdom, but there cannot be enough earth-hours to learn all that is needed. Therefore, what good is wisdom if there is no continuation of life?

She next addressed resolutions that had been passed earlier in the convention giving women and men equal rights and privileges—socially, religiously, and politically:

> At the present, your government declares that woman is neither a person, citizen, nor member of a race of people. Though she is the mother of all the nations of the earth, yet society treats her as a mere toy, a plaything, something beautiful to look upon, adorned and decorated with ribbons, flowers, plumes, feathers, and styles of every class and kind, until her body is deformed and her intellect in a state of nudity. How unsafe is this condition of human society when we know that maternity stamps all life with its future destinies? Every mother loves every other mother's child because of the love she bears her own, whether it be dressed in purple and fine linen or in rags and tatters. No mother but that knows that every baby has been baptized in the sacred fountain of a mother's love.[150]

Amelia then returned to the Spiritualist view of death and the afterlife, which conveyed a beautiful idea of life's changes from the low to a high form of intellectual and spiritual growth. She rejected the notion that life ended with only decomposition and destruction. She concluded by stating:

> The great thinking population of the globe has sought the presence of a God, for whom, through prayer and supplication, they might obtain the knowledge necessary for life and happiness; but all in vain ... silence reigned, and God refused to speak. Hence, I offer to these, the children of human life, my prayer: I would prefer the sunshine of human life rather than the dazzling brilliancy from the throne of a God.[151]

The Truth Seeker lauded her speeches as exemplary and included addresses by Mattie Krekel and Juliet Severance, the only other women who spoke at the conference. There is no doubt that Juliet shared her story of Lake Pleasant with Amelia, and in turn, Amelia shared the account of her interaction with Beals. There were many similarities between the two women—both were devout Spiritualists, freethinkers, and believers in free speech and individual sovereignty. However, one significant difference was that Severance had formal educational training while Amelia was apparently self-taught, and another was that their view of Christianity differed. Amelia adamantly opposed any semblance of Christianity as a formal religion while Severance was willing to give the churches their due. However, she believed that by educating people, the church would eventually die out as people grew in wisdom and discovered there was no need for institutionalized religion.[152]

After the convention, Amelia and Olive worked with J. Frank Baxter in Georgetown, New York, then traveled 220 miles to Springfield, Massachusetts, where they spent two months. Amelia's first lecture in Gill's Hall—"What Will Be the Result of the Present Decline of the Influence of Christianity?"—addressed the liberal belief that orthodox churches were losing their hold on the population. She believed this was primarily due to Spiritualism and liberal freethinkers who emphasized education and social freedom, and concluded that the "churches would become schools for adults, and the clergy be changed to philosophers who should instruct the people in the practical truths of science, and the worship of an unknown God passes away."[153] Unfortunately, no other summaries of her lectures are available. However, the titles give an indication of her topics and approach. Her lectures—"Man's Inhumanity to Man Makes Countless Thousands Mourn," "Bread for the Starving Millions," "Psychology and Mediumship," "The Irrepressible Conflict," and "Is Spiritualism True?"—show the depth of her ability to address not only the philosophy of Spiritualism but also the political and social concerns of the day.

As Amelia finished her time in Springfield, she received word that her old friend Ed Wheeler had died. Letters to the *Banner of Light* and

Mind and Matter pointed an accusing finger at the administrators of Lake Pleasant as being culpable in his demise. The accusation of being a liar and guilty of conspiracy in front of 10,000 people created such distress that it affected Wheeler's health. In addition, he suffered the indignity of being labeled a free lover and accused of attempting to adversely affect the election of the NES officers by Col. John Bundy, who placed a front-page editorial in the September 1 issue of the *Religio-Philosophical Journal.* The editorial also cautioned other camp meetings against engaging Wheeler in the future.

Following his experiences at Lake Pleasant, Wheeler had left for home in distress. Becoming ill on the way, he could get no farther than Boston, where he took a room in one of the hotels with his wife attending him. J. William Fletcher wrote that Wheeler had been disgraced and insulted by his treatment at the lake. He wrote, "always delicate, broke down under this weight of misrepresentation and falsehood, and remains here in Boston in a state of physical prostration and suffering that defies the skill of the physicians ... his life is rapidly slipping away."[154] Wheeler remained at the hotel through September and October, and appeared to rally. He claimed typhoid fever was the culprit, but in a letter to the *Banner of Light,* his wife said he had trouble seeing and could not write, so she "was catching up" on correspondence to well-wishers. While typhoid fever was possible in the late 1800s, the symptoms described are more indicative of a stroke. This is plausible since great stress from the Lake Pleasant episode could have induced the condition.

By the end of October, Wheeler had seemingly recovered and attended a public reception held in his honor at Horticultural Hall in Boston. Amelia, who remained in Springfield, could not attend but sent a letter supporting the recognition given to her old friend.[155] Friends and supporters packed the hall, and multiple speakers referenced the poor treatment of a worker dedicated to truth, the well-being of humanity, and Spiritualism. They did not go so far as to name Lake Pleasant or the derogatory articles written in the *Religio-Philosophical Journal* or *The Olive Branch.* Still, those present, and those who read the reception report, understood what was being implied. The reception itself could not have been more timely. Three weeks after this giant show of support and love, Ed Wheeler suffered a stroke while speaking to the Ladies Aid Society in Boston and died within days. He was fifty-one.

The fallout was immense, but none more so than with his friend, co-worker, and fellow freethinker J. William Fletcher. Making his feelings very clear, Fletcher announced his old friend's death in *Mind and Matter* and the *Banner of Light*. He placed the blame for Wheeler's death squarely on the shoulders of the Lake Pleasant administration and the horrible treatment Wheeler had received there. In the November 17, 1883 issue of *Mind and Matter,* Fletcher said, "It is my painful duty to inform yourself and readers that the noble worker Edward S. Wheeler passed on to the higher life Monday, Nov. 12th, watched over by his loving wife and friends. As your readers are aware, he has never recovered from the shock received at Lake Pleasant. The funeral will take place on Thursday. Dr. Storer and the writer, with other speakers, officiating."

Fletcher was more critical during his oration at the funeral service by pointing to the event that he felt had precipitated his friend's death. He reminded the attendees that Wheeler had advocated free speech to 10,000 people and the conservative administration at the campgrounds. Fletcher said Wheeler was "the *people's* friend, the *truth's* friend, *liberty's* friend" and that he was an "earnest and impartial truth-seeker, an inspired and fearless worker" and would always say what others were afraid to speak. Fletcher complimented Wheeler's honesty, his love for humanity, and "unbounded charity for his fellow man." He concluded there "were only two words that Wheeler knew in his public work: Liberty and Truth."[156]

A large portion of the Spiritualist community blamed the events of Lake Pleasant for Ed Wheeler's death, and community newspapers also took up the refrain. Buffalo's *The Evening Telegraph* reported his untimely death with the following account:

Edward S. Wheeler of Troy, who was buried on Friday, is now said to have died of a broken heart. He was wedded to Miss Marie Lester of Troy a year ago. When at the spiritualistic camp meeting at Lake Pleasant last summer, Mr. Wheeler advocated free speech and a free platform and was denounced as a free lover and was finally driven from the platform. Though a spiritualist, Mr. Wheeler was in no sense a free love advocate. These accusations preyed upon his mind, and he became ill, pined away, and died, his attending physicians assert, from mental rather than physical anguish.[157]

Amelia wrote and published a pamphlet titled *The Colby Bombshell* three days after the *Banner* report of the funeral service for Wheeler. Her temper and sense of outrage were the fires that lit the match for this controversial document. The pamphlet did not list her as the author under the title, as most pamphlets were written. Instead, Amelia signed and dated it at the end of the pamphlet, giving it the appearance that it had initially been written as a letter to an unknown recipient. She detailed how she was rudely treated at Lake Pleasant, including the attempts made to suppress her speech. It was only seven and one-half pages long, and in typical Amelia style, her writing was blunt and to the point.

Amelia recalled her initial reception at the camp and how Beal refused to let her speak, without explanation. She outlined her meeting with camp leaders and the length of time that elapsed before she was permitted to speak. All would have been well if she had stopped there—but she did not. Making her feelings known, Amelia wrote that "very little spirituality" was found on the grounds:

> There is too much contention. The people were wrought up to a fighting pitch. The officers elected last August are very dissatisfactory to the great mass of Spiritualists I met at the Lake. After the election was over, I met hundreds who said they were disgusted with the corruption of the election and detested the use of money, slanders, and lying about good men who happened to be in the minority. The tendency of the Camp is too much in the line of money-making; too much time is devoted to dancing and frivolity, amusements crowding off lectures and seances.
>
> There is too much beer drinking, for there should be none at all at a Spiritualist Camp meeting. There is too much seeking for power in order to keep certain people in office. Another objection is

the nearness of the tents and cottages to each other. Such nearness prevents privacy of homes, engenders hostile magnetisms, and enables busy-bodies to retail gossip, which engenders hatred. The sanitary condition of the Camp while I was there was very bad—and I wonder that more people were not sick.

After denouncing the camp's administrators, Amelia advocated creating a new camp. But it was not enough to call for a new camp, and she continued to attack Camp Pleasant:

Let the money makers, the office seekers, the medium catchers, the fraud exposers, the scheming self-seeking hypocrites, the devotees of frivolity, and constant dancing, the beer drinkers, and the shams whether in Mediumship or in Journalship and the secret yet REAL "free lovers" remain at Lake Pleasant.

Amelia claimed the new camp meeting could be "truly spiritual" with freedom of speech, and new ideas offered without criticism. She added that the camp could teach morality "by people who are themselves moral" and no beer, rum, "or any other thing which can debase the body shall be sold."[158]

The pamphlet was sent out nationally, and it would be an understatement to say that it landed like a bombshell in every Spiritualist community. Amelia's temper overtook her common sense, and her statement concerning the "lying and slander about good men" could only reference the treatment received by Ed Wheeler. Her additional criticism of the camp was so notable and scathing that it is surprising she was not sued for slander herself. However, there were repercussions.

Nearly every large Spiritualist camp meeting blackballed Amelia for several years. Large camps, such as Lake Pleasant, Onset Bay, Neshaminy Falls, and even her beloved Cassadaga, refused to engage her. She ultimately returned to Cassadaga in 1888 and Neshaminy Falls on occasion, but none of the other larger camps invited her to speak for the remainder of her professional life. Smaller camps and those who enjoyed a liberal audience continued to engage her for their platforms. Nevertheless, she did not enjoy the same popularity after her stark criticism of Lake Pleasant. The restrictions lasted for several years before she branched out to more Spiritualist societies.

Six years later, Amelia made good on her recommendation to start a new camp, becoming a founding member of Camp Chesterfield, in Indiana. As far as Lake Pleasant is concerned, the diatribes against it continued until as late as January 1884, when free lover Moses Hull weighed in. He recalled how Ed Wheeler, when he was secretary of the Neshaminy Falls camp meeting, had canceled Laura Kendrick's speech after the administration discovered Kendrick was her new, married name. In fact, she was the notorious Laura Cuppy Smith, an advocate of free speech who had served as a caregiver and character witness for Victoria Woodhull during her obscenity trial (for exposing the Beecher-Tilton affair). She had also advocated for and won a presidential pardon for Ezra Heywood, convicted of distributing materials favoring "free love." Hull alleged that while the treatment of Ed Wheeler could be seen as "murder" by the New England Association, he also wondered if it was retribution for Wheeler's past behavior toward a fellow freethinker.[159]

J. William Fletcher responded quickly by saying that while the story was true, Ed Wheeler, as secretary of the Association at Neshaminy Falls, was only acting at the orders of the president. He had a "warm regard" for Kendrick and "often spoke with regret of the part he was obliged to take in the affair." Fletcher continued by saying the two examples were not comparable. Wheeler spoke with Kendrick privately, while Beals denounced Wheeler in front of 10,000 people and canceled the remainder of his speeches:

A more cowardly proceeding was never seen in the days of the antislavery movement, when advocates of reform were hounded from town to town, than disgraced Lake Pleasant last year, and I know that Mr. Hull, who has personally endured so much at the hands of those canting hypocrites, would be the last to throw a shadow over the fair name of a man who gave his all in the cause of human liberty.[160]

Controversy between conservative and liberal Spiritualists continued to dog Lake Pleasant for several years. By 1887, the Fitchburg Railroad had lost patience and refused to lease the grounds to the Association. The Association then attempted to purchase the grounds but was unable to raise the money—and a group formed as the Lake Pleasant Association purchased the land and took over the management. However, Lake Pleasant continued to experience chaos and controversy over the years and never seemed to regain its reputation as the "best" Spiritualist camp meeting. It is tempting to consider that karma visited Lake Pleasant in the end.

TIME TO CHOOSE

AFTER A SUCCESSFUL ENGAGEMENT in Springfield, Amelia returned to Boston, where she lectured at the Spiritual Temple in December 1883. Sadly, her travel schedule was limited to just three organizations from then until the end of March 1884—likely due to her criticism of Lake Pleasant.

Amelia's first lecture, given on December 2, 1883, had no title, but she began in trance, saying, "I have not come here to tell you what to do; that you must know for yourselves." What followed was a call to become better people—better in action, thought, and compassion. Her control continued:

> It is our duty to learn from within the power and possibilities of ourselves. If not, where shall we go for it? Never can we be happy with our powers inactive; never happy until they are brought out into usefulness. When sorrow is found arising from oppression, the heart of man feels it, and so long as free thought is crushed, it calls for an effort on our part to liberate it.[161]

Although entranced, it appears that some of Amelia comes through, as her reference to crushing free thought makes clear. The tone is far milder when compared to past lectures. Urging the audience to strive to live the "higher life." She states that the higher life is "that which elevates our fellowmen." Education is the proper lever that allows an individual to help another, and it is not a property that makes the true man, but rather an education to help others. The lecture ends with Amelia urging the audience to "be true to thyself; then the world will be benefited, and you can be just to others."[162]

Amelia's lecture the following week—"Does Phenomenal Spiritualism Merit Our United Protection"—addresses mediumship, how phenomena are possible, and what makes for successful mediumship. In effect, she chastises the audience and argues that they are just as responsible for a medium's success as the medium is. She states that the medium is surrounded by conditions that "place them beyond any control of their own." Members of the audience arriving with negative energies adversely affect the medium and bring negative energies through the unconscious trance speaker. It is not just the wise, honest, pure, and moral who come to their loved ones—"the ignorant, the false, the impure and revengeful may express themselves to their ... loved ones as well." Amelia does not pull any punches with her audience—she says she knows they think mediums should be above reproach but asks why they would expect that of mediums if they cannot be above reproach themselves?

Amelia points to the educational opportunities in Boston and New England, believing they afford citizens the expectation of a higher standard of morality. However, it seems the people do nothing but try to make others think "what they know they are not," inferring that some people will purposely pretend to be something other than who they are. She accuses the nation's rulers, state leaders, and churches of this failure, and concludes, "Can you reasonably expect more of the poor, uncultured, and uneducated, who have not had these advantages?"

Amelia reemphasizes that spirits from the earth plane fill the spirit world, including pure and impure spirits. She argues that a medium, whether in a trance or not, has no control over which spirit comes to them. It is the sitter or the audience who controls which spirits present themselves to the medium. She again urges her listeners to improve their lives, educate themselves, and act in a manner that will attract spirits who can bring spiritual growth and wisdom to them.[163]

The correspondent omitted a summary of Amelia's evening lecture for the *Banner of Light*. The lecture's title, "Some of My Reasons for a

Total Abolition from the Influences of the Church," provides a likely reason for the omission. However, the correspondent added that the audience was "even larger than in the morning," demonstrating the freewheeling, liberal nature of the Boston audience.

On December 16, 1883, Amelia presided over a memorial service for Prof. William Denton hosted by the Boston Spiritual Temple. Denton was a naturalist, explorer, geologist, Spiritualist, and liberal freethinker who had little use for orthodox religion. He owned an extensive collection of butterflies from all over the world (and, as of this date, it remains on display in the St. Louis Science Center in Missouri). His death came during an exploration trip to New Guinea (with two of his sons) after he fell ill with a fever. He was best known in Spiritualist circles for his experiments in psychometry with his wife, Elizabeth, and his sister, Annie Denton Cridge, and his work *The Soul of Things: Psychometric Researches and Discoveries* remains a classic in the field of Spiritualist writings today. Amelia's funeral oration was a beautiful tribute to Denton, recalling his past accomplishments and offering comfort to his family and friends. She called Denton "one of the noblest, one of the truest, one of the most manly of men" and said that the world was better for his having lived in it. She closed with an eloquent passage urging all present to strive to live their highest life, as Denton had, reminding them that he still lived in their hearts and the afterlife. She concluded that he would welcome them all in the afterlife, "a united family once more, to the bright home which he was preparing for them."[164]

As beautiful as her tribute was, a member of her evening audience still asked, "Does physical science prove that William Denton is not dead?" Her answer was clear and to the point. "Nothing in nature is lost. If there is one thing that can be struck out of existence, then all can be … what you call death is change." She explained that all nature changes in some way, and all things hold life. The mineral kingdom and the animal and vegetable kingdoms all have life and experience constant change. A child is born and grows into youth, adulthood, and old age. Ultimately, death occurs, but the will remains. "Your will continues its existence separate from the body" and results from a law of nature that changes the relationship between will and body.

The physical body is a clothing to the spirit within—and you clothe the physical body. You do not, when you make a change for new garments, think it necessary to destroy the body with the old garments; neither does the spirit die because the physical body (its clothing) cannot hold the two together longer ... Physical science says "there is no death," therefore William Denton still lives.[165]

Amelia's conclusion that physical science proves there is no death was a simple statement following an extensive explanation of the laws of physical science and natural law. Spiritualists believe the body is a mere covering for the spirit, and when the body decomposes, the spirit is unaffected.

Amelia's next lecture for the Boston Spiritual Temple was called "The Effects of Influences," where she discussed the different races of people. She stated there were "five distinct races of people on this earth, and each one different, because of the composition of the soil and the action of the sun." Unfortunately, Amelia displayed a racist attitude, reporting that the African region has slow soil growth, and African people are similar:

> The Caucasian race sprung from a soil where vegetable life is more compact and quicker, and they, therefore, are more positive. The positive will always control the negative; hence the Caucasian will always rule. When the Caucasian crosses the African, the result will be a weakening of the former, and the succeeding generation will be feeble or die in childhood.[166]

Not only did Amelia insist on the supremacy of Caucasians, but also argued, in the same lecture, against mixing the races. Native American tribes were vastly different, however, and reflected the position of all Spiritualists. She claimed that "the Indian of our country illustrates the same truth regarding soil and vegetable life; he cannot be enslaved; he knows no man as master. The earth, air, water, and sunlight produce his characteristics."

Amelia's racism was not unusual for the time. James Peebles, Hudson Tuttle, Andrew Jackson Davis, and William Denton tackled the Darwinian theory of natural selection. Some were monogenists, which posits a single origin of humanity, while others upheld a polygenist theory of human origins, believing the human races had different origins. Nearly all believed in the superiority of the Caucasian race.[167] But it was not just scientists or Spiritualists who subscribed to this view. The women's suffrage movement had been using the supposed limited intelligence of black male voters as an argument for women's suffrage, although some were more indirect than others. Elizabeth Cady Stanton used names like "Sambo, and the gardener, and the bootblack, and the daughters of Jefferson and Washington..." much to the dismay of friends such as Frederick Douglass. While disconcerting to modern feminists, Stanton's apparent racism was no different from the broad swath of Northern, white society of the day.[168]

Amelia was no stranger to the issues and arguments surrounding Darwinism and certainly no stranger to the issue of black enfranchisement over and above women's suffrage. She ended her lecture by observing that some people exert more influence over others, and that governments exert power and control citizens similarly. Amelia concluded that "family government is the first and most important" and that family is where children learn self-control. Women's equality with men would influence the family and raise "the whole condition of mankind to a better and purer life."[169]

Amelia's December 30 lecture, "The Laws of Psychology and Their Necessitated Utility in the Work of Mediumship," addressed the importance of understanding natural law. Reviewing the theory of cause and effect, and its effect on the human condition, she reported that everyone who wished to understand natural laws must first understand themselves and the universal power within each person. She added that individuals who work at harmonizing themselves with nature would create the perfect conditions to attract spirits on whom they could depend.[170]

Amelia urged her listeners to educate themselves concerning these universal laws and apply them to the world and the individual. Her afternoon lecture, "Bread for the Starving Millions," was purely political and addressed the nation's poverty. It had been given to other societies before and was likely not delivered in trance. Following her series of lectures at Boston Temple, Amelia and Olive traveled to Norwich, Connecticut, to give eight lectures through January for the Spiritual Union, a liberal Spiritualist organization. The hall remained packed with people who relished Amelia's comparisons between Spiritualism and orthodox theology. Byron Boardman, the correspondent for the *Banner of Light*, wrote in the March 1, 1884 issue that her lectures again proved successful financially.

It was a testament to the readers of the *Banner* and the organizers for Spiritualist lectures that Amelia's criticism of Lake Pleasant, and her presumed blackballing, did not influence the people who wanted to hear her speak. She may even have been elevated in their eyes by her courageous dedication to the truth. After a brief engagement in Somerville, Massachusetts, she returned to Boston to lecture at the Spiritual Temple again from mid-February to March 5, then traveled to Norwich, Connecticut, where she remained through March.

Amelia's final lecture at the Boston Spiritual Temple was so well received that she was asked to repeat it on March 5, and special arrangements were made for her appearance. The lecture, "Experiences on Entering Spirit-Life, and His Contact with That Most Perfectly Systematized Catholic Power," was a trance lecture by her control, Thomas Paine. The March 15, 1884, edition of the *Banner of Light* recorded the address. In this lecture, Amelia's control defined the spirit world as composed of more refined substances thrown off by the material world, and it included ten spheres. The different spheres "were largely to be construed as classes or conditions of mind rather than localities in space." The control described the first sphere as being closest to earth, and said every living form, whether animal, vegetable, or mineral, exists in this sphere and finds its expression on the physical planet. The control claimed that children often existed in this initial sphere.

Amelia's control discussed the purpose of all ten spheres and stated that individuals gravitated to the sphere that best fitted their needs for progress. The control reminded the audience that every condition of life, every act or thought they expressed while living, had its counterpart in the spiritual life. All actions or thoughts were registered somewhere, and at some time, everyone would be brought face to face with the record for personal review. The control added there was no room for a savior in the spirit life, but each individual required individual atonement for their shortcomings. There was no vicarious release of error; instead, everyone could affect "salvation" individually. Each sphere was progressive, and none was absolutely dark, unpleasant, or unlovely. They each had their own center and their own light, and each person—even infants—could progress as their nature enabled them to do so. She (Paine) concluded by saying that no one should ever lose their love or trust for humanity's better instincts and should always work toward the highest good for all individuals.

Amelia traveled to Somerville for an Anniversary of Modern Spiritualism celebration on March 29, 1884, and then immediately returned to Boston for its celebration on March 31. The highlight in Boston was the appearance of Maggie Fox, now Mrs. Margaret Fox-Kane, who featured alongside Amelia. Fox-Kane's appearance came eight months before her testing at the Seybert Commission in November. The Seybert Commission was a group of faculty members at the University of Pennsylvania who in 1884–87 investigated a number of respected Spiritualist mediums, alleging fraud or suspected fraud in every case that they examined. In one of Fox-Kane's tests, the commissioners required Fox-Kane to stand on four glasses and produce raps. She attempted the exercise twice before raps were produced on the third try. An investigator holding onto her feet acknowledged they didn't move, but the Commission ultimately reported the test inconclusive.[171]

Amelia's appearance on the same platform as the celebrated medium was likely the highlight of her life. Fox-Kane attended only briefly and did not remain for the entire event, but the audience was delighted. She left in the middle of Amelia's speech for unknown reasons, and Amelia pointed her out as she left the hall, calling her "one of the children who started the fire thirty-six years ago."

Amelia reminded the audience that "two little girls—not boys, remember—girls" were the pioneers of the Spiritualist movement. Telling them that women were becoming a great power in the land, and that Spiritualism began and continued with them, she argued that "no minister can meet one of these mediums and withstand the power and intelligence that is manifest through him or her." Mothers could reconnect with their dead children, and the efforts of mediums reunited family and friends. However, she cautioned the audience to remember that spirit raps were like the child who had to learn the alphabet before reading. They preceded phenomena, and people trying to learn mediumship should make this their simple beginning. Spiritualism was a movement without restraint, no matter how hard critics wanted to contain it: "No doors can hinder it; no chain can bind it." She added that love was the only energy that elevated those who encountered it [referring to Spiritualism].

The speaker closed with an eloquent passage, in which she impressed upon her audience the power of life, especially of a pure one, and the necessity for making this life surrounding them so lovely that they would not need a Peter to open the gate for them at death, as they would already have within them all they could bear of heaven.[172]

Amelia ensured that the audience understood the importance of women in general but asserted that the entire Spiritualist movement resulted from women's continued efforts. Referring to the Fox sisters, she also argued that critics of Spiritualism pointed to raps as just another spectacle and fraud perpetrated on unsuspecting believers. Amelia saw raps as a stepping stone toward mediumship and the ability to receive more philosophical wisdom from the spirit world. Her final remarks, urging her audience to a more noble life, reminded them that spiritual work was most successful when the medium and recipient worked cooperatively to bring about higher vibrations.

In the April 29, 1884 issue of the *Banner,* Amelia outlined her coming schedule. It was a circuitous route that had her visiting Boston, Somerville, and Norwich. She ended by telling readers that her address for May would be Muncie, Indiana. Amelia's daughter Lillian and son, Augustus, lived in Muncie. Augustus was expecting the birth of his first child, and it may be that Amelia hoped to be present for the birth. To all outward appearances, she seemed to have little interaction with her children due to her heavy traveling schedule. However, since no extant letters are available, it is difficult to determine the true extent of their relationship. Still, significant gaps in her travel schedule indicate her return to the family in Indiana and New York, so it is possible she maintained a close connection with her children despite appearances. Her lectures on family and children's upbringing make it seem so.

Amelia could not be present at the birth of her granddaughter, Echo, born in late May—she had returned to Clarendon, New York, to fulfill her commitment to lecture in May and June. From August 31 to September 7, she lectured at the Niantic camp meeting in Connecticut to 1,500 people. While there, her Spiritualist and freethinker friends created a controversial split that ultimately forced Amelia to choose between the two groups.[173]

The National Liberal League had a contract with the executive staff at Cassadaga to hold their Eighth Annual Convention on the grounds from September 3 to 7, 1884. Cassadaga graciously allowed the convention attendees to use their grounds free of charge. Freethinkers, as a whole, included a wide swath of people who criticized Christianity, the authority of the Bible, and dogmatic belief. At that time, it included atheists, agnostics, materialists (or rationalists) and liberal Spiritualists. Although Spiritualists and freethinking materialists were divided about proof of the afterlife, nearly all subscribed to social reform and understood the necessity of working together for a common purpose. Therefore, the criticisms of their different platforms remained primarily civil. Unfortunately, the rift between them continued to grow wider as more and more letters to *The Truth Seeker* saw a running debate about the validity of Spiritualism that, at times, grew quite heated. The division was rendered almost complete following the events at the convention.

George Chaney, an ex-Methodist minister turned Unitarian minister turned materialist, came to Cassadaga a few days early and participated in seances and Spiritualist lectures. The Spiritualists were ending their camp season before the Freethinkers Convention, and Chaney had a chance to join in some final activities. To the surprise of his materialist friends, Chaney became a Spiritualist convert and announced it during his opening address at the Freethinkers Convention. Materialists might have ignored his conversion, surprising as it was, except that he committed an unforgivable act. He criticized and attacked Materialism during his lecture—likely a remnant of his old Methodist need to convert everyone to his new belief. His criticism of materialists continued when he delivered a second lecture the following day.

The lecture was summarized in the September 13, 1884 edition of *The Truth Seeker,* and the full address appeared in the following week's edition. Although he complimented the freethinkers, it appeared more backhanded than sincere, and his criticism was outrageous to the leaders who had invited him. The response from the materialists was swift. Charles Watts, a secularist and journalist from the U.K., and Thaddeus B. Wakeman, an attorney, editor and president of the National Liberal League, made severe statements against him and Spiritualism, and the ensuing conflict became more heated between the hundred or so Spiritualists who had remained for the convention and the materialists who were present.

At the time, 25 per cent of *The Truth Seeker*'s readership were Spiritualists, although 90 per cent of those Spiritualist readers had been arm-in-arm with D.M. Bennett when he was fighting for free press and mail.[174] Consequently, Spiritualist readers were outraged when Samuel Putnam, an ex-Unitarian minister turned atheist and president of the Bennett Liberal League, wrote his convention report in the September 13 edition of *The Truth Seeker.* The rift between the two groups widened to such an extent that few would find a reason for cooperation in the future.

The convention was not as successful as previous conventions had been, for unknown reasons. However, Putnam criticized both Spiritualists and their beloved Cassadaga as if they were responsible for the low turnout at the convention. Acknowledging that approximately one hundred Spiritualists had remained to listen to the liberal speakers, he reported that the one railroad, the Dunkirk, Allegheny Valley & Pittsburgh—the only railway going to the camp—was "a most miserable apology for a railroad, with infrequent trains, uncivil employees, and wretched rolling stock." In other words, if anyone planned to go to Cassadaga, they could count on a miserable trip there—not the best advertisement for a budding Spiritualist camp competing with other more established camps. Putnam then acknowledged that the

Cassadaga leaders had generously donated the grounds to the New York State Freethinkers Association and the National Liberal League, and the grounds were well managed. He continued:

> ...with the exception of the poor hotel accommodations, there can be no fault found. A moderate influx of visitors, however, swamped the resources of the manager of the only hostelry within the limits of the camp, and the place must suffer in popularity unless the building and restaurant are improved.

Putnam's criticism against one of the youngest Spiritualist camps (only five years old) showed a complete lack of grace. Further, it alienated their Spiritualist leadership as the rift between Spiritualists and freethinker materialists widened to immense proportions. The fallout between the two groups did not limit itself to the convention at Cassadaga. Editors at *The Spiritual Offering* wrote a scathing op-ed against Charles Watts, one of the men who responded to Chainey on the platform. It attacked not only his ideas but his person as well. *The Offering* editorial was reprinted in *The Truth Seeker* and condemned as an outrage. It described Watts as a bull: "He bellowed, he stamped with his hoofs, he gored with his horns, he tore up the earth about him, casting the turf and stones into the faces of the Spiritualists." The editorial continued by pointing out the numerous misrepresentations in his speech and his unfair description of Chainey as "too womanly." Watts attacked Spiritualism, and the editorial suggested that he was unsuited to speak of Spirit; therefore, he could never communicate with one: "Let the beef-consuming, ale-guzzling Englishman talk of something for which he has a capacity." The editorial added that he had addressed an audience full of intelligent women and had offended them as if "he was the pope of Rome." The editorial ended with a final insult:

> It is he who should never, in this life, again attempt to enter woman's domain of spirituality unless he puts himself in training and upon a diet calculated to reduce his surplus corporosity. Any pure spirit could not get within one sphere of those dreadful eyes, and it is small wonder that he spoils all the conditions.

The letters began to fly between the *Truth Seeker* and other Spiritualist papers, including the *Banner of Light, The Spiritual Offering, The Religio-Philosophical Journal,* and others, until the division was nearly complete. Amelia was an avid reader of all the newspapers and found herself conflicted as she had old friends in both camps. The decision to choose between the two was painful but inevitable. It seems that since D.M. Bennett's death, there was less willingness for the two groups to afford each other freedom of belief, and letters in *The Truth Seeker* grew more critical of Spiritualism without a shred of diplomacy.

Amelia chose. She no longer acted as an agent for *The Truth Seeker* nor advocated for subscriptions to it. Leaders of the National Liberal League stopped inviting Spiritualists to lecture, or perhaps Spiritualists simply refused invitations presented to them. In either case, the attacks from the materialists on the platform were more than they were willing to tolerate. Amelia no longer lectured at freethinker conventions and restricted her speaking engagements to liberal Spiritualist societies.

Amelia's relationship with Olive Smith also appeared to end. Records show that the pair were together as late as January 1884, but there is no mention of Olive again until she surfaces in California in the late 1880s. Olive, who always sang before and after Amelia's lectures, was no longer identified in news reports covering Amelia's engagements. It is possible Amelia's reduced schedule and income was not enough to cover Olive's travel costs, or perhaps Olive—who originally came from California—simply couldn't take another winter in the snowy, cold northeast where Amelia spent most of the season. Finally, a simple falling-out, as often happens with relationships, may have been the cause. Whatever the reason, Amelia traveled alone for most of the remainder of her professional life.

Amelia's schedule, limited mainly to Massachusetts and Connec-ticut for the remainder of 1884, was full through October 1885. She returned to Boston to speak at the Spiritual Temple in December 1884 and again in March 1885; made a side trip to Portland, Maine in February of 1885; was in Springfield, Massachusetts in April; spent May in Indiana with family; and returned to western New York from

June until September. She reported that she was entirely engaged until the first Sunday of October 1885. Amelia, who rarely advertised herself or her travel schedule, appeared to be telling the blackballers that their slander, criticism, and attempts to keep her from working had been unsuccessful.[175]

Following her visit to the Niantic camp meeting, Amelia returned to the Boston Spiritual Temple in October 1884. Some of her lectures were philosophical and others were more political, emphasizing women's equality and rights. On October 5, Amelia's morning lecture, titled "The Origin of Man," discussed the difference between the biblical account of origin and Darwin's theory of evolution. She walked the audience through creation and pro-creation and said, "Mothers are the molders and builders of the world; they are the highest ideals of the universe. They mold children for the next generation. Fathers are not molders—they *think* they are, but it is the mother's love that molds." Her evening lecture continued the theme, "The Destiny of Man."

Amelia told the audience that everyone has a destiny, and as we move toward that destiny, we are constantly growing and unfolding in wisdom. She reminded her listeners that science was the result of inspiration, and with inspiration we realize that our destiny is to "unfold as much of the power one possesses." Humanity compares the past to the present—consequently, we can define the future with our power. Claiming that the physical body comprises food and drink consumed, but the spirit body contains deeds carried out in this life, she concluded that the body holds the grandest combination the world has ever seen—the physical structure, how it moves, thinks, and acts, but all are "governed by spirit." The implication is to realize one's destiny by working at good deeds in this life so that the spirit grows strong and more supportive of human life.[176]

Amelia's following lecture—"What Action Should Be Taken by the United States Citizen to Protect and Perpetuate His Citizenship?"—was political and utterly radical. The November 1, 1884 issue of the *Banner of Light* provided a summary:

The meaning of citizen has been given by a Judge of the Supreme Court of the United States to be a male person over twenty-one years of age. That excludes all women; mothers and children under twenty-one are not citizens. Who are citizens? All men. Their families are subject to them and not to the government.

Amelia admitted that the Emancipation Proclamation of 1863 changed matters since men could no longer sell their offspring by African American women. But this did not completely address the Constitution's idea of freedom, and she reminded the audience that the Declaration of Independence was "infidel" because the document did not mention God. The Declaration allowed the freedom to worship all religions and mandated total equality. She claimed that America was politically diseased since it did not follow the Constitution's mandate for equality.

Further, she claimed that the country was financially diseased, with lobbyists obstructing a free-flowing republic. Criticizing the banks and the government of the day, Amelia accused them of affecting the country's destiny. She supported the Legal Tender Act, saying that America should not return to the gold standard for currency. Claiming that "the ignorance of the voter" was another illness, she called for removing lobbyists and adding intelligent voters to cure a diseased republic. Voters should send men to Washington who would be beyond the corruption of lobbyists.[177]

Amelia's 1884 lecture could be applied today or at any time in the nation's history. Democrat Grover Cleveland was running against Republican James Blaine for the United States presidency (Cleveland won in November). Amelia's discussion of money referred to Cleveland's support of the gold standard and his opposition to Free Silver, which alienated the farmers, miners, and laborers. She had denounced the gold standard in the past, claiming it only served the rich, who would hoard it, and that farmers would have difficulty paying their debts. The Legal Tender Act was passed to help finance the Civil War, and Amelia connected paper money with the gold vs. silver debate. The summarized lecture makes it difficult to catch the entire strain of Amelia's thoughts, but it is clear she fully supported the poor working men and women, all disenfranchised to one degree or another. Amelia was likely speaking inspirationally rather than in trance during this lecture. Her evening lecture, "Man's Destiny in the After-Life," was delivered in trance as a philosophical treatise on the afterlife and the need to embrace change. It is almost poetic at times:

> The spirit world is opening to you to show that change is necessary, and I know no place where change is not. We see that while we have repeated ourselves in our children and children's children, we have not lost our own identity. When we open the telescopic power of sight in this life, worlds on worlds open to our vision. So, in spirit life, the telescopic vision in Spirit opens fields and worlds beyond. I must be true to myself, and then I shall be true to all around me.
>
> The law of love goes on increasing and deepening. The record says that there we shall not be given in marriage, but a love deeper and purer than marriage here can give and will grow with our growth there. We are daily writing our destiny. If I do not know my own, how can I tell of another's destiny? Be true, be just, be kind, and the great power will give you the life and the growth in love. The work here to feed, clothe and shelter the needy twill open the door of our soul so that the spirit world can assist you in that labor. When we know that we write our own destiny day by day, we shall be careful how we do it.[178]

Amelia's comparison between marriage in the afterlife and marriage in this life is interesting. She reflects the free lovers' idea that marriage in this life is tarnished if it is done out of necessity. In fact, "a love deeper and purer than marriage here can give" sounds as if all marriage in the physical, whether of necessity or not, is found wanting—she makes no secret of her distaste for the marriage laws that suppress women. Again, she urges the audience to embrace a moral life of justice, kindness, and care for the less fortunate, and promises that the spirit world will support those lofty desires.

Amelia lectured in Connecticut during November and returned to the Boston Spiritual Temple in December. The *Banner's* December 13, 1884 issue summarized her first trance lecture, "Human Progress, or the Old and the New." Amelia advised that there was "an immutable law of human progress" based on the power of growth, and said that "within us exists a power awaiting development in order to give higher and nobler manifestations." She continued that Spiritualism came to reveal great truths to humanity, and though humanity has existed in ignorance and superstition in ages past, Spiritualism was the vehicle that opened the door to freedom. Spiritualism moves all things onward, and "those who do not move with it will be crushed by the movement." She instructed the audience, saying:

> Man gravitates to the place and association as his own condition demands and affiliates with high or low. We are making up our lives even by our secret thoughts, for these have their record and influence. Every expression and touch is magnetic and imparts something to those around you. You are recording in your life-book your own condition and imparting good or an otherwise effect on others.[179]

Amelia calls attention to the inherent power in every individual and speaks of the ability to effect others based on positive or negative energy, or what she calls magnetic energy, from thoughts, speech, and touch. It is an early rendition of the philosophy of interconnectedness with all things. However, magnetic energy was widely seen as a primary influence on people and its use in healing.

She delivered her next lecture, "Personal Characteristics and Their Effect Upon Our Future Life," in trance. She began by stating that each person's "peculiarities" constituted the individuality of humankind and that these differences were the result of design. If there was a design, there must be a designer. However, it was not a lecture intended to prove God's existence but to establish each soul's responsibility for the coming generations.

She claimed that regulating antenatal conditions had been regarded with suspicion, and some felt that humankind might be accused of prying into the mysteries of God. Indeed, Amelia may have been discussing an early version of eugenics. However, she noted that God's characteristics, as recorded in the Bible, were jealousy, revenge, hatred, and delight in inflicting punishment. Unfortunately, man imitated this God—children grew up with the same characteristics, and generations followed with similar traits. She then asked how the child could be at fault for following their parents' teaching, or how women could be responsible for laws they did not make. Amelia's control ended by stating:

> ...our apartments in future life are hung with pictures representing acts of our past, and these are ever-present with us. We may pray to have them changed, but it must be a prayer of actions, and that action must be our own ceaseless efforts, for, without work, nothing can ever be accomplished; therefore, we pray unto ourselves and answer our own prayers.[180]

It is as if Amelia is saying that God made this mess, so there is no need to send your prayers there. It is better to make your prayer of desire, and work to accomplish it.[181] Her evening lecture, reported in the same edition of the *Banner*, was a continuation of the afternoon lecture, and she addressed diversity, saying:

> The flower or leaf growing on the same stalk are not exactly alike; the flowers have not the same color and shape. The sunlight, the rain, the air, and the earth do not produce the same effect on the different processes of formation. Some persons are slow in growth, others fast. You pass from this sphere by natural law. The laws of physical life demand their fulfillment. Decomposition of the body releases the spirit and is natural. We still retain our own identity and express our characteristics in every stage of being. Every transgression of natural law has to be met and paid for in spirit life.

Amelia claimed that actions by individuals in this life affect the conditions of the spirit in the afterlife. Mediums who are obsessed with financial success will bind themselves to earth conditions. Consequently, they cannot rise to a higher sphere when they cross to Spirit. "None, however, are lost. The child never lived whose life on earth was so low as to prevent it from rising into the higher." Amelia verbalizes the philosophy that would later become part of the Declaration of Principles composed by the early National Spiritualist

Association of Churches, that "the doorway to reformation is never closed against any soul here or hereafter." She also points to the need for living a moral, pure, and true life so that the spirit will cross to a higher sphere at death. This veers closely to the orthodox belief that to do good will send one to heaven, but it departs from the idea that to do wrong will send one to hell. Instead, people who live a less than savory life still have an opportunity to improve their lot in the afterlife. It also reinforces the Spiritualist idea of the afterlife consisting of various spheres, each higher in knowledge than the previous, and removes the fear of death.

BOSTON, ALWAYS BOSTON

As 1884 DREW TO a close, Amelia completed her time at the Boston Spiritual Temple with four additional lectures that demonstrated the breadth of her ability and the reason for her popularity. The topic for her lecture on December 21, 1884, was chosen by an audience member. This was not an unusual act. In some Spiritualist societies, an audience member asked a question or posed a subject unknown to the lecturer at the beginning of the service. The speaker then spoke inspirationally or in trance on the topic. The subject chosen for Amelia's afternoon lecture was "The Science of Being, or the Power of Mind Over Matter." Her lecture, delivered in trance, was a complex philosophical treatise on what constitutes truth and how the mind, influenced by the past, addresses the present.

Amelia compares truth with individual perspective and argues that truth is nothing more than perspective based on past and present experiences. She asserts that man has a body composed of all forms of matter in the universe. The mind advances the truth of one's being, and the mind enacts the ability to choose what is truth or not truth. The mind then is the vehicle for understanding the processes of matter, and the mind is the only organ that allows humanity to advance in knowledge. She argues that science is only valid if demonstrated to her consciousness but may not be accurate to another if it cannot be shown to them.

Consequently, the mind is the only vital organ for humanity. Amelia concludes by saying that "psychological law" is a science that underlies all others. A human being's character can be read in their aura, and everyone has the power to use it, but few do. In other words, everyone has the inherent ability to influence the world around them.[182]

Amelia's evening lecture, a continuation of the same theme, was titled "Self-Government vs. Elective or Representative Government." In trance, she stated that "the human family knows but little," primarily because they bow to a power outside of themselves that compels submission. Her criticism of God and church teachings pointed to the church's idea that humanity is depraved, possesses original sin, and that "everyone belongs to and owes obedience to God, and yet all they could do will not appease his anger." She reminded the audience of how the Puritans first came to America out of a desire for freedom, yet oppressed others with scripture when they arrived. Arguing for "self-government" through control of the self with mind and reason, she described how few self-govern because they prefer to be governed by others. She pointed to Demosthenes, Socrates, Galileo, Copernicus, John Brown, and Abraham Lincoln as examples of people who "governed" themselves, and were thus able to affect an improvement in human conditions.[183]

Amelia's final lectures were delivered in trance the following week and reported in the January 8, 1885 edition of the *Banner of Light*. The control who delivered the lecture was an entity named "Solon," who had been an Athenian statesman, lawmaker, and poet. History remembers him as a reformer legislating against Athens' political, economic, and moral decline. He reversed all his predecessors' laws, which had stated that all crimes were punishable by death. It is not surprising that Amelia would bring this entity forward in her two-part lecture titled "The Seen and the Unseen; the Touch and the Untouched; the Heard and the Silent."

In the first part of the lecture, given in the morning, the control tells the audience that what they can see is a natural result of the unseen forces of the universe. "In all nature, the unseen power is the force that brings to view the seen." Solon, via Amelia, describes the galvanic battery as an example—it could not be "seen" or created into material form without the power of the "unseen," and the forces of copper and zinc trying to create an equilibrium. Lightning could not be visible without an equalizing electrical disturbance. The human body is composed of all the elements of nature and holds an "unseen" power within it. This unseen power is the battery for mediums to express the ideas of spirit. However, few understand these laws of nature and create conditions that prevent this internal power, or spirit, from giving full expression.

Amelia's control explained that each person's aura holds a "photographic plate" recording all their life events. The world may see a prominent person as inherently good, but the history of his actions may show his spirit differently. A servant could have a brighter aura than the master based on the servant's charity, kindness, and good deeds. "The blessings you give to humanity are from your motives. Motives are the expression photographed and not the outward, ostentatious act." In other words, a person who acts without love, kindness, or charity makes the act unworthy, and their photographic plate reflects this.

Directly addressing the audience, Solon via Amelia then acknowledges that not everyone who consults a medium receives visits from family and friends or obtains truthful information. The control lays the blame on the individual: "They cannot reach you sometimes because there is so much deceit that covers you." People must change their mode of living if they want to change the events reflected in their aura. Unless they change their motives and lifestyle, "the love of your friends," or spirit communication, will never reach you:

Do not charge it to spirits or the medium, but to yourself. If you wish communion with your spirit-friends, purify yourself and make such conditions that they can come to you, and they will give to you the truth as they see it. Remember, the unseen forces are greater than the seen, and they produce it.[184]

This astounding finger-pointing toward her listeners, accusing them of having auras filled with deception, boggles the mind. Amelia's control comes perilously close to mimicking the very ministers she, herself, criticizes. However, even more people attended the second part of her talk, given in the evening. It is curious to note that in this lecture, Amelia's control perceives the spirit as more significant than the mind and reason—an idea reversed in other lectures, where mind and reason take precedence over everything. However, the control's criticism highlights the need for the audience to improve their lives, improve humanity, and understand that the power or spirit that fills the universe also fills them.

The same control, Solon, reaffirms that "the unseen," or Spirit, gives us our greatest strength. Reviewing some of the history of humanity filled with ignorance and superstition, the control advises that Spiritualism exists to "tear away these obstructions and open to the light of truth the powers of the universe." Amelia's control reminds the audience of the Inquisition and other civilizations that supported a master over a slave, concluding that now "is a beautiful time to live upon the earth." Solon via Amelia believes a beautiful life results from an individual's freedom of expression and ability to choose how to live their life, and adds that individuals hold the key to moving forward from the past and using their knowledge to do good in this life and the next. Amelia's control concludes with a beautiful statement concerning death:

Should you fear death? Ah no! It is but the rising sun after the darkness and bears you on to the noonday. It brings beauty; it gives power to scale the walls of the past. When I merge from one life, I enter into the beauties of another. It is not necessary to forget the labors and acquirements of yesterday to enter upon and obtain those of today, for all that has been attained will always remain with and of us ... Everywhere is motion, growth, life, experience. Your mediums require your help to sustain them. If right conditions were given by you, we of the spirit world could talk with you as you do to one another. I close with the best wishes and the blessing of Solon.[185]

Amelia's control is less accusatory in the second lecture but continues to urge the audience to improve their lives and humanity. The beauty of the statement "Should you fear death? Ah, no! It is but the rising sun after the darkness, and bears you to the noonday" highlights the draw Spiritualism held for its adherents. Tearing down the idea that death is something to be feared releases people from a life of oppressive dread. As Amelia points out, a person may work to do good, but is doing good motivated by fear or love? If by fear, then how can it be good? She emphasizes that unseen power exists throughout the universe and must exist in humanity despite past church teachings. The audience only needs to learn lessons from the past and improve the present by tapping into their own unseen power.

Following the Boston series, Amelia traveled 100 miles south to Norwich, Connecticut, where she lectured on "The Political Outlook of the Country" in trance. The *Banner* correspondent, Byron Boardman, reported in the January 31, 1885 edition that Amelia was creating a decided sensation in the Spiritualist community by pointing out the political actions, intrigues, and corruption against the rights of the people. Rebuking party corruption in "the most scathing terms," she urged the audience to use their reason to see the truth. Following her engagement in Norwich, she traveled 200 miles north to Portland, Maine, where she stayed at the home of an old friend, Thomas P. Beals. Although she served the Spiritualist community in Portland on Sundays, she made a special trip to Farmington, 90 miles farther north, to deliver two weekday lectures. The report in the March 21, 1885 edition of the *Banner of Light*, by Dr. P. Dyer, reflects Amelia in classic form:

Orthodoxy has just received one of the most vigorous shakings up in this town it has ever experienced. Mrs. Amelia H. Colby has been here, and the Christian community knows it ... The first lecture, though Mrs. Colby was a stranger here, was listened to by about eight hundred people; and at the last lecture, the house was packed to its utmost capacity. Mrs. Colby has the honor of being the pioneer speaker upon the subject of Spiritualism in this section; and as the people were nearly all born in the fold of the Church, and were reared upon the milk of Orthodoxy, her advent among them, and her bold and crushing criticisms of their religious notions, were well calculated to startle and confound them. Such was the effect. Today nothing is talked about but Mrs. Colby's lecture. The ministers are mad, the laity are excited, and the liberals are rejoicing ... The ministers did all they could to keep people away from the lectures, and they are now doing all they can to counteract their effect. When called upon personally by myself the Sunday morning previous, with a request that they give notice of the lectures, they promptly refused to do so. Such is Christianity in Farmington. It is staggering under the sledgehammer blows dealt to it by Mrs. Colby, and it will be a long day, if ever before it can assume its equilibrium again.

Amelia returned to Boston in March 1885, where she stayed the month with Mr. M.S. Ayer, the president of the Boston Temple Society. Her first lecture addressed the current attempts by the Medical Society in Massachusetts to regulate alternative medicines. Medical licensing laws were a hot topic nationally, and Spiritualists opposed those laws almost universally. Amelia compliments Boston for its love of truth and concerted efforts to suppress attempts to curtail human rights, and acknowledges the recent "Doctor's Petition," which argued for restrictions on alternative medicine and giving doctors exclusive rights to treat patients. Many people sought treatment from alternative practitioners, such as medical mediums and spiritual healers, who advocated hydropathy, herbs, tinctures, and other home remedies. The alternative practitioners also called for proper diet, exercise, and loose clothing for women.

Physicians, who often prescribed medicines to treat symptoms rather than the illness, were avoided by many—and for good reason. Drugs, including purgatives, stimulants, and narcotics such as opium, frequently made the individual worse than before. Amelia delivered a scathing rebuke of licensed physicians by stating that they are "filled with egotism and think that the world must come to them for help and not to any others."

Ridiculing the idea that textbooks and education alone make a good physician, she saw an "educational aristocracy" holding power over others. Amelia accused physicians of attacking all forms of treatment until theirs was the only one left, and added that "nature makes true physicians" while education alone does not make an effective one. She saw mediums as true healers simply because they followed nature's laws and received their advice from the spirit.[186]

Amelia's attack on education is surprising if nothing else. The constant refrain of all female reformers was that women should be afforded the same opportunities in education as men. Without education, women were stuck in the same rut as before—unable to earn an adequate income and thus required to look for a husband to support them. However, the issue Amelia condemns is not education in and of itself but rather the restrictions against alternate medical practitioners and the public's inability to choose what was best for themselves. Amelia saw this as usurping the Constitution's promise of freedom and liberty. She concluded her lecture by telling the audience that they knew themselves better than anyone else and had the right to choose when it came to the health and well-being of their own bodies. The argument rages on in the twenty-first century—in today's world, Amelia would likely have been the first to say, "My body, my choice."

Amelia's second lecture, "Where Are You Drifting?" (reported in the same issue of the *Banner of Light*), continues the theme of the morning lecture and touches on several subjects related to human rights. She argues that truth never fears investigation, but all nations tend to create a master-slave relationship with their populations. When thinking men present the truth, bigotry and ignorance attempt to crush it. She sees the correlation between the attempts to regulate medicine and physicians making themselves a privileged class:

> If your child dies under their treatment, it dies according to law, and no questions are asked; the next shares the same fate, and is dismissed with "The Lord gave," etc. The hand of a nurse, a mother's care, and applications are forbidden, or if not by this law, it is a long stride toward such restriction. You have rights, and you should not, under any pretext, surrender them.

In other words, the "mechanical physician," or those who follow textbook remedies, get a free pass if their patient dies. Those who rely on home remedies or alternative medicines, such as water-cure treatments, magnetic treatments, herbal potions, and even the mother's care, can be brought to the courts if their patients do not respond and die. Comparing the attempts of physicians to the church's efforts to control people, Amelia points out that the church "has been praying for the spirit to be poured out upon all people,"—but now that Spiritualism has brought it, the church won't acknowledge it.

By the Constitution, we worship according to the dictates of our conscience. Yet chaplains are appointed in both army and navy to enforce their religious opinions on the minds of others. According to state and national laws, everyone belongs to himself but has no right to encroach upon another's rights. The legislative bodies are for the protection of the whole state and not to make any privileged classes. Amelia concludes that the time is coming when everyone will be his own physician. This is the ultimatum for the American people.

The attempts by the Massachusetts Medical Society to regulate the practice of medicine were not new and had been attempted in multiple other states as well. Amelia, and most Spiritualists, saw the bid to restrict homeopaths, spiritual healers, and other alternative practitioners as a violation of their rights preserved under the Constitution. Amelia's comparison to church oppression is a provocative but telling argument and one that Spiritualists agitated against at every turn. While ministers saw disease of the spirit in women specifically, medical men "alleged that a disease-prone reproductive system governed women's physiology, resulting in inevitable physical frailty." It was as if both groups collaborated to oppress women and control all people.[187]

The following week, Amelia's lecture addressed the inequality between men and women. In trance, she observed that women were superior when they had equal advantages with men. However, the childhood training of women was far from being similar to men, and it affected their health and well-being:

> The boy is allowed to exercise freely and fully in the open air, in climbing, running and jumping, etc.; the girl is refused these exercises because it is claimed they do not look well. Alluding to the dangers that the boy and girl meet with as they grow up and mingle with the world, it was said that while the unfortunate daughter is cast aside, the man who has made her such is honored by society, and maybe

placed in some honorable office ... Woman stands man's equal and should be allowed equal advantages as legislators, jurors, and lawyers. When a woman has these and other rights, she will be true, and man will be as true as he desires a woman to be.[188]

Amelia rightly acknowledges the cause of women's frailty—not a diseased reproductive system, as the doctors believed, but a lack of exercise in nature. She points out that women are more often intuitively capable of making clear, sound judgments and should command respect with their presence. Unless there is a change for women's equality, "man will be compelled to pay in full" in the spirit sphere. There will be no escaping "all the wrongs to women" in this life or the next. Amelia's control said the very thing that most women thought—women had been wronged for centuries, and men would not escape the consequences of their inability or unwillingness to correct those wrongs. Again, her comments come perilously close to orthodox views of punishment and sin.

During Amelia's tenure at the Boston Spiritual Temple, several societies came together to give a reception in honor of her work in Boston. The party was hosted by Mrs. E.R. Dyar, the settled speaker for The Working Union of Progressive Spiritualists at Berkeley Hall. The party included leaders from College Hall, the Spiritual Temple, and several from the Ladies Aid Society. In addition, the group included John Wetherbee, a noted lecturer and the author of *Shadows,* which was a compilation of experiences in Spiritualism. In actuality, the reception was a "working" reception since several of the mediums gave lectures in trance and clairvoyant messages to the group. For Amelia, it was a welcome respite from traveling and lecturing, even though she gave a short lecture, in trance, during the gathering.[189]

Amelia's next lecture for the Boston Spiritual Temple addressed a subject on which Spiritualists articulated various views. None agreed with each other. The issue of reincarnation generally elicited a healthy debate, but most Spiritualists denied the existence of reincarnation.

Amelia's lecture titled "Evolution and Reincarnation" fearlessly addressed the issue. She reaffirmed what most Spiritualists believed at the time—that reincarnation was impossible, and that evolution occurred in the physical and spirit worlds. It was contradictory to say that the spirit world was composed of spheres where individuals progressed upward, and at the same time believe that individuals would return in a different form and different personality. The Spiritualist idea that the individual's character was retained in the spirit world did not cohere with reincarnation. However, Amelia points out that we are constantly involved in the process of evolution and reincarnation or "re-embodiment." She rejects the concept of reincarnation promoted by Helena Blavatsky, founder of Theosophy, although she does not mention Theosophy itself in her lecture.[190]

> ...our experiences constitute our individual lives; they make us what we are and foreshadow what we may be when ages upon ages shall have elapsed. Re-embodiments are constantly going on; bodily, you are not this year what you were last; you will not be next year what you now are.

Amelia spoke at The Working Union of Progressive Spiritualists in Boston on Sunday, March 22, 1885. The Union was a group of liberal, freethinking Spiritualists and one of many in Boston. The *Banner of Light* records her lecture a week later. Telling her audience that Spiritualism came to earth and found superstition and ignorance, she identifies superstition as orthodox church teachings and states that Spiritualism arrived to wage war with them "and anything that hinders human advancement."

> ...It brings a tidal wave of justice and kindness to overcome all oppression; it unlocks the door of mystery of your immortal life. Underlying all human life, there is a spiritual progression laid out, an evolution of power and progress for the human family. How favored are the people of these United States; they are far advanced beyond other nations. See what a great amount of power and liberty you have

in politics and religion and the right of investigation; no clanking of chains, no usurpation of power for you here in this country.[191]

Again, Amelia's nativism is apparent. She sees the United States as the greatest nation on earth and believes that Spiritualism came to America first because her people had more wisdom, intelligence, and progressive thought than any other nation. Pointing to the fact that "spiritual manifestations" are becoming prominent throughout the country and that "friends are returning to you in full form," she acknowledges the possibility of deception. It was hard to ignore it— when Spiritualists entered the darkened seance rooms, it opened the door for many frauds in the movement. Amelia acknowledges fraudulent activity but then asks her listeners if they have always lived an authentic life with no element of deception. She then states a repetitive strain among Spiritualist apologists—if there is deception in the audience, it will only attract deceptive spirits. "Do you always expect spirits to be honorable and just if those good qualities do not exist within *you*?"

Interestingly, Amelia gives the audience a prescription for growing into more spiritual life, and in doing so, her Quaker background comes through:

> I want each family to sit in silence one hour out of each twenty-four, with an aspiration and desire for something purer, higher, and nobler than is generally found in earth-life; do so for three hundred and sixty-five days, and you will progress in spiritual development far beyond your present comprehension. Try it, and your progress will astonish you. There is something within your nature which at times demands of you something higher; can it be obtained by reading the Bible? Not often, but the truths of Spiritualism will reveal it to you, and your longing will be satisfied. Let us be true to ourselves; our surroundings make it almost impossible, I suppose, but do be true one day out of the week; choose not Sunday for that is the hardest day in all the week to be true, because so many of you go to church three times that day, and you do not take your church with you, for you leave your true life at home.[192]

Amelia ended her lecture by saying that Spiritualism was the bridge to communication with the spirit world. She added that it would continue to tear down old beliefs until "the churches are toppled over," and reminded her audience to "live one day in the week true, and thus far you will help to destroy crime, end war, sorrow, etc.; then joy and sunshine will follow, and the cries of the poor unfortunate no more be heard to arise even to the seventh heaven." Her reminder to sit in silence, waiting for Spirit to give direction and knowledge, is one of the few instructions she gave explicitly and one that many people probably attempted to practice.

Amelia's final lecture for the society, "Belief and Catholic Influence Upon Mediums," touches on the negative side of belief. Claiming that "Catholic" means "universal," she compared the entire Christian church to the Jewish faith. Belief without knowledge begets ignorance, and ignorance allows the church to control the populace. Belief passes from parent to child, and ignorance continues. She tells the audience that whenever someone speaks out against church beliefs, they are labeled an infidel and persecuted. Claiming that knowledge overcomes belief and therefore destroys superstition and ignorance, she warns them not to accept the words of Spirit without reason, for spirits must stand the test of reason.[193]

Amelia celebrated the Anniversary of Modern Spiritualism with the Boston Spiritual Temple and shared the platform with J. William Fletcher, a popular clairvoyant since the age of seventeen, and his wife, Susie, who had been a clairvoyant and public lecturer since the age of fifteen. The couple were set up as professional mediums at the Lake Pleasant camp meeting in Massachusetts in 1873. Four years later, Fletcher traveled to England but was poorly received and heavily criticized by *The Spiritualist* magazine. In 1881, his wife, Susie, met more than criticism when an English court sentenced her to twelve months of hard labor for unduly influencing Mrs. Hart Davies to give up her home and possessions to the Fletchers. It is possible that the charges were accurate. Sadly, some Spiritualists were known for using spirit communication to unduly influence unsuspecting victims in this same manner. At the time of Susie's arrest and conviction, Fletcher was in Boston, lecturing to an audience of 3,000, and refused to return to

England since he would suffer the same fate. Susie Fletcher ultimately published her experiences of prison in 1884.[194]

Amelia's lecture discussed the beauty and necessity of death— no progress could be accomplished without the change of death. She claimed Spiritualism would narrow "the domain of creedal gods and widen that of natural law." The truth of natural law and Spiritualism would "disrobe the priesthood," disprove vicarious atonement and trinitarianism, and "extinguish the fires of creedal hell." Asserting that Spiritualism would destroy "a fear-cultivating theology" and bring humanity forward from their "darkened condition" to truth, knowledge, and liberty, she concluded that greater materializations were coming, and future generations would lift man higher into spiritual excellence than any prophet had ever dreamed, "and place by his side on the very pinnacle of successful achievement, his sister woman."[195]

During April, Amelia lectured for the Spiritualist Society in Springfield, Massachusetts. It is doubtful that she spoke in trance since they were lectures already presented in Boston. They included "The Seen and the Unseen," "Standing on the Threshold," and "The Cause of Human Life" delivered by the control "Solon." While lecturing in Springfield, Amelia sold her home in St. Louis. The local paper only records it as "Amelia H. Colby, et al., to Jas Weston—Lots 6, 7, and 8, city block 1610, 155 feet on Arkansas Avenue—warranty deed."[196] The question is who "et. al." signified, but there is no further information. However, since Amelia had not returned to Missouri since her departure in 1879, Olive Smith may have used the home as a halfway stop on her way back to California. In any event, Amelia received a cash influx that helped with travel and living expenses.

Before leaving for Worcester, Amelia was given a farewell reception in the home of two women who were using their home to offer "Light and Color Cures" to patrons. Amelia likely obtained healthcare services from these ladies before traveling to Worcester since she fully embraced alternative medical treatments. The Light and Color Cure was a technique authored by Edwin Babbitt, an American physician who pioneered the science of chromotherapy in his book *Principles of*

Light and Color, published in 1876.[197] Chromotherapy is still practiced today by some alternative practitioners.

Amelia spent May in Worcester and was planning to return to New York for lectures in various cities when tragedy struck. Receiving word that her daughter Lillian was deathly ill, she canceled her engagements and rushed to be by her side in Muncie, Indiana. Amelia arrived at Lillian's home just twenty-four hours before she passed away in June 1885. The correspondent for the *Banner of Light* reported that Lillian was thirty years old and left a husband and three young children. Amelia must have returned to New York soon after the funeral since it was reported that despite her grief, she "gave one of the most soul-stirring lectures we have ever heard."[198]

By July, Amelia had returned to the lecture circuit, appearing in Clarendon, New York, and the Cape Cod camp meeting at Harwich, Massachusetts. Her daughter's death took a greater toll on her than she presented to the public, though, and at the end of July she went to see Dr. Abbie Cutter at the Wickets Island Home. Dr. Cutter had opened the home in Onset Bay, Massachusetts, specifically for Spiritualist mediums and trance lecturers. According to Cutter, mediums required rest and care if they were to continue their work—the spirit could come close and strengthen the medium during rest periods. The home was also "intended as a spiritual school where teachers from the spiritual sphere can come and chemically change the organism and develop the various phases of mediumship that each person may possess."[199] Starting with nothing, Cutter had somehow managed to create a large home on Wickets Island—by the time Amelia arrived, it was fully functional with private rooms, a cafeteria, and various treatments, including electro-therapeutics and magnetic treatments.

Following her respite, Amelia returned to the lecture circuit with appearances at the Cape Cod camp meeting in Harwich, Massachusetts, and in Mount Pleasant Park in Clinton, Iowa, where she lectured with her old friends Dr. Juliet Severance and Moses Hull. She then traveled to Neshaminy Falls in Pennsylvania to speak before an audience of 5,000 and to Niantic, Connecticut camp meeting to finish the summer season. During September and October, Amelia was in Portland, Maine, where she gave fourteen lectures. Annie D. Fisher, the corresponding secretary for the society, wrote in the *Banner:*

> Mrs. A. H. Colby, the well known radical speaker, has been with us the past six weeks, giving our society fourteen lectures, all of which have been acceptably received. The subjects were well chosen and handled in a manner showing not only intellectual power but great force and decision of character. Thomas Paine, whose name is spoken with pride by every lover of American liberty, has been the source of the waves of inspiration that have thrilled our large audiences, bearing them upward to the highest unfoldment. It was thought by many that Mrs. Colby's radicalism would not call our people together and that her engagement might result in financial embarrassment, but the facts are, the lectures have been well attended by the best intellects of Portland, the audiences coming from all classes of liberal thinkers, hence financially a success. Mrs. Colby is engaged to return to us at her earliest opportunity, which is not until February and March of 1887, her entire time being engaged until then.[200]

Amelia's radical political discourses and her attacks on Christianity continued to give societies pause, but liberal Spiritualists and freethinkers were enthralled with her work and clamored to attend her lectures. The societies' financial success gave Amelia open doors to return in the future, keeping her busy and financially solvent.

"ALL PERSONS ARE BORN FREE AND EQUAL..."

In November 1885, Amelia returned to the Boston Spiritual Temple to give a series of lectures. Her first, "The Relation Existing Between All Classes of Spirits in the Spirit-World and This," denounced superstition, ignorance, and bigotry as the great enemies of human progress, and asserted "mere belief in a theory does not make it true." Humanity's beliefs and ignorance have generally thwarted spirits who have tried to enlighten humanity in the past. She argued that humans could not accomplish anything by building on ignorance, and continued to urge the audience to trust in and use their reason and internal power. "There is a power beyond our consciousness and within it ... and the channel of enlightenment is through mediumship. So, we should utilize all the powers given us, be they in whatever direction."[201]

She continued to address true and false mediumship by telling her listeners that to be a good medium, they must be "true to themselves and set an example worthy of the emulation of every true and aspiring soul." When Amelia talks about superstition and bigotry, she presents a milder version of past lectures where she forcefully denigrated the church. She believes that mediumship is the vehicle that will right the wrongs of society, but correspondingly, mediums should not fall prey to the baser temptations of life. Amelia is not only a radical freethinker but an idealistic Spiritualist as well.

The following Sunday, Amelia spoke to a packed house in Horticultural Hall on "Ancient and Modern Materialization Compared." Comparing modern materialization with multiple examples of phenomena in the Bible, she reminded the audience that human history is full of occurrences that have never been explained because the laws in which they occur are unknown. She pointed to the angels who appeared to Abraham at his tent in Mamre; the woman of Endor who summoned the spirit of the prophet Samuel for Saul; and the experiences of Shadrach, Meshach, and Abednego as evidence of materializations. Then she considered the materialization of a hand writing on Belshazzar's wall and compared it with appearances in seance rooms of hands writing communications to loved ones.

Amelia concluded that the Christian world must come to Spiritualism to prove materialization throughout the modern world. She claimed the appearance of Moses and Elijah to Jesus, Peter, and the rest of the disciples was evidence of materialization, and the story of the angel appearing to Mary at the Annunciation and the tomb of Jesus was further evidence. The comparison was evident to Spiritualists, even if it was not evident to Christians. The paradox of refusing to recognize modern materialization while accepting the stories of materialization in the Bible could not be more apparent in the lecture.

The Boston Spiritual Temple enjoyed a special event the following Sunday when the popular Cora Richmond joined Amelia for a double trance session. The November 21, 1885 edition of the *Banner of Light* recorded the session. Amelia spoke in her usual radical fashion with a lecture titled "What Must Be the Result of the Unreliable and Unsatisfactory Manifestations Given Through the Mediums of the Present?" The title is surprising since she had lauded manifestation to the skies in her previous week's lecture. Nevertheless, she discussed (in trance) the confusion that sometimes occurred when mediums presented clairvoyant messages and the messages were inaccurate. Her control observed that he did not know how much Spirit influences the medium or how much the medium influences Spirit. He said that a spirit "can say his name is Smith," but without additional evidence, there is no proof of identity.

Amelia's call for proof and the control's inability to determine who influences who are interesting. Mixed audiences accepted most early female mediums because of their passivity and ability to be controlled by spirit entities. Now, Amelia, or her control, suggests that Amelia herself may control the spirit entity. This reversal of roles was eye-opening and gave Amelia credit for her innate intelligence on the subjects being discussed. The comments also highlighted the possibility that the spirit might be in error—only the recipient of the message could ascertain the statement's accuracy. Amelia points to the necessity of "testing the spirits" and acknowledges the possibility of deception within the spirit. She explains that just because a spirit says "I am Mary" does not mean they are the Mary who is the recipient's loved one, but instead may be a spirit attempting to deceive the recipient. She adds that the recipient might have a deceptive personality themselves, thus attracting a deceiving spirit.

Amelia added that mediums should not offer their services unless they could present convincing evidence of true Spirit. She urged the audience to "give mediums a good surrounding aura, a truthful atmosphere" to receive reliable spirit communication. In addition, a medium who works on their communication before appearing in public will demonstrate manifestations more convincingly and develop "a band of strong forces" for his or her protection. Individuals who attend meetings and seances should use their judgment and discernment in determining whether to accept or reject a message from the spirit.

Amelia's blunt assertion that mediums have no business performing in public if they are incapable was an honest observation. Mediums without the ability to produce convincing evidence, and who relied instead on broad, vague, or general statements, were not helpful to Spiritualism. They allowed critics to argue that there was no proof of spirit communication. Her address was one of the most instructive lectures possible and touched everyone who heard her.

Later that evening, Cora Richmond was greeted by a large crowd who had come to hear her lecture "Are There New Beginnings in

Spiritual Growth?" Comparing Spiritualism to the springtime caused by the sun, she stated:

> Spiritualism was recognized as one of the spring-times in spiritual life; many others have preceded it. There are many spring-times in the spiritual growth of every individual, and then was the time to sow the seeds of knowledge and experience. Like the sowing of seed in the earth, the growth is gradual and continuous. When we first entered Spiritualism, we thought we had all that was wanted, viz: proof of immortality, but as we progressed, we found more and more to learn. In fact, Spiritualism is like ancient Rome, where the highways were made to radiate from it to all parts of the empire. So does truth radiate from Spiritualism into all life. If there is one medium untrue, there are thousands who are true. You who are in the light of the spiritual sun should rejoice to see this day.[202]

It was a poetic and beautiful tribute to Spiritualism and echoed Amelia's lecture in a way that was pure Richmond. The two women complemented each other—Amelia, bold and blunt; Richmond, poetic and soft. It would not be the only time the pair worked together to bring Spiritualism's voice to the public.

Amelia's next lecture for the Boston Spiritual Temple was one previously given to other societies. In the November 28 edition of the *Banner of Light*, the correspondent wrote, "Although Mrs. Colby physically was not as strong as usual, her discourse seemed not to lose its vigor nor the arguments any of their points." The comment regarding Amelia's health may have been the first indication that the years of travel were beginning to weigh on her. Still, she met her commitment to her work despite her physical ailment. Her final lecture for the society was inspired by a question from the audience. Someone asked, "Who was the author and who was the writer of the Declaration of Independence, and what is the result of the present condition growing out of the country?" In reply, she said:

> America has bestowed upon her children a condition never before enjoyed by any people. We find a people more intellectual and more

just because of the liberty they possess. There are opinions that cannot be changed by what may be said here, but those who have read Thomas Paine's published works and compare them with the Declaration will find a similarity. His "Common Sense," "The American Crisis," and other publications were referred to it. He advanced the thought of making this new country a free one with the broadest ground for everyone fleeing oppression, whether civil or religious.

Amelia alleged that Paine was the author of the Constitution, but his draft was criticized and severely edited. She added that if his draft had remained intact, "Woman would not now be suing for the equality she is asking for." She concluded that Paine always acknowledged the rights of the minority but accepted majority rule. The greatest liberty in a country brings the most splendid harmony to the people—and while oppression still existed in America, she firmly believed that following the Constitution would lift this oppression.

Thomas Paine was indeed influential in those early years of drafting the Constitution, and his fall from grace came only after he attacked Christianity in *The Age of Reason*. While the upper echelons of society and the church condemned him, the working man, the farmer, and the lower classes never forgot what he had done for America and continued to hold him up as a national hero. Amelia reminded her audience of that while emphasizing that no political party could give them the freedom they desired—oppression is only defeated by the freedom of individual sovereignty. Amelia addressed the second half of the original question by looking at the country's current state. The correspondent summarized her thoughts:

All persons are born free and equal of whatever sex, race, color, or previous condition. The male judges of the Supreme Court of the United States say "all persons" mean "all men." In this view, a female child is a slave and remains one from the cradle to the grave.

Amelia compares the oppression of women to the oppression of the working class by the capitalist in America. When labor and capitalists work together, "harmony prevails," but when either tries to oppress the other, nothing but conflict will ensue. Amelia believes both have demands to be met with fair and equal results. "The prosperity of a nation depends upon a healthy, harmonious state of its people." Eliminating oppression of all people and creating a fair and equal relationship between capitalists and workers, men and women is the only solution.

Amelia's attitude borders on socialism or, at the very least, verbalizes a mild form of anarchism. The idea of harmony between capitalists and working men was not new. Spiritualists voiced it before her, including Juliet Severance and Victoria Woodhull, who both advocated labor reform. However, unlike her earlier instructions on attaining accurate mediumship, Amelia identifies the solution but sees no path for harmony between the working classes and the capitalists. It was an error that most Spiritualists in the late nineteenth century made. Their disdain for authority, unwillingness to organize, and insistence that the "highest form of government was inferior" failed to bring concrete societal reforms.[203]

After her successful engagement in Boston, Amelia traveled to Brooklyn to speak for the First Brooklyn Society of Spiritualists during December and then back to Worcester, Massachusetts, for January and February 1886. At the end of her two-month engagement in Worcester, she returned to Boston.

The society at Worcester had nothing but high praise for Amelia and again noted that her lectures drew the biggest crowds and had the most financial success:

> During the two months she has been with us, we have had the largest and most intelligent audiences assembled in our hall since the association was formed, and I can truthfully say that none have had any but words of praise to speak of her, and she will leave here with the respect, esteem and best wishes of all who have listened to or met her. We regret exceedingly that our engagement with her cannot be prolonged from two months to two years.[204]

This correspondent's letter suggests that the leaders asked Amelia to remain with the society as a "settled speaker." By the late

1880s, many societies were hiring mediums to act as their "pastor" or routine speaker. Cora Richmond accepted a permanent position in Chicago, stipulating that she could take travel breaks. Others, such as W.J. Colville and Nellie J.T. Brigham, came off the road altogether and settled into permanent positions. Amelia turned down the possibility—like other itinerant lecturers, she preferred travel to remaining in one place. The reasons were varied, but for many, there was the feeling that the work was too important to be confined to one limited area. Amelia believed that spreading the news of Spiritualism as far as possible was her duty and her chosen field.[205]

Amelia returned to Boston in March. Her first lecture began uncharacteristically in a more poetic fashion than she had ever used before:

> We had hoped to present to a Boston audience a vivid description, and with them make a visit to the reality of spirit-life, and observe the rising and setting sun in the realm of thought; to see the glistening drops as they hung on shrub and tree, and feel the rest that comes from the dim twilight, and the rising of the sun pouring forth its early mellow rays. Then to stand upon the Mount of Reason, view its surroundings, and go down its sides into the valleys and hamlets below, there to educate and assist those who dwell on the broad plains around. But however pleasant this might be, and however instructive, we must come down to the realities of life here, with all its trials, its duties and its labors that surround us; and we take for our subject, "The Issues to be Met."[206]

Amelia couldn't help herself. What came next was a lecture addressing the inequities found in the world, her warnings about the loss of freedom in America, and her denunciation of the church if change did not occur. She told the audience that America needed to learn from the rise and fall of past empires, and "in politics, in religion and in social life, the aggrandizement of one to enslave another must be changed, and all stand upon one common ground of liberty." She asserted that Calvinism was not dead, and the oppressive dictates of the church were not lifted; the cry of humanity was still freedom, and women deserved their rights. "No political health can be where woman has no voice." Asking how the government could erect monuments to the dead while leaving their "living neighbors, a soldier's widow and children in suffering and want," she argued that a "united action of man and woman is necessary"—but that men only desired power and could not exercise clear judgment because the desire for power was too overwhelming. She held up women's voices to combat this male power grab and argued again for harmony between labor and capital. If men and women worked together equally, "justice will rule the land and America will become what she has set out to be—a place where all are free and equal."

Leaving politics behind for the next few Sundays, Amelia attacked the Bible and the church with such fervor that the correspondent for the *Banner of Light* was forced to summarize it very briefly. Beginning with a history of Christianity, she examined a story attributed to the Council of Nicaea, an assemblage of bishops formed by Constantine to establish church doctrine. She told the audience that the assembled bishops of the Council allegedly selected a large number of manuscripts (fifty) and put them under the communion table. The books to be chosen miraculously appeared on the top of the table and the bishops then voted, identifying Matthew, Mark, Luke, and John as the sacred canon. Amelia concluded that this story was pure myth. The primary source of the story came from Voltaire, who took the fictional account from the *Synodicon Vetus,* an anonymous, pseudo-historical account of early Christian history, and denounced it. It is not surprising that Amelia echoed Voltaire's work since most freethinkers held him up on the same pedestal as Thomas Paine. Voltaire was a deist who denounced the church, ministers, and the Bible as being based on myths, and who argued for people's civil rights.

Amelia's evening lecture, "The Champions of the Church," continued her attack on the church by reviewing the achievements of Alexandria and relating the horrific details of the murder of Hypatia at the hands of the Bishop of Alexandria. Although most scholars determined that Hypatia's death was politically motivated, Voltaire saw it as a Christian effort to extinguish a pagan and used it as an anti-Catholic argument. Hypatia, a female Neoplatonist philosopher, astronomer, and mathematician, was a brilliant teacher, author, and inventor who lived in Alexandria. She was cruelly murdered by a mob of Christians, with most historians believing that the order came from Cyril, the Bishop of Alexandria.[207] Her killing was far more horrific than Amelia recounts—or the correspondent was prepared to report:

> Hypatia, while in her carriage going to give one of her lectures, was assaulted by a mob, taken to a church under the direction of this Bishop and before the altar murdered, and the flesh from her bones scraped off and burned. This Bishop drove forty thousand Jews from the city. He stopped the investigation of science. Alexandria fell with her two libraries and schools of science, and no other city has taken her mantle.[208]

Amelia returned to her earlier attacks on the church's hypocrisy and its persecution of any who did not follow its theology. She recounted horror tales of the Christian Roman emperor Theodosius, who slaughtered 17,000 men, women, and children, presumably referring to the "Massacre of Thessalonica" and that emperor's campaign to stamp out paganism. Moving through history, she recalled Charlemagne, Mary I of England (or "Bloody Mary" as history recalls her), John Calvin's persecution and slaughter of Michael Servetus, and the witch hunts of Europe and America. She warned the audience that "champions of the church are here and now as much as at any time previous." This change from Spiritualist philosophy to her former freethinking, radical attacks on the church may have resulted from the Boston audience welcoming the liberal nature of her lectures. On the other hand, perhaps she was simply being true to herself, resuming her arguments against orthodoxy and advocating for equal rights and freedom of conscience. It also reflects how informed and educated Amelia was at this stage in her life.

The following week, she tackled the character, attributes, "the abode and throne of God, and the worshipers that surround and prostrate themselves before that throne." It may well be that her lecture was so radical and severe that the correspondent would not summarize the address as in times past in an attempt to avoid controversy within Spiritualist circles and the general public. Her evening lecture—"If

There Is No God, What?"—was only briefly mentioned, likely for the same reasons. The April 17, 1886 edition of the *Banner of Light* reported her final speech to the Boston Spiritual Temple on the Anniversary of Modern Spiritualism. It began with the more lyrical and philosophical tenets of Spiritualism.

> Oh! beautiful Death, you did not close the portals so tightly after you that the prayers of earth's children are ever unheard over there! The angels have left the gates ajar: they have proven to humanity the immortality of the soul, and man's unfolding reason bids him no longer fear demons and tortures.

Amelia summarized the history of Spiritualism by stating that there was "so much to tear down" to bring freedom to the people. Asserting that Spiritualists had defeated the idea of the Bible being the infallible word of God, and the belief that an omnipotent God was seated on a throne in heaven, ruling over humanity, she next points to the Spiritualist argument against heaven and hell as real places in the universe—reminding her listeners that they only exist in the individual's mind. She states that Spiritualism came to give hope to humanity where there had been none before:

> Spiritualism came not to teach the human family how to die, but how to live correct, just, and true lives; not that God will damn them if they do not, or bless them if they do, but that, by a wayward course, they will damn themselves, and the blessings which they require will be further away than they otherwise would have been.

In other words, the concept of heaven and hell, damnation and blessing were solely within the individual. Most Spiritualists could not condone a place called hell, alleging the idea was inconsistent with a benevolent God. Amelia rejects the concept of God altogether and points instead to the natural laws of the universe. If God exists in all things of nature, it only stands that God exists within humanity. Therefore, humanity holds its own key to blessing (heaven) or damnation (hell). She continues more philosophically about the benefit of Spiritualism:

> ...it has long held you in its tender embrace; it has brought to you your loved ones, and filled the vacant chair: Bibles can be lost, and no one be sorry: churches can go down, and no one mourn; but when you think of the mother who has passed away, still loving and caring for her own, of the father who has left the earth sphere of action, still mindful of the welfare of his dear ones, of the babe who goes to spirit-life in its infancy, protected by the laws of growth and lavishing its love and tenderness on those who remain upon earth—what could you do without it? It has tinged the clouds of life with the sunshine of immortality and taught you that when you pass from this sphere to another and unfolded sufficiently, you shall find rest from the sorrows and cares of earth, and the burdens you have born; the shackles of time shall fall from your soul, and you shall be free in a world of purity and holiness.

In the final part of her lecture, Amelia reminds her audience of the continued oppression of women and the laboring classes. She reports that according to the 1880 United States Census, 1,280,000 children under the age of sixteen were working from early morning until nighttime, nearly seven days a week. She states that this destroys children's health for nothing but the sole purpose of building up millionaires, which is not consistent with Spiritualist philosophy. Her observation may well be accurate. She urged her listeners to work at enacting laws to protect child labor and reminded them that Spiritualism came to America precisely because the Constitution promises freedom from oppression—including freedom from oppressive labor laws and liberty from priestly and religious rule. "The Church is endeavoring to unite itself with the State, and you need to watch your rights at midnight as well as at noonday, for when you put God into the Constitution, you put the American citizen out."

The correspondent's summary makes it appear as if Amelia's thoughts were disjointed, jumping from topic to topic. However, there was probably a line in Amelia's thinking, that the correspondent failed to record, which led from the oppressive labor laws to God in the

Constitution. Nevertheless, Amelia's lectures in Boston highlighted her knowledge of world affairs and religion, and her ability to bring financial success to an organization.

Following her Boston service, Amelia traveled to Norwich, Connecticut for April, then to Brooklyn, New York, where she lectured to the First Society of Spiritualists during May. She planned to lecture at various camps during the summer months, but illness prevented more travel. In an uncharacteristic letter to the *Banner of Light*, published on July 3, 1886, she admitted to exhaustion and illness, canceling all engagements through August.

> Allow me through your columns to say to my many correspondents that my seeming neglect in replying to their letters of congratulation and kindness is occasioned by a severe illness of ten days at the home of Amy Post, Rochester, N.Y., during the second and third weeks in June, entirely unfitting me for any duties of a mental character. For the first time in my twenty-six years on the public rostrum have I been compelled to cancel an engagement, but my entire nervous energies had become so exhausted that I have been using for two years past more physical strength than I was able to generate, hence there was no other alternative but to drop down.
>
> I hope to be able to commence my work at the Camp-Meeting of the First Society of Spiritualists of Philadelphia near the middle of August. Till then, all engagements are cancelled. My time is entirely engaged until one year from September next. Shall be very glad to hear from my friends, all of whom belong to the great humanity. My address till further notice will be 176 Terrace Street, Buffalo, N.Y.
>
> A . H . Colby.

Amelia's stay at Amy Post's home is not surprising. Post was well known for her hospitality, but more so for her healing skills. Her late husband, Isaac Post, had owned an apothecary shop in the 1850s, and Amy was skilled in using herbs and tinctures. Her home provided a welcome spiritual or medical respite for a diverse group of friends, family, and even strangers, whether Quaker, Spiritualist, or freethinker.[209] Amelia, a long-time friend and co-worker, felt no qualms in allowing Amy to give her medical care. She and Amelia likely had long discussions about the conflict between Spiritualism and their materialist, freethinker friends.

Despite her promise to resume lecturing in August, Amelia did not return to the circuit until September 1886, when she traveled to Iowa for a month-long engagement. Still needing rest, she traveled back to Crown Point, Indiana, where she stayed with an old friend, James H. Luther, during November. They had been friends since the 1860s, and Amelia had spent time in his home with fellow Spiritualist E.V. Wilson, where they gave entranced lectures to Luther's friends and family.

In December, Amelia returned to the Boston Spiritual Temple, giving lectures twice daily on each Sunday of the month. She quoted John 10:20 as the basis of her first lecture, stating, "He hath a devil and is mad, why hear ye him?" She then counted off the men and women in history who had been thought mad but, in truth, had helped the world to progress in both spiritual and material ways, so much so that they could be labeled saviors of humanity. For example, she pointed to Galileo's hypothesis of the earth traveling around the sun—which opened humanity to astronomy and broadened their perspective—and noted Benjamin Franklin's accomplishments, James Watts' invention of the steam engine, and Samuel Morse's invention of the telegraph. She pointed to how Amy Post was accused of madness when she took the Fox girls to Rochester for a demonstration, and then tongue-in-cheek said, "But Mrs. P was an anti-slavery woman and was used to being called mad."

In her evening address, Amelia discussed Spiritualism's progress, urging the audience to actively unite. Spiritualists were notorious for their failure to organize into a cohesive body. Her argument for organizing was surprising given her absolute dislike of authority and promotion of freedom of conscience. However, she believed liberty was only possible if those liberal minds banded together. She paid tribute to those who advanced freedom for others, including William Denton, abolitionists Wendell Phillips and William Lloyd Garrison, and many others who worked to free the oppressed.[210]

The following week, Amelia's lecture promoted the philosophy of Spiritualism and the freedom it presented to humanity. The same control delivered her evening address, but rather than a lecture, the audience was given a guided meditation—something Amelia had not done in past lectures. The meditation took the audience into the world of Spirit.

> As we cross the line of mortal life, a guide takes us and places us in a car, the seats of which are like a cloud for softness. We start, and as we advance, the perfume of flowers fills the air. When we stop, we are welcomed by music and by friends. We pass on until we reach the foot of a mountain. The plain is filled with beautiful villas; the whole laid out in grandeur, and we are enraptured with the lovely scene before us.
>
> Proceeding, we approach the Mount of Reason and, ascending, find a city. He who is one of its residents has said, "The world is my country, and to do good my religion." The air is filled with music, and the people are in the enjoyment of the most refined pleasures. Before us is the great unknown realm of space; behind us are the experiences of a life within the power of progress. There is no death. Life exists here today, goes on, and will always continue. To the city on this mount, Thomas Paine has taken under his care many a waif, the oppressed, regardless of color or nationality, and he welcomes them to his home. Be true and just. The spirit world cannot do all the work; it must have your assistance. Mediums who are negative must have a strong protective power around them, and you must give it. Will you do this? If spirits are to come, they demand proper conditions. Will you provide such conditions?[211]

Unsurprisingly, Amelia took the audience to meet her hero, Thomas Paine. The words "The world is my country, and to do good, my religion" was the typical quote given by lecturers of the day, but it is not the complete original statement. In Paine's commentary on the French Revolution, *The Rights of Man,* he writes, "Independence is my happiness, and I view things as they are, without regard to place or person; my country is the world, and my religion is to do good."[212] Paine argued for liberty for the oppressed in whatever form it took against an individual in all his works, and Amelia revered him throughout her life.

Amelia's final lecture to the Boston Temple, "The Approaching Revolution," was pure Thomas Paine. Reviewing the early history of America, she reminded her audience that patriots had fought in the revolution for freedom from an oppressive aristocracy. The original impetus was freedom for all people—religious freedom, freedom of speech, and a free press. While the young nation began to grow with ideals of liberty and freedom, and without aristocratic rule, two classes appeared nevertheless—the wealthy and the poor. Telling her listeners that there was only "one of the first and a hundred of the other," Amelia argued that the way to equalize the disparity between the wealthy and the poor was at the ballot box. However, individuals must exercise their reason when voting. Too many say, "I vote with my party," without giving thought or reason to the policies that party represented. They would remain enslaved as long as they remained ignorant; thus, freedom was only a delusion.[213]

Amelia warned the audience that "a great revolution is before us. Such come, not always by bloodshed, but by the power of thought," and the result of the exercise of thought or reason had initiated some of the greatest revolutions ever known. She added that "powers that elevate the mind accomplish revolution." Arguing that religious wars had been the most destructive in the era of humanity, for they are led by the ignorant, she told the audience that studying past mistakes in history allowed them to move forward. It was their responsibility to understand the policies and laws of the nation and how it affected the country—and they were also responsible for ensuring that their children learned to think and reason for themselves.

After the lecture, she received a vote of thanks from the society, who felt it was her grandest lecture yet—radical and revolutionary. Amelia left Boston and returned to Crown Point, Indiana, where she shocked every Spiritualist and freethinker on the planet. She married James H. Luther on January 5, 1887, at the age of sixty. True to form, at least as far as the church went, she and James were married by a Justice of the Peace at Allman's Abstract Office in Crown Point, Indiana.[214]

NEW BEGINNINGS

AMELIA'S MARRIAGE TO JAMES Luther must have seemed shocking to many, but perhaps not to those who knew her well. There are no extant letters between the two, but by connecting the dots, they likely first met in the 1860s when both were living in Crown Point, where James was the postmaster. In addition, he was a long-time, active Spiritualist. He wrote letters to the *Banner of Light* and the *Religio-Philosophical Journal*, with the earliest correspondence printed on June 11, 1864, in the *Banner of Light*. In addition, he and his wife attended the first National Spiritualist Convention held in Chicago in 1864.

Amelia had lectured in the Crown Point area since the 1860s and had stayed at James' home during her travels to Chicago on speaking engagements in the late 1870s. James opened his home to any medium who was traveling through the area. In a letter to the *Banner of Light*, he noted, "I would also extend very kind remembrances to Mrs. Colby and Dr. Peebles, and all other lecturers whose company in my own house has given me so much pleasure, and from whom I have learned much."[215] It is clear they had been maintaining contact throughout the years. He was not only a Spiritualist, but also a freethinker like herself. When his wife died in 1882, he refused to allow prayers at the graveside, nor did he allow a minister to conduct the service.

James was Amelia's senior by thirteen years and a prominent businessman in the area. When making her decision to marry him, perhaps Amelia's recent bouts of illness swayed her thinking, or perhaps she was just getting tired. On the other hand, she may have realized that James was her spiritual affinity, and true to her Spiritualist beliefs, she agreed to marry him. Whatever the reason, the marriage surprised most of her friends, and Amelia immediately limited her speaking engagements, again suggesting that her health was a factor. She attended and spoke for the Chicago Association of Universal, Radical, Progressive Spiritualists and Mediums Society for the Anniversary of Modern Spiritualism on March 31, 1887, then traveled to Philadelphia in April.[216] It is not known whether her husband traveled with her, but Amelia announced in the May 7 edition of the *Banner of Light* that she had canceled all her engagements until September and would be at her home in Crown Point until that time. Although she did not elaborate, poor health was the likely culprit.

Amelia did not return to the lecture circuit until November 1887. However, she did not stop supporting Spiritualist organizations. On November 5, 1887, she and James signed as two of fifty founding members of the Indiana Association of Spiritualists, newly organized by Dr. John Westerfield. The latter had promoted Spiritualism and free thought since the 1860s at his hall in Anderson, Indiana. She and James had been friends with him since the mid-1860s, and it seemed natural that they would support the new organization within their state.[217] After pledging her support as a founding member, Amelia traveled to Boston for a month-long engagement at the Spiritual Temple in November, and then to Providence, Rhode Island, in December. Following these commitments, she returned home to Crown Point, a distance of 945 miles, where she remained until March 1888.

Her Boston lectures drew big crowds, and she remained one of their most popular speakers. She continued to speak on the nation's political state, and her first lecture at the Spiritual Temple addressed the Haymarket Affair, also known as the Haymarket Riot, an event that had consumed the country for the past year.

The event had started as a peaceful protest rally for atrocities committed by the Chicago police. On Monday, May 3, 1886, workers rallied at a plant in Chicago to agitate for the eight-hour workday. Although the rally was peaceful, police attacked and killed several picketers. A protest rally at Haymarket Square, in Chicago, was organized for the following day by Albert and Lucy Parsons—who were well known in labor reform circles. The protest was not as large as hoped, and when several engaged speakers did not appear, Albert stepped in with Samuel Fielden, an English-born Methodist lay preacher.

The event was nearly over when someone threw a dynamite bomb—the first time this had ever happened at a peaceful rally in United States history. Before the bomb, reports claimed that 176 police had gathered to break up the meeting, even though the governor of Illinois had approved the event. It was almost dark when the bomb was thrown, and most of the crowd had already dispersed. Seven police officers and four civilian workers died in the aftermath. The bomb itself killed only one officer—the remainder were mistakenly shot by fellow officers in the dark.

Martial law was declared nationwide, with several state governments using the Haymarket Affair to crush local labor unions. Officials arrested labor leaders across the city, and it did not matter whether they were at Haymarket or not. A total of eight men were charged, including Albert Parsons and Samuel Fielden. Although the attorneys agreed that no one could determine who had thrown the bomb, the eight men were nevertheless judged guilty. Officials seemed to be sending a message to labor activists when they sentenced seven of the men to hang as anarchists convicted of conspiracy, and gave one a fifteen-year sentence. The governor commuted the sentences of two men, a third committed suicide in jail, and four were hanged on November 11, 1887—even though there was no evidence that they were guilty of throwing the bomb. Albert Parsons was one of those four.[218]

Amelia addressed the issue directly in both lectures on her first Sunday at the society. She pointed to the need for justice and stated that the workers' rights had been trampled, but it was more than that. The real issue was freedom of speech, the right to assembly, the right to a fair trial, and the right of workers to organize. All these constitutionally mandated rights had been violated. She added that hanging alleged anarchists did not destroy anarchism, and it was the duty of every "friend of liberty to guard against further encroachments" of our rights. She rightly pointed to the court's acknowledgment that it was not known who had thrown the bomb, and while it "might be law, it could not be justice that condemned these men to death." She appealed to the spirit for justice and urged the audience to do so as well.[219]

The remainder of Amelia's lectures to the society focused on Spiritualist philosophy— some, such as "Belshazzar's Feast," had been given to other societies previously. Amelia may have been starting to tire. She spent December in Providence, Rhode Island, giving lectures repeated from other engagements, then stayed in Indiana until March 1888. Amelia then traveled to the Boston Spiritual Temple to assist at a memorial service for her old friend W.A. Dunklee, the society's treasurer. She gave the society an additional eight lectures, and at the close of her final speech, a resolution of thanks was offered and approved unanimously.

> Whereas the present is the last Sunday of Mrs. Colby-Luther's engagement, and as it is probable that *circumstances may not admit of her accepting another in Boston* [italics mine], it is but just that some expression of the highly appreciative sentiments of her Berkeley Hall hearers should be officially made.[220]

It is a telling statement given by the society. The reasons for the "circumstances" are not known, but Amelia's poor health or a lack of stamina may have played a part. She finished her tour with them at the Anniversary of Modern Spiritualism with a beautiful tribute to Spiritualism, which appeared in full in the April 14, 1888 issue of the *Banner of Light*.

Following her successful Boston engagement, Amelia traveled to Newburyport, Massachusetts, a short 40 miles away. While she was there, a traveling evangelist minister, Rev. Mr. B. Fay Mills, denounced Spiritualism, specifically women who were mediums, from the pulpit of every church he visited. Amelia responded on behalf of the Spiritualist community in Newburyport, and her reply, in the form of two lectures, was printed in Newburyport's *Herald*. The *Herald* article was reprinted in the *Banner of Light* on April 28, 1888:

It is an established fact that the ministers of all ages have been, are today, a hierarchy. This is a great power all over the world. I speak of Christians, and I use the word as I do that of Spiritualists. We may differ in our opinions, but this does not change facts. No matter whether you accept or deny it has nothing to do with the facts or truth. As the church teaches, the less we know the more we believe, and the more we believe, the less we know. If your Rev. Mills has facts, all I say cannot change them; they may be against my ideas, but all heaven or hell cannot change them. Spiritualism is a great principle, and as God is said to wink at ignorance—allow me to do the same with the reverend gentleman's (ignorance). It is a pity that a man should so debase himself as to deny and talk about that which he knows nothing of. I do not ask you to accept what I say, but if the newspaper reports are true, he debases himself. In his address, he brings up what he calls a witch; the Bible nowhere calls her a witch or hag, but somebody heads the chapter "a witch"—some clergyman probably. She is called "a woman."

Amelia then recounted the story of Saul, who consulted the woman of Endor to summon the spirit of Samuel and asked if he would be victorious in the battle of the Philistines. She questioned how Rev. Mills knew the woman was an "old hag" and doing the devil's work.

Instead of ridiculing women mediums as base [and] vile, let the pure mothers, wives, and daughters answer. Instead of ridiculing Spiritualism, the Bible is full of it, from Genesis to Revelations. The lecturer instanced Moses and Elijah on the Mount. How did Jesus know it was them? One had died thirteen hundred years before, and the other ten hundred; their history had not been written; how could Jesus know who they were? Were they really there at all? I don't know; your church and clergy say they were; what will he do with the story if it is true? Spiritualism answers.

Amelia moved to the divine conception of Jesus and asked how the clergy knew it was a true story. She wondered if they had bothered to investigate it as critically as they had investigated Spiritualism—or whether they had investigated Spiritualism at all.

> Today the reverends all talk about the misfortunes of Spiritualists. If I put on green goggles, everything is green; if I put on blue or white glasses, all is blue or white. If I use the eyes of those who are decrying this doctrine, does not all look to me as through their own medium? I can prove that he had false eyes upon the rostrum and could not know anything about Spiritualism for want of mental caliber. One cannot be a wise man in the true sense of the term and be a minister. I know they have much knowledge, but they are deceivers. Is this reverend ready to stand the test Jesus puts in a text like this: Go into the world and preach the gospel to every living creature?

The ridiculousness of the statement is the point itself. In arguing for the truth of the Bible, Mills contradicts himself by not following its tenets. Amelia very pointedly states that he cannot preach the gospel to "every living creature." Therefore, he is both a failure and a sinner by his own standards. Amelia continued to point out the numerous cases of materialization and prophecy listed in the Bible to show the hypocrisy of the church's rejection of Spiritualism or its inability to understand it. She argued that while "the church and the Bible remain the same, Spiritualism moves on and has fostered the arts, sciences, literature, poetry."

Amelia's evening lecture, "The Origin of the Bible," continued to criticize Mills. She began by asking where the Rev. Mr. Mills got his authority for referring to the woman of Endor as "a hag? In his creed? In his articles of faith? In his love of Jesus Christ? No, the word comes from the lowest slang and the vilest people." Amelia not only condemned the preacher's own words with corresponding arguments taken directly from the Bible, but she issued a challenge to him via the newspaper to a formal debate. She argued that ministers who believed in the infallibility of the Bible should be able to stand up to the tests that Jesus gave.

I ask the ministers to lay their hands on the sick and heal them—
the simplest test used by Christ. Hundreds of mediums are used for
that purpose, and thousands of human beings in the United States
are healed of diseases which had been pronounced incurable by the
medical fraternity.

Amelia finished her lecture by telling the audience that
Spiritualism came to redeem the world from ignorance, thus implying
that the church and its ministers worked to hold the populace in
ignorance. She stated this was the worst sin. In addition, the church
specifically and purposefully oppressed women—the mothers of
nations—which was another great sin, whereas Spiritualism lifted
them higher. Pointing out that Spiritualism had withstood the test of
the scientific community while Christianity had not, she prophesied
that as mediums were allowed to continue their work unmolested,
some of the most extraordinary phenomena of all time would appear to
the world—and "the reverend gentleman knows that as Spiritualism
marches on, his business is gone."

The war was on. The following Sunday, Rev. Mills' sermon was
titled "Diabolism and Demonology." He focused his address on the
devil and his imps, and evil, fallen angels, or spirits. The references to
Spiritualism were explicit. Amelia responded with "Christianity vs.
Spiritualism," sharply attacking the Bible, the church, and its ministers,
and claiming that Spiritualism was vastly superior to Christianity.[221]

The evidence seemed overwhelming. Amelia began by citing all
the acts of Catholic and other Christian rulers from earliest recorded
history, describing in blunt language the deeds of cruelty and bloodshed
committed in the defense and interests of the Christian church. She
argued that the Bible's claims could not be supported by any rational,
thinking human mind, and said that biblical justification of cruelty
and bloodshed in the name of God defied scientific investigation and
human advancement. Accusing the priests and the church of being the
foe of "mental progress in every department of literature, science, art,
and poetry," she was especially severe on the Christian doctrines of
vicarious atonement and forgiveness of sins, and argued against the

idea of heaven and hell. In typical Amelia fashion, she sarcastically denounced ministers:

> ...[heaven] was just about large enough to hold the seventy thousand ministers and priests who are living in luxurious idleness off the earnings, mainly of the wives, mothers, and daughters of the land.

Amelia spoke at length on the power of the clergy and priests over the women of this country, and declared that the time is nearing when women were beginning to think for themselves:

> ...to realize the tyranny of the Church—and they will ere long emancipate themselves from priestcraft, and force the representatives of the latter class of the community to shift for themselves and support themselves, as they should long ago have been forced to do.[222]

Amelia concluded her lecture by reviewing the benefit Spiritualism brings to the world, and its aims, principles, and objects. She continued to assert that Spiritualism, unlike Christianity, uplifted people—especially the nation's women—educated them, and argued for reforms, including temperance, public morals, woman suffrage, and labor reforms. That evening she repeated an old lecture, "What Shall We Do to be Saved?" and again drew comparisons between the scientific community, reason, and logic with the superstitions promoted by the church.

After returning home, Amelia made a short trip to Chicago to lecture for the First Society of Spiritualists during May. She did not travel again until August, when she returned to her beloved Cassadaga to speak on August 5, 7, and 11 of 1888. Following that, she and James worked on building the budding Indiana Association of Spiritualists.

Amelia's travel itinerary remained limited, but she connected with Lucy Colman, Dr. Juliet Severance, and Thaddeus B. Wakeman when she attended the Twelfth Annual Congress of the American Secular Union (previously the National Liberal League), held in Pittsburgh, in early October. Although she did not speak, she enjoyed the company and the discussions with all her old freethinking friends. The only friend missing, Amy Kirby Post, remained at home due to frailty and ill health. She would die on Thomas Paine's birthday, in January 1889.

Despite the announcement that she would likely not return to Boston, Amelia returned to its Spiritual Temple for a series of lectures in December 1888. Evidence shows that her husband traveled with her this time as she toured the northeast. Her lectures to the Boston Society were a mixture of Spiritualist philosophy, the beauty of the afterlife, and current political issues. Her final lecture was delivered in trance by the spirit of Thomas Paine and echoed his observations from *The Age of Reason.*

Paine (via Amelia) observed that reason was the most formidable weapon against error. Every age of humanity required someone to speak against bigotry and superstition, and those who reasoned least were the most superstitious and bigoted. He said that someone should write an *Age of Reason* for the modern world, and then addressed the new "Sabbath day laws" the church was attempting to pass. Urging the audience to keep a close watch on these attempts by the church to govern, Paine added that "If all the proposed measures should be carried, not a decade of time would pass before blood would run in your streets."

Sabbath day laws were instituted at the urging of the church to prevent people from working on Sundays so that they could attend church. Amelia accused the church of using the Bible for monetary profit. She explained that when people attend church, they give their money to the church rather than spend it at a store, on entertainment, or at other venues. The Sabbath day laws would restrict all trade on a Sunday, as well as travel, entertainment, mail, military and naval drills, and virtually anything that was not connected to the church.

Amelia was severe enough in her lecture to cause some of the male members in the congregation and those who embraced Christian Spiritualism to take issue with her ideas. She did not care. The evening lecture was the largest of the season. It was as if most of the congregation knew a battle was coming. Responding to her critics, Amelia did not mince her words:

Knowledge is the groundwork of wisdom. No man can use his best thought and subscribe to [religious] creeds without being a hypocrite. If the church has its say, in a few years only, you will have to put out the fires of the Inquisition. Can America lose her freedom?

I want to ask this intelligent audience, who shall I hold responsible for all the vices and crimes that flood our land? Who wields the scepter of government? Who fills your halls of legislation today? Is it possible that we can ascribe to woman any of the great prevailing evils? Who shall we hold responsible for the death of three hundred thousand men—victims of your late war? Was woman consulted in the matter? You answer, no; I answer no. Has woman any voice in closing the drinking saloons and places where crime is committed? You and I answer, no. If mothers could be consulted, they would put up the barriers of prevention against the ruin of their boys and girls. You are satisfied that this organic life is just what your surroundings and conditions have made it. Study the conditions of self-hood from a standpoint of right. Dare to be true. Dare to be just. If, as a Spiritualist or freethinker, I have a principle, that principle I must give thought to. If I think at all, that principle I must live, if I live at all. Arouse into action and set your houses in order. Soon the call will be sounded, and you will be obliged to leave your accumulations. Shall I again ask you to protect American liberties?[223]

It is no wonder that women flocked to hear Amelia speak, and in this response, she was brutally honest and accurate. Women had no control over state or federal laws created or enacted. They had no say in decisions related to war or peace, or to saloons, bordellos, or other places frequented by men, and where crimes were often committed. At the very least, men committed "social crimes" in the home where their spending on entertainment disrupted the family finances, or their drinking produced abusive behavior. In conclusion, Amelia let the audience know that if they had a principle or held a belief, they had to consider that belief or principle carefully. If they determined the principle was true, they must live that truth if they were to live at all.

Perhaps Amelia was giving the audience a bird's-eye view of her motivations and purpose. She knew that not everyone agreed with her, and life would probably have been easier if she had told people in flowery language what they wanted to hear. Trance lecturers who gave ornate but vague lectures may have been popular but they rarely rocked the boat. They gave no substance for the thinking public to consider. Amelia could not and would not compromise her truth nor her stated mission to deliver that truth as she understood it.

Amelia and James traveled to Worcester for a series of lectures, where she continued her radical and persistent attack on Christianity. She made a side trip to Stoneham, where she thrilled the audience and a correspondent for the *Banner of Light* reported her delight with Amelia's presence and lectures. Complimenting Amelia's reason, the correspondent wrote that people "may well be astonished to see a white-haired woman stand before an audience for more than two hours pouring forth the most profound reasoning and radical truths." The correspondent added that if more women fearlessly opened their mouths and spoke truthfully, "the world would be the better for it." The audience was so pleased they asked Amelia to remain in Stoneham as a constant, settled speaker. Again, Amelia declined, preferring to retain the option of travel.[224]

After her engagement in Worcester, Amelia traveled to Providence, Rhode Island, where she spent February. Her lectures included the subject of prison reform, arguing that those incarcerated could only realize reformation if the states initiated an educational process that included moral codes of conduct. She said male legislators had failed to reduce crime:

> ...you shut men up in prison for life; you hang men for murder; you put them in vile dungeons, and yet you don't stop murder and crime. How would I check it? I would not let such men be at large, but I would have institutions for the development of their morals. Have such an institution—one of learning and not one of degradation—and have it graded, and let a man go through it until he goes out of the highest department, and then he will be capable of being a citizen and should go free.[225]

Acknowledging that people would argue "it couldn't be done" or there wasn't enough money to implement such a program, her reply was typical Amelia. She noted that a thing "can never be done until it is tried." It could be accomplished, she impishly replied, by taking half of the millions of property and income from the churches to finance it. If the church was genuinely interested in redeeming people, she argued, they shouldn't mind contributing vast sums for that purpose.

Amelia gave several lectures on the Spiritualist concept of the afterlife, again noting Swedenborg's idea of the various spheres of enlightenment—these were all reported in local community papers. She also gave several lectures against Catholicism, of which nothing appeared in the local papers. It seems the press was willing to cover her until she began to attack Christianity and Catholicism, and then it prudently stopped reporting.

Her next stop was Philadelphia, in March. The corresponding secretary praised her lectures as grand and eloquent, reporting that their great hall was overflowing with people eager to hear her. "She is a true woman in every sense of the word and believes in the advancement of her sex. She has joined our 'Women's Progressive Union' of Philadelphia and indicated in many ways her liberal, progressive, and beneficent nature."[226] It should be no surprise that Amelia found a very progressive and liberal group in Philadelphia, and again, she was so popular that the society's treasury was "replenished." It was not just her ability to pack the house every night but her attitude. Her belief in freedom of conscience endeared her to friends for the remainder of her life.

Amelia's most radical lecture was given to the Philadelphia crowd on the forty-first Anniversary of Modern Spiritualism. *The Philadelphia Inquirer* reported the proceedings, and newspapers across the country repeated the article—its tone was less than complimentary. Amelia shared the platform with J. Clegg Wright, a Spiritualist minister and author. The paper described Wright in dignified, glowing terms while referring to Amelia as "a tall, gaunt medium from Chicago." Her address was delivered "in a deep, masculine voice" and was generally an attack on the Bible. Reporting that the audience loudly applauded her most blasphemous points as she delivered the lecture under the control of the spirit of Thomas Paine, the article claimed she ridiculed the immaculate conception of Christ and declared there was no God. Amelia stated that Spiritualism had "taken Christianity by the crown, sloughed off its Gods, closed the doors of Heaven and shut hell forever." She added that there was only one more task for Spiritualism: "To put all the ministers of Christianity in coaches and send them to their hell." This might not be done anytime soon, but it would eventually be accomplished. While the local paper may not have appreciated Amelia's lecture, the vast body of liberal Spiritualists in the audience certainly did.[227]

Amelia and James returned to Crown Point for April, where they planned to remain through the summer. However, an event occurred that put Amelia on the road again almost immediately. Prof. William M. Lockwood, Prof. James S. Loveland, and Dr. Juliet Severance notified her that Morris Pratt had built a Temple of Science in Whitewater, Wisconsin, dedicated to investigating all subjects that affected humanity. The temple was a substantial brick building with three floors above the basement. The space was to be used for popular meetings, entertainment, and dancing on the lower floor, with the upper floors devoted to investigating "all questions involving the welfare of humanity." Upper floor rooms were intended as a sanitarium, and equipped with electricity and a furnace. The entire building cost $20,000 [over $600,000 in today's dollars] and was dedicated as a Temple of Science by Pratt and his wife.[228]

Amelia was asked to dedicate the building during a two-day celebration along with Loveland and Lockwood April 26–28, 1889. Giving the dedicatory address on Sunday afternoon, she said she regarded "that occasion as being among the most important of her thirty-one years of public life as a speaker." Loveland reported that the crowds were phenomenal, and many people were turned away for lack of space.

While successful for a few years, the temple had trouble with organization and management. The Pratts presented a letter to the National Spiritualist Association in 1893, offering the temple as a gift for educational purposes. Only nine years in organizational existence, the Association did not feel it could support the academic enterprise. Consequently, the Pratts renamed the temple the Morris Pratt Institute in 1901 and established it as a Spiritualist educational center. Moses Hull was appointed its president, to begin educational endeavors in Spiritualism, science, philosophy, and theology. Today, the temple is known as the educational arm of the National Spiritualist Association of Churches and continues to offer Spiritualist education in Whitewater, Wisconsin.[229]

Amelia returned home after her dedicatory exercises in Wisconsin and remained there through the summer, with only one short excursion to Vicksburg, Michigan, in late August. Her lectures were so popular that the camp administrators invited her to stay four days beyond her scheduled contract. She spent most of her time working for the Indiana Association of Spiritualists and was the main speaker at their annual meeting in late September 1889. At that meeting, she was most severe in her denunciation of the Catholic parochial schools "and advocated, amid applause, that all children should be required to attend the public schools without respect to the religious preferences of the parents or the dictation of any church, whether Catholic or Protestant."[230]

Parochial schools were not new but had remained localized to community parishes. The current push was national, with the Catholic church angling to receive tax dollars as part of their funding. Most states had already passed laws preventing public tax dollars from funding parochial or other types of church-related educational systems. This did not stop the church from advocating for public funding at every opportunity.

The parochial push gave Amelia a new battle to fight in her ongoing war with the church. In addition, she denounced Postmaster General John Wanamaker for denying postal privileges to the *Banner of Light* and other Spiritualist papers.[231] A staunch Christian, Wanamaker appeared to follow in Comstock's footsteps by restricting mail privileges. The Indiana Association of Spiritualists developed a series of resolutions during their meeting in Dr. John Westerfield's Hall in Anderson. The resolutions have Amelia's mark all over them.

After the usual resolutions relating to spirit communication, a resolution was included to maintain the separation of church and state. While they denounced fraud within Spiritualism, they pledged to support mediums as needed. The 12th Resolution was pure Amelia:

> That we emphatically and with the spirit of liberty incorporated in the U.S. Constitution, denounce the anathemas of the Pope of Rome, Leo the 13th, as read from his encyclical letter of a recent date against the free institutions of this country—the liberty of press, of speech, of conscience and of religious worship with the right to employ force as the means to that end.[232]

Amelia advocates sedition against the Catholic church in response to the *Quamquam Pluries,* an encyclical delivered by Pope Leo XIII on August 15, 1889. The encyclical appears relatively benign on the surface since it promotes adding a prayer to St. Joseph at the end of the rosary. However, the document urges the poor to accept their lot such as it is, avoid falling into companionship with those who spout sedition and violence (referring to labor parties), and be as holy as St. Joseph in his poverty:

> For Joseph, of royal blood, united by marriage to the greatest and holiest of women, reputed the father of the Son of God, passed his life in labor and won by the toil of the artisan the needful support of his family. It is, then, true that the condition of the lowly has nothing shameful in it, and the work of the laborer is not only not dishonoring, but can, if virtue be joined to it, be singularly ennobled. Joseph, content with his slight possessions, bore the trials consequent on a fortune so slender, with greatness of soul, in imitation of his Son, who having put on the form of a slave, being the Lord of life, subjected himself of his own free-will to the spoliation and loss of everything.[233]

Amelia saw this piety as an affront against every freedom listed in the Constitution, including men's rights to agitate for labor reform. The final sentence in the resolution, stating "with the right to employ force as the means to that end," is astounding. However, her response was not surprising given her radical defense of liberty, her reverence for Thomas Paine, and her family history related to the American Revolution. The Indiana Association of Spiritualists approval was more surprising and an indication of the liberal minds who initially formed it. The resolution is still an astonishing reaction to a benign encyclical. The only other encyclical by Pope Leo XIII that could have elicited the same knee-jerk reaction was the one given on December 25, 1888, when he denounced rationalism, socialism, materialism, and atheism, identifying reason without faith as an attack against the church.[234]

Amelia remained at home, working with the fledgling Indiana Association of Spiritualists, until October, when she returned to Whitewater, Wisconsin, to meet her old liberal friends. Spending the month in Wisconsin, she remained long enough to attend the Wisconsin State Association of Spiritualists Annual Convention at Omro. She was one of the prominent speakers, and a local paper reported that she was "without doubt the ablest lady orator on the Liberal Platform."[235]

Following this engagement, she returned home, remaining there until August 1890. While she continued to work with the Indiana Association of Spiritualists, ill-health may have restricted her participation and, certainly, her travel itinerary. Nevertheless, she participated in quarterly and annual meetings of the Association, using her many contacts in the lecture field to bring notable liberals and Spiritualists to Indiana, such as Cora Richmond of Chicago, Prof. William M. Lockwood of Ripon, Wisconsin, William Colby of Florida, and Will Hodge of Wisconsin.[236]

DISSENT AND RESIST

AMELIA TRAVELED TO Mount Pleasant Park in Clinton, Iowa, in August 1890 to attend and participate in a camp meeting. Generally supported by the Wisconsin State Spiritualist Association, it drew Spiritualists and liberal thinkers from multiple states. The headliners for the opening day listed Cora Richmond and Amelia. It was Richmond's first time at the camp, and she attended with her husband. Amelia, however, was alone as James remained in Indiana. Some of the day's most radical freethinkers (and free lovers) attended, including Lois Waisbrooker, Juliet Severance, and Moses Hull.[237]

Amelia's lectures were similar to previous addresses, where she denounced Spiritualist "fraud-hunters" and provided admirable instructions on the laws of mediumship. She lectured nearly every day for a month, and even attended a dance one evening with Richmond and her husband. One correspondent reported in the August 23, 1890 edition of the *Banner of Light* that "some think her a little too radical; at the same time, we have never had a more popular speaker with the whole people than she is." Amelia lectured and took an active interest in the business side of the Wisconsin State meetings, including the elections held on August 15. Prof. James S. Loveland was elected president, and Amelia was unanimously elected vice president, with Will C. Hodge as Secretary and a Mrs. McCarrol as treasurer.[238] The position was not Amelia's first office in an organization; she acted as one of the vice presidents for the National Liberal League years earlier. However, it was the first Spiritualist office she had held.

On Sunday, August 17, 1890, Amelia gave her lecture on "The Future Republic," by special request. It was a talk she had given before, and she spoke in her normal voice. Two thousand people were present for the address and loudly applauded their approval. Scheduled to lecture on August 31, Amelia found that her health prevented her from giving her standard, lengthy lecture. Prof. Loveland stepped in to cover for her and began a speech on "Aristocracy." Amelia followed with brief comments related to his address. It was all she could manage.

Amelia returned home for a much-needed rest and made short trips to lecture in Indianapolis during October. She did not travel again until November, when she returned to friends at the Society of Spiritualists in Pittsburgh and the Pittsburgh Secular Society. The only record of her lectures was reproduced in the Pittsburgh local press when she addressed "The Origin of Royalty and Nobility" to the Pittsburgh Secular Society. It should be no surprise that her lecture addressed the country's status.

Amelia argued that initially, there were two classes of people—first and second classes. She stated that the first class of people "tilled the soil, had homes of their own, and tended their little flocks and herds in contentment." They were happy, industrious, and governed by a spirit of kindness to each other. The second class included those who lived by the labor of others. They loved luxury and banded together to achieve that luxury. She called this second class "freebooters." This group enslaved the laboring class—they realized the benefits of slave labor and created a hierarchy system that allowed their children to inherit their luxurious lifestyle. Amelia claimed that the monarchies of the world were freebooters and bandits.

She compared early foreign monarchs, whom she called "freebooters," to America's politicians and church leaders, who wanted Sunday laws enacted and created an exclusive banking system for state money. She pointed to multiple other atrocities conducted by the church and politicians, and told her audience to be watchful of ignorant people, stating it was up to them to stand up for true liberty:

Our present government is not satisfactory. Protestants are crying for God in the Constitution; freethinkers are crying to keep him out, and the pope is taking advantage of the religious turmoil to get a still stronger hold on this country. You, citizens of the United States, who have so long been slaves to a dastardly priesthood and an arrogant aristocracy, will you do nothing for yourselves? I think you will. The man who goes to the pope of Rome to get his vote should not be allowed to cast it in free America. We are threatened on all sides. People are coming to this country by thousands who know nothing more about the principles of representative government than a pig does about the geography of the heavens, and yet they are being raised up to positions of honor within three years of their arrival. Its end in this country will cost many a drop of blood.[239]

In today's language, Amelia could be called a nativist. It was the first lecture in which she argued against immigrants' eligibility to participate in "representative government." However, she was not alone in her belief. She echoed the suffragists, who were outraged that male immigrants could vote after a specified time when educated women born in America could not. The outrage surrounded the idea that "ignorant male foreigners" were more capable of choosing the leaders of America than women who had educated themselves in the world of politics, medicine, and science. It was a difficult idea to swallow, and neither Amelia nor the suffragists were having it.

Amelia returned to Indiana and remained there for the next year, participating exclusively in the Indiana Association of Spiritualists events. Significantly, she brought some of the most radical freethinkers and free lovers to the annual and quarterly meetings, including Lois Waisbrooker, who lectured at the annual meeting in October 1890. Waisbrooker was notorious as a free love author, editor, and women's rights advocate, who firmly rejected Christianity as oppressive to women. She wrote on taboo subjects such as "women's sex servitude," rape, wartime rape, prostitution, and syphilis. In 1894, at the age of sixty-eight, she was arrested on obscenity charges for publishing taboo articles in her newspaper *Foundation Principles*.[240] Waisbrooker opened the eyes of some of the more conservative Indiana Spiritualists since her lecture on "finances" was most likely a lecture titled "The Sex Question and the Money Power," a speech she had been giving since 1873 on sex, power, and money. The conservative secretary for the Indiana Association of Spiritualists simply recorded the lecture: "Mrs. Waisbrooker made a short address on finance."[241] Waisbrooker was not the only freethinker that Amelia brought to Indiana.

Although Amelia remained at home, she still managed to ruffle feathers and create controversy with her lectures. She was invited to participate in an anniversary celebration of modern Spiritualism in Cincinnati, Ohio, on March 30, 1892, where she shared the platform with Prof. J. Clegg Wright. All went well until Amelia rose and, controlled by the spirit of Thomas Paine, proceeded to attack the Christian church. She claimed it was the "destroyer of truth and liberty" and that "it kept the world in ignorance, and ignored the rights of all human beings," at which point a woman rose from the audience and said that an assault on the church was wrong. Indeed, she argued, it was "the platform of liberty and the very basis of Spiritualism." The interruption caused a great sensation until Amelia calmly said that if the lady wished to occupy the rostrum, she could do so, "but you will have to wait until I get through." A newspaper reported that Amelia continued her denunciation of Christianity, its preachers, and its false teachings and "was possibly more bitter than ever, owing to the interruption..."[242] Amelia finished her lecture undisturbed, but it is probable that Tom Paine was no longer controlling her.

In July 1891, the Indiana Association of Spiritualists held its fifth annual meeting at their newly acquired campgrounds in Chesterfield, Indiana. Amelia gave the opening address and dedicated the grounds to "free speech." The next few months saw a decided interest and increased participation on the campgrounds, so much so that the ministers in the neighboring town of Anderson grew concerned. People were coming by the thousands to Camp Chesterfield, and the local ministers were furious. In a front-page article, *The Muncie Daily Times* reported the dispute between the Spiritualists and the Anderson churches. The article celebrated the camp's success and noted the local ministers' dismay:

This has aroused the jealousy of the churches, and a merry and relentless war is to be waged against the Spiritualists. Last Sunday, Anderson ministers hurled denunciations against the doctrine of Spiritualism from the pulpits of all the churches in the city.

And now comes one brave minister who proposes to annihilate the doctrine and banish the spirits. The ministerial David, who is to slay the Goliath of Spiritualism, is Rev. Hunter McDonald, a Christian minister of Middletown, who has challenged Mrs. Luther, the Nestor of Spiritualism in Indiana, to a joint debate. Mrs. Luther has accepted, and the debate will occur at the Spiritual camp meeting ground near Chesterfield next Saturday. The outcome will be watched with much interest by the Anderson church people and the Spiritualists.[243]

The Spiritualists chose Amelia as their mouthpiece for multiple reasons, primarily because she had an acute understanding of the Bible, as she had already demonstrated in numerous lectures. In addition, she was a woman who would further pinch the noses of the conservative Anderson clergy. On August 9, 1891, the debate took place before a crowd of 3,000 people at Camp Chesterfield. The group consisted of Spiritualists and local ministers from the surrounding area. The question for discussion was "Resolved, that the teachings of Jesus Christ as found in the New Testament scripture, King James' version are immoral in their tendencies."

The Muncie Daily Times reported the debate in full. Describing Amelia as a competent, experienced debater, the paper recalled her work for the Republican National Party during Lincoln's campaigns. It described how she opposed slavery and provided such excellent service to the party that "her name became national among politicians and her services in demand in many of the States." Her experience as she debated with the young minister definitely stood in her favor.

Amelia began the debate by reminding the audience that Jesus wrote nothing himself other than once—and then those were only a few words in the sand that were washed away. The only writings available then are those that come secondhand from others. To argue that the teachings of Jesus are immoral, she points to the scriptural phrase, "If any man come to me and hate not his father and mother, and wife and children and brethren, yea, and his own life also, he cannot be my disciples." Her argument is concise. Pointing to the effect this would have on families—the sacred institution that the church holds dear—she argues that Jesus could not have possibly taught man to hate his mother or his wife. Such a person, if Christian, would be anathema to the church itself. Consequently, if someone preached this doctrine today and practiced it, he would be labeled insane. Therefore, this particular teaching is immoral. Amelia was given thirty minutes for her part of the debate, and she used the entire time allotted to her. Then the young minister stepped up to the podium.

He was welcomed with generous applause, indicating there was a large group of Christians in the audience. The paper reported he preached for the Christian church in Middletown, Indiana, but was an Ohioan by birth. A young man of around thirty-five years of age, he spoke for eighteen minutes of his allotted thirty minutes. His opening remarks addressed the point Amelia made for only six minutes—he said that the teachings of Christ were not immoral, and it was true, "Christ taught men to hate ... but only to impress the people of that day and warn them to keep pure, and to hate all that was sinful, and follow him." He urged everyone to "take upon them the life of purity" and denied the quote that "all men would go to hell if they did not follow Jesus." Arguing that Jesus said that "every man would be judged according to his deeds," he asked, "Is that not justice?" Then he added that Jesus was only talking to his disciples—his specially appointed people, and "don't she know this?"

Amelia had thirty minutes to respond and used every bit of time she was given. She noted that the young minister did not touch the scriptural passage she addressed, so she offered a second, relating to the comparison between Lazarus and the rich man. "Lazarus, it is said, went to heaven and the rich man to hell. Was there justice in sending the rich man to this place of torment? Is there anyone here who feels that he will go to hell just because he is rich?" Amelia argued that this was not justice and was grossly unfair to men who worked hard for their earnings. She added that the young minister stated that Jesus made no effort to send people to hell but pointed to the scripture that said, "He that believeth shall be saved, and he that believeth not shall be damned." Amelia claimed this was not only coercive but also immoral in its tendency.

She poked at the ministers just a bit by pointing to the scripture where Jesus says, "In my name shall they cast out devils."

> I will not ask my brother here to cast out devils, for if he can, and did, he would have to cast out so many that are within the church that there would not be a sufficient number left to sustain the ministry in the pulpits of this country, and then there might be a few vacancies in the pulpits, for there are men filling positions in the pulpit who were never intended for the places they occupy.

After that nose-pinch, Amelia started to roll. She began with the Inquisition and accused the Catholic church of murder and theft. She introduced Constantine and the Council of Nicaea as evidence that man wrote the Bible, and argued that no substantial structure could have these beginnings as its foundation. The Presbyterian and Methodist hells were "cooling off a bit" and did not affect intelligent people. She then ridiculed the immaculate conception, and pointed to the scriptural passages that indicated that Jesus was humanly born—Mary says, "Behold, thy father [Joseph] and I have sought thee sorrowing." Amelia continued, "Now then, is there anyone who knows better than a mother who the father of her child is?"

Amelia finished by arguing that if Jesus was indeed who the Bible said he was, and the ministers were urged to follow the path of Jesus, then today's ministers should be healing the sick, raising the dead, and casting out devils—and as far as she knew, not even the pope of Rome could do those things. Therefore, the entire Bible was a myth and immoral in that a corrupt church used it to accumulate wealth and property. She urged the taxation of all church property because "Jesus Christ, if a reality, according to the teachings, can be worshipped in less costly structures. The accumulation of property by the church, other than that directly used for the purpose of worship, is a menace to this free republic."

Rev. McDonald addressed the story of Lazarus and the rich man by arguing that "it was the manner in which the rich man accumulated his wealth" by taking the proceeds of others and living "sumptuously upon it." This, he argued, was why the rich man went to hell—though McDonald failed to note that nothing in the Bible accuses the rich man of victimizing others. In addition, he could not identify the similarities between the rich man and the church, as Amelia had less than subtly pointed out. McDonald used only twelve minutes of his time and declined to discuss anything further as he believed he had addressed the issue.

The afternoon session was just as bad. McDonald continued to use only small portions of his allotted time and addressed none of the points that Amelia raised during her time on the platform. According to the reporter, many people in the audience left during this afternoon session due to McDonald's "display of egotism and his derision of his opponent, Mrs. Luther."

> The clergymen present felt deeply chagrined at his style of argument. The debate closed in an uproar caused by the refusal of Mr. McDonald to listen to a question and answer the same, desired to be put to him by Mrs. Luther. When asked why not give the question attention, he replied: "I am tired of this balderdash coming from an ignorant woman."[244]

Amelia's debate with the young minister was not her first debate with clergy, nor would it be her last. As the clergy in Indiana continued to denounce Spiritualism, she was the chosen defender of the faith in debates. The people loved her for it, and even newspaper reporters knew she was the best Spiritualist debater in Indiana. She continued to participate in the events of the Indiana Association of Spiritualists, lecturing at quarterly meetings and serving on multiple committees to assist in the organization's leadership. It seemed that her idea of creating a new camp in response to her negative experience at Lake Pleasant, in 1883, had come to fruition. She was so pleased with the new organization that she planned to "build a neat two-story cottage" on the campgrounds.

In May 1892, however, Amelia responded to a call from friends in Pittsburgh, and traveled there for a two-month engagement with the Pittsburgh Secular Society and the First Church of Spiritualists.

However, her motive for making the trip may have been something other than her work. Her husband, James, was embroiled in a family disagreement regarding his property. His heirs tried to take him to court to test his sanity and obtain his income and property. Sadly, this tactic was used by many nonbelievers against their Spiritualist family members. James circumvented their efforts by appointing an administrator of his estate, who distributed his property, valued at $75,000 [over $2 million by today's standards] according to James' wishes.[245] Amelia wanted no part of this family drama, so she gladly left for Pittsburgh. Her lectures were tailored to the needs of each society, arguing for liberty to the Secular Society, and promoting Spiritualist philosophy for the Spiritualist Society. She remained with them until mid-June and returned home to find her old friend Dr. Westerfield embroiled in controversy at Camp Chesterfield.

The mediums who visited the Indiana campgrounds and set up tents for business wanted more seance time and less lecture time. They were starting to perform materializations, and not only did they want more time, they also wanted to increase their fees. Furthermore, they were not opposed to scripture as their guiding force. They wanted fewer attacks on Christianity made by Amelia, Westerfield, and a host of other lecturers, including invited lecturers such as free lover and radical feminist Dr. Juliet Severance, and freethinker Hon. A.B. French, an author and attorney. A battle ensued between the visiting mediums and the leadership of the camp, with the leadership prevailing. At the close of the camp meeting, Dr. Westerfield retained his presidency, and Amelia was elected first vice president. They continued to uphold their policies with no increase in fees to the public.[246]

Amelia continued to involve herself in the organization of the Indiana Association of Spiritualists. By 1893, she had built a two-story home on the grounds of Camp Chesterfield, and formed the Ladies League, using her home as the headquarters. The Ladies League was dedicated to women's rights and, according to camp history, was controversial at times in their efforts to defend women's rights.[247] She remained at home for the majority of 1893, declining to travel except for short trips to Indianapolis and other surrounding areas. It may have been a combination of James' ill health and her own poor health that caused her to restrict her travel itinerary.

However, she did not stop attacking the church. It began to create a division between the radical, liberal, and conservative elements within the Indiana Spiritualist community, as the following report from *The Rushville Republican* demonstrates:

> Mrs. Colby-Luther, one of the leading lecturers at the Chesterfield Spiritual campmeeting [sic] denounces Christianity as a humbug, ridicules the divinity of Christ, and pronounces the Bible a tissue of falsehoods. She has done much to widen the breach which already exists between the radical and liberal wings of the spiritualistic organization, and a split is threatened.[248]

The divisiveness between the mediums and the camp leadership began to affect even liberal trance lecturers. Still, Amelia remained steadfast in her criticisms of the church, holding it accountable for the oppression of people, and in particular women. She would not change her principles—not even for the organization she helped form.

Returning to the road in September 1893, Amelia traveled to Chicago to speak at the first National Delegate Convention of Spiritualists. This meeting was convened to create a national organization of Spiritualists. Notable Spiritualists came from nearly every state in the Union, and included many of the biggest names in Spiritualism, such as Cora Richmond, Dr. Juliet Severance, and Thomas and Marion Skidmore. This vast arena of Spiritualists represented a broad spectrum of philosophies and beliefs, which showed in the three-day disputes over language.

The Spiritualists haggled over the use of the word "belief" rather than "knowledge," the use of the word "religion," the use of the word "citizen" rather than people, and multiple other words and phrases. They even argued over the title of the proceedings and who precisely the organization represented. Amelia threw her two cents in a few times. She objected most strenuously when one of the resolutions stated, "whereas several million citizens of the United States are avowed advocates of the philosophy of Spiritualism, and entitled under the Constitution of the United States to protection in any form of worship, teaching, or practice of their knowledge and belief, consistent with the rights of others." Amelia rose immediately with her objection:

> You have used the word "citizens," which, under the laws of the United States, cuts out every woman in this house or in the world. I am not a citizen. There is not a woman in this town that is a citizen; not a woman in the United States that is a citizen.[249]

Amelia's statement "I am not a citizen" references her lack of voting privileges—something that is supposed to be a right for all American citizens. The convention immediately understood her meaning, and the word "citizen" was omitted without argument and replaced with "people." She objected again when "religion" was used as a defining term for Spiritualism. Amelia stated that religion, as defined by Webster, was "the performance of a duty that we owe to God. As I have no God, of course, I could not go to Him."[250] Multiple Spiritualists supported her, including Juliet Severance, who wanted the word stricken from the amendment. However, a few of the attorneys and judges in the convention argued that the organization had to define itself as religious for legal purposes, including receiving the benefits of donations and other financial resources. The word remained part of the definition, which ultimately stated, "It is the purpose of this Convention to organize upon a scientific, philosophical, moral, and religious basis."

By the end of the second day, there had been so much argument over language that Amelia's patience had run out. When the chairman announced that they had made arrangements for the janitor to keep the lights on so they could continue throughout the night, she rose. She told her fellow participants she had been in Spiritualism for more than thirty-five years, and when Spiritualists gather together, they should know the difference between the words "tweedle-dee-dee and tweedled-dee-dum. I am almost 100 years old now, and I can't sit up as late as some of you." She suggested they cancel the ten-minute speeches scheduled for the next day and resume the business at hand,

and added tartly that they were acting like Congress who couldn't seem to get anything passed. She urged them to show that they could function better than that and advocated ending the day's proceedings. The audience applauded loudly, signaling their agreement.[251]

The convention adjourned with no further arguments. The final day of the convention found the participants continuing to argue over language, purpose, and place for most of the day. When they had finally agreed on the most critical matters, a motion of thanks was offered for the tireless work of the convention leaders, including the secretary and, more specifically, the chairman, H.D. Barrett. It was then that Amelia rose with some delightful, tongue-in-cheek remarks, and the convention minutes recorded this brief interaction:

> Mr. Chairman, my grandfather, an old Revolutionary soldier (he didn't pass away or die, just passed over), when thanked for anything would always say: "Thank yous would starve a cat." I think so too. We are all of us thankful to this wonderful chairman. This is the most remarkable man I ever saw in a chair. I understand, from good authority, that he has no salary for doing all this work. Now, we can thank him a thousand times, and he could not get a meal of victuals with it if he should try or take a single ride on the streetcar, and if each one of us will give him a few dimes, it will take him home. If you will allow me the privilege, if I am in order, and I am always getting out of order, because I don't know what order means, and you can call me to order at any time...[252]

Another convention-goer rose and suggested that Amelia could do whatever she wanted. Amelia continued to speak and ask for donations for H.D. Barrett as thanks for his efforts in organizing and chairing the convention. The assembled Spiritualists (approximately 200), each representing their local Spiritualist societies, had finally agreed to form the National Spiritualist Association by the end of the convention. The title was later changed to the National Spiritualist Association of Churches, and it remains the largest Spiritualist organization today.

Amelia returned home and continued to lecture for the Indiana Association of Spiritualists. Unfortunately, within two months, James died in December 1893—after just six years of marriage. Although there is no concrete evidence, he likely left Amelia in comfortable financial shape and still provided his heirs with their fair share of his estate. Four months later, tragedy struck again when her son, Augustus (Gus), died from pneumonia at the age of fifty-two. Amelia was by his side and comforted his grieving wife and four young children through his illness and death. It appears that she helped his widow financially for the remainder of her life.

Devastated by the loss of her husband and son within four months of each other, Amelia remained in Indiana, alternately living at her camp home or her home in Muncie. She continued participating in the activities of the Indiana Association and the camp meeting in Chesterfield through 1894. However, in January 1895, at the age of sixty-seven, she returned to the lecture circuit. She traveled to Philadelphia to meet with old friends and lecture to the Spiritual Conference Association, combining two Spiritualists societies. Her old friend Lyman C. Howe shared the platform with her and wrote to the *Banner of Light*:

Today (Jan. 20), she treated the question, "If there is no God, how did man originate?" She said no theological system had attempted to tell how or when space and time came into existence, and it is presumed they had no beginning; that there could be no vacuum, therefore space was always occupied with something. Spirit always avoided matter and kept as far from it as possible; hence matter sought its own. Spirit surrounds force and acts on matter through force as its medium. Without spirit, force could do nothing; without force, matter would be eternally still and dead. In answer to the question "What is the greatest need of humanity?" she said, wisdom, the knowledge of laws, and disposition to obey them which are the secret of happiness. Her peroration carried a magnetic enthusiasm to the minds of the audience and left them aglow with the inspiration of her free-flowing psychological oratory.[253]

Amelia's efforts to define what most philosophers and scientists could not was a testament to her individual educational efforts. She acknowledged Spirit as the driving force that acts on matter and thus creates matter, but failed—or refused—to identify God as the creative force of Spirit. Nevertheless, it pointed to her willingness to address philosophical questions that many trance lecturers refused to tackle.

Following her engagement in Philadelphia, Amelia traveled 315 miles northeast to Lynn, Massachusetts, where she spent February 1895. She gave lectures addressing the philosophy of Spiritualism and the country's political and economic health, and ended two of her lectures with improvised poems, which was unique for her. The poem "America" followed a lecture titled "Human Life and the Impression of Thought Through Spiritualism on Religion and Politics in this Country." Her second poem, "Love," came after her lecture titled "Wherein is Spiritualism Superior to Materialism and Creedism?" Unfortunately, the correspondent recorded neither poem.

One lecture, "The Origin of, and the Power, which Syndicates Hold Over Labor, and Its Application to the Present Times," was a review, and rebuke, of the syndicates and monopolies who not only embraced the power of money but controlled it as well, all to the detriment of the common laborer. One of Amelia's solutions was to curtail immigration for the next twenty years, and the other was to eliminate money for bonds. She refers to America's depletion of gold in the government treasury and the international economic crisis, which brought scores of immigrants to the country's shores. Her reference to syndicates relates to the government's recent abdication of its monetary stability to a private syndicate of businessmen, known as the Morgan-Belmont syndicate, "one of the most crucial and controversial interactions of government and business in American history."[254] Once again, she demonstrates the breadth of her knowledge of governmental processes and laws.

Amelia continued her assessment of the government the following week in her lecture "Wealth: Which Shall It Be, a Servant or Master?" The correspondent to the *Banner of Light* reported that, for more than an hour, she gave "thrilling word-pictures" of the existing evils of the social, political, and financial systems that were all operating against the best interests of society. She concluded with a "high tribute to woman and recognizing in her influence more largely developed morality and spirituality, in the solution of these weighty problems which affect the welfare of the human race."[255]

The remainder of Amelia's lectures were both political and spiritual. She spoke on "Liberty and Spiritualism," "Our Country and its Heroes," and ended with "If There is no God, What Power Organized Matter," which was a repeat of her lecture to the Philadelphia crowd. Her success in Massachusetts was evidenced by the many letters of congratulations and compliments sent to the *Banner*.

Amelia next traveled 450 miles to Washington, D.C., where she lectured for the National Spiritualist Association in March 1895 and took part in the forty-seventh Anniversary of Modern Spiritualism exercises. The compliments abounded, specifically for her ability to raise money. Francis B. Woodbury, Secretary of the Association, reported for the *Banner of Light*. He said Amelia "was instrumental in raising two hundred and seventy dollars for the National Spiritualist Association [and] eight hundred people attended the evening service." Two hundred and seventy dollars is approximately $9,500 in buying power today and was an astounding amount of money at the time.

The celebration lasted the entire day, and several local mediums participated in the exercises. Before Amelia gave her opening address, she notified the audience that she had spoken with Theodore J. Mayer, who was in the audience. Mayer was a prominent businessman who was active on the committee to form the national Spiritualist organization. Years later, the National Spiritualists' Association moved their headquarters to a building owned by Mayer in Washington, D.C. He ultimately deeded the Washington property to the Association. At this meeting, he agreed to match the donations made to the National Spiritualist Association. Consequently, the amount collected amounted to $540, or $19,000 in today's buying power. Amelia's farewell address to the assembled crowd was perhaps more premonition than a simple goodbye. The correspondent summarized her final remarks:

Mrs. Luther then made an eloquent farewell address; this noble instrument of the spirit world eloquently pleaded with the people to be true to the cause of human liberty and requested them to keep upon the rostrum after she was gone the bust of Thomas Paine, and have inscribed over his head, "There is nothing so sacred as Truth." She eloquently pleaded with them to stand true to the principles of Spiritualism, the Constitution of the United States, and the flag of our country; the enthusiasm was intense and was manifested in rounds of applause; a large proportion of the audience pressed forward to take her hand and bid her farewell at the conclusion of her address.[256]

Unbelievably, Amelia then traveled back to Boston, a distance of more than 430 miles, and spent the month of April lecturing and socializing with her friends at the Boston Spiritual Temple.

"WRAP MY BODY IN THE FLAG
OF THE UNITED STATES"

AMELIA'S STAY IN BOSTON would be her last. If she sensed it, however, she wasn't about to give in to the thought of it, and her lectures during April 1895 drew enormous crowds. She began with a lecture titled "Spiritualism as a Reformatory Force in the World" and stated that no reform was ever achieved that did not come from liberal thought. She compared liberal thought to the freedom of nature, and as humanity belongs to nature, humanity must develop their own innate freedom of thought. She added that if any person wanted God, they must find God within themselves. This statement sounds closely related to her Quaker upbringing and "inner light." Comparing God to nature brings the audience into a creation story where divinity exists within creative nature and, therefore, within themselves. It also echoes the ideas of Andrew Jackson Davis in his work *The Principles of Nature, Her Divine Revelations and a Voice to Mankind,* published in 1847. Amelia alleges that even for those defined as "bad," an understanding of Spiritualist philosophy can overcome any darkness within the individual. She includes fraudulent mediums in this assessment as well.

Never one to avoid an unpleasant topic, Amelia states baldly that both she and the audience know there are fraudulent mediums or those who are "not pure." Her solution is concrete. If they wish a medium to be pure, they must strive to be pure themselves. The adage "like attracts like" is a fair comparison, and she continues to argue that if everyone were as pure as we wanted them to be, there would be no need to seek a medium for guidance. Therefore, enlightenment begins within the self, and the energy of purity and light moves outward toward others. This new-age wisdom of 1895 applies the same standard to attorneys, ministers, and politicians. There are fraudulent professionals in every walk of life, and working on the self is the only solution.[257]

Amelia replayed old favorites for the next several weeks, including "Some of the Saviors of the Liberties of the People." She reminded her audience of the inventions and scientific progress that were the true saviors of humanity. Reviewing each century from the thirteenth to the nineteenth, she claimed Spiritualism was the savior in the nineteenth century. Her following lecture revisited "The Origin of Aristocracy and Royalty and Its Application at the Present Time." Her opinions had not changed since she first gave the speech, several years previously—apparently, her audience did not mind the rehash. Amelia argued, "what was called robbery in olden times is called revenue and taxes today." Complaining about the poor, tax-paying laborer and the rich man who does nothing but benefit from the labor of the working man, she compared bond houses and banks to the "Robbers' Castles" of the past:

> Banks are made to circulate credit, not money. Credit is the circulating medium for business [now]. Have you thought of that? Banks grow rich and make the poor poorer. Banks form rings and make plans, and they are loaning more money than you have in circulation. Banks never did protect bodies, but certain individuals.[258]

Amelia addressed immigration, stating that America was in poor shape but large enough to embrace anyone who wanted to come to its shores. However, she placed a caveat on that idea. People could come to America only if they became citizens:

> If they wish to remain French, German, Italian, or anything else but American, let them stay in their own country. We have had too many of the paupers of other countries who have never become citizens of the United States. Let us put a stop to this; let us work together as a united

body. Just as sure as Massachusetts and the other States do not work more in unison together, there will be an eastern and western republic. Do not let this happen; respect your states and work together, and you will have a better and a grander nation.[259]

The lecture was met with a "storm of applause," showing the audience's understanding of the financial crisis in America as well as on the international stage. It also demonstrated public sentiment concerning immigration—at the time, the worldwide depression had caused huge increases in immigrants entering the country. Amelia's lecture merely reflected what the majority of Americans thought and felt.

Amelia's next lecture to the Boston Spiritual Temple, "The Wonderful Power of Spiritualism as Incentive to Right Living and Right Doing," objected to the idea that Spiritualism was only concerned with phenomena. She argued that Spiritualism did provide proof of the continuity of life, but most importantly, it came to the world to teach people what was practical for life. She stated that those who believe only in phenomena are not Spiritualists but "phenomenists," and that those who come only for clairvoyant messages or seances, without understanding the philosophy of Spiritualism, were not true Spiritualists. She claimed they were no different from those who attended church but failed to understand that higher knowledge and wisdom are available. Spiritualism took a practical approach that encouraged people to live as authentic, honest, and good a life as possible in order to reach higher wisdom with knowledge rather than simple belief.[260]

In this lecture, Amelia acknowledged that some only cared for the phenomenal aspects of Spiritualism, and in doing so, they remained static and failed to progress spiritually. Although she had participated in past seances, it appears age had given her some wisdom concerning what was important and what was not in the world of spirituality. It also points to the division that Spiritualism had been experiencing for some years, and many of her colleagues, such as Moses Hull and Cora Richmond, expressed the same thoughts.

The following week, Amelia spoke at a special convention of the Massachusetts State Spiritualists' Association. She reviewed Spiritualism's progress over the years and stated that the Massachusetts Association was necessary for people's liberty. Claiming that the Spiritualists of Massachusetts should be leaders working toward freedom and justice, and that greater patriotism was needed, she stated that if the Massachusetts Association were a strong body, none would fear losing liberties such as freedom to worship, free speech, and equal rights for all. She denounced the "medical and church despots" and advised that no Spiritualist should patronize medical doctors or the church elite; they should instead take care of each other. Amelia ended her lecture by making an earnest appeal for cash funds and new subscribers, or members, and set an example by becoming a member herself. She raised $100 in collection and membership fees, equivalent to $3,200 in today's purchasing power.[261]

Amelia's final lecture to the Boston Spiritual Temple, "If There is no God, What Force in the Universe Creates Matter," was a repeat of an earlier lecture, but people were so impressed, it was forwarded to the *Banner of Light* with an appeal to have it reproduced in full. It appeared in the June 1, 1895 edition. Her talk traversed through astronomy and molecular theory to theories of time and space. It was an astounding lecture that included an assessment of Darwin's theory, concluding that it was only partially correct since the spirit of man cannot be similar to that of an animal. However, she claimed that Spirit, force, and matter existed before God as they knew Him, i.e., the biblical God. Therefore, since man as Spirit holds the wisdom of the ages within the human consciousness, humanity contains a greater force than God today. She argued that communication with a tree, a pebble, and Spirit was possible when humanity grew in consciousness, and concluded with a tribute to life itself:

What a beautiful thing it is to live; what a beautiful thing it is to think and express your thoughts. How beautiful and how grand is this great, vast universe of mind and matter, though darkened here and there by clouds of ignorance and superstition! Do not submit and do not conform to that which you know is unjust to yourself. Be true to yourself, and you will be true to this great, infinite spirit power, and this great force that you and I have been talking about, and then you are true to the mighty minds and philosophers that lived here one time in the past and have outgrown this condition and gone into a world far, far, far away, into the great regions that you and I, perhaps, can know but little of for ages yet to be. How little you can afford to be idle, then! Breathe not the spirit of ignorance. Regain the confidence in yourself that you have lost in the past.[262]

Following a much-needed rest at home, Amelia participated in the summer activities at the Indiana camp. She was reelected as first vice president, with Dr. Westerfield continuing as president during the Indiana Association of Spiritualists Annual Convention, in August 1895. During that convention, the executive board met with a representative of the National Spiritualist Association, Mary E. Cadwallader of Philadelphia, to discuss taking a charter from the national organization. After a brief discussion, Amelia, Westerfield, and the rest of the executive board agreed to the charter. In addition, the Indiana Association chose Amelia and Prof. William Lockwood of Wisconsin as delegates to the October 1895 National Spiritualist Association convention.[263]

The celebration of Westerfield's return as president was short-lived. He became ill while on a trip to Michigan and returned to Indiana, only to die on September 29, 1895. Amelia gave the funeral oration for her old friend and fellow liberal. After the funeral, Amelia traveled to Norwich, Connecticut, for a series of lectures in October. She was expected to present the response on behalf of delegates to the Third Annual Convention of the National Spiritualist Association in Washington before traveling to Connecticut. However, for some unknown reason, she never arrived in Washington. She did arrive in Norwich, Connecticut, for two lectures on October 20 and 27 and then traveled to New Bedford, Massachusetts, to lecture through November.[264] Unfortunately, Amelia suffered a stroke and collapsed on the platform during one of her lectures at New Bedford. She recovered enough to make it as far as Philadelphia, and one of her old friends brought her the rest of the way home. When she arrived back in Indiana, the news immediately picked it up:

> Mrs. Colby Luther, the well known Spiritualist lecturer, is in a serious condition from a stroke of paralysis. Mrs. Luther was in the East on a lecture tour when she was stricken with the dread disease. Mrs. Luther is well known in spiritualistic circles in Muncie, and her friends are worried about her condition as she is quite advanced in years, and the attack may prove fatal.[265]

Amelia was expected to return to the Boston Spiritual Temple in December but canceled that engagement and all others planned. By all accounts, she worked on her recovery at the home of her oldest grandchild, Olive Powell. Amelia minimally participated in some minor events at the Indiana Association of Spiritualists during 1896 and returned to lecturing at its camp meeting that summer. Although her lectures were not as long as they used to be, she continued to lecture after the manner of Thomas Paine, and her radical comments did nothing to heal the division within the Indiana Spiritualists.

The division was most noticeable at the Indiana camp opening in July 1896 when Amelia's lecture denounced Catholicism and the Bible. A second lecturer contradicted her and argued that the Bible was critical to Spiritualism, saying "It was woman's first duty to fully occupy woman's sphere in domestic life."[266] The comment could not have been more odious to every female freethinker and liberal Spiritualist in the area or the nation for that matter. This urging to return to an early 1800s-era definition of a woman's sphere discounted not only Spiritualist reformists but suffragists as well. The speaker, Marguerite St. Omer, was a medium from Cincinnati, Ohio, who did not practice what she preached—since she gave lectures, clairvoyant messages, and psychometric readings in the Cincinnati area, she clearly was not staying at home in the "woman's sphere."[267]

The division at Camp Chesterfield culminated in a split between the conservative and the progressive leadership. The membership elected a moderate as president following Westerfield's death, and Amelia was reelected first vice president at the 1896 August convention of the Indiana Spiritualists. However, her participation was nominal, and she made only a few brief speeches that summer. St. Omer, a conservative, and E.W. Sprague, a liberal, were that year's primary speakers. Consequently, the division did not dissipate as more moderate Spiritualists had hoped. Amelia continued to minimally participate in all the activities related to the Indiana Spiritualists for the next year and attended only one executive meeting of the board in April 1897.

She returned to a geographically limited lecture circuit in May of 1897. Unfortunately, her lecture to a group of Muncie Spiritualists was so "rambling, broken, and unconnected" that only the faithful appreciated it. During the speech, she trashed the country's newspapers by stating they "were hardly fit to grace a water closet," severely criticized President McKinley, and "patted William J. Bryan on the back and said he was a genius."[268] The reporter returned the "compliment" to his newspaper by trashing her lecture in the paper. In June, she fared better when she lectured to Spiritualists in Hartford City, Indiana, a short distance from Muncie. *The Muncie Morning News* provided a more objective report of her lecture on "Spiritualism in the Bible." Once again, Amelia used the Bible to justify modern Spiritualist materialization. She pointed to the woman of Endor's materialization of the prophet Samuel to Saul's benefit and discussed the materialization tests that Gideon demanded of God (Judges 6:33–40).[269] It seems contradictory that Amelia denounced the Bible as fantasy in one lecture and used it to prove the truths of Spiritualism in another. The contradiction remains a mystery since she left no written documentation on her stance.

Amelia remained at home until Indiana's camp season in July 1897, where she participated in the opening-day ceremonies at Camp Chesterfield. She shared the platform with old friends J. Clegg Wright and Mrs. H. S. Lake (Sarah Genevra Lake), who were prominent speakers in the national Spiritualist community. Wright remained a traveling lecturer on the Spiritualist circuit, while Lake was a settled speaker for the Boston Spiritual Temple. By now, news reports and members of the Indiana Spiritualists were calling Amelia "Mother Colby Luther." Sadly, her final lecture was not printed. The newspaper report only documented that she claimed a physical inability to give a good speech and then lectured quite eloquently for the next half hour.[270] However, her lecture was noticeably short compared to previous occasions where she talked without notes for one or two hours.

When the election of officers was held during the first week of August, Amelia did not run for her old seat as first vice president. She did not interact with camp leaders until October 1897, when she requested payment on a loan she had provided to the Indiana Association of Spiritualists. The loan, for $880, had been given to help sustain the camp's depleted finances—a problem for most Spiritualist camps. It also documented that Dr. Westerfield, Amelia, and Carroll Bronnenburg, a wealthy Chesterfield resident and board member, kept the Indiana camp afloat for years with loans and outright gifts. Amelia's request for payment resulted from her belief that she had little to no money and was destitute. Nothing could have been further from the truth.

Amelia died on December 26, 1897, likely due to heart issues resulting from her past stroke. She must have known that she was failing as she met with Moses Hull on two separate occasions before the Fifth Annual Convention of the National Spiritualists Association in October 1897. At that convention, her name was brought before the convention body by Thomas Locke of the Spiritual Conference Association in Philadelphia. He stated that he had heard she was in dire straits and desperately needed money. Locke elaborated by saying that he had received a letter from a friend who was caring for her. The caregiver stated that she only received $2 per week and did not think she could care for Amelia any longer. He continued, "If there is anyone on the platform today whom I revere, it is Mrs. Colby-Luther," and argued that Spiritualists should not forget to honor their workers. He asked the convention if anyone had further information on Amelia, including whether the stories of her destitution were true.

Locke told the convention that two or three years ago, he was told that Amelia was financially well-off. However, she took care of "ten to twelve family members" and had been doing so for several years. Now her savings were depleted to such an extent that Amelia could not afford her living expenses, including those of her caretaker with whom she lived. Cora Richmond said she had seen a report in one of the Spiritualist newspapers confirming the story and that the convention should discuss the best way to help her.

Moses Hull spoke next. He reported that he had recently spent two Sundays with Amelia. She told him she had spent $3,500 on surgery in the past year and now "only had about $600 left, but it was loaned to the Spiritualist camp." She hoped someone would take up the note and help her with her finances. He stated she was very feeble and had been providing for thirteen people. The issue was referred to a committee for further consideration.[271]

When the committee returned at the end of the convention, they noted that the National Spiritualist Association, while wanting to help, simply did not have the funds to do so. The committee recommended that the individual members of the convention return to their home societies and endeavor to raise funds for Amelia. They decided that all funds raised would be sent to a trusted Spiritualist, Benjamin Lukens of Anderson, Indiana, to be delivered to Amelia.[272]

There is conflicting evidence in the reports made by Moses Hull at the convention and the statements made by Thomas Locke. The true story did not come out until after Amelia's death. By then, multiple society representatives had returned home, and funds for Amelia were raised by Norwich, Brooklyn, Boston, Philadelphia, and many other societies. The monies were sent to Lukens, who agreed to deliver them to Amelia.

Following Amelia's death, Moses Hull gave the funeral oration in Muncie to hundreds of mourners. He submitted his speech to multiple Spiritualist newspapers throughout the country, and the *Banner of Light* published the complete address on the front page of their January 8, 1898 edition. Hull told the attendees that Amelia must have known her time was near because she had made all the arrangements for her funeral "in as systematic and business-like manner as if she were preparing for a pleasure trip." She wanted nothing but patriotic songs at her funeral, particularly "America," and wanted her body wrapped in the United States flag. For that purpose, a friend in Philadelphia sent a beautiful silk flag to her caregiver, Mrs. Lydia Marks. In addition, she refused to allow Hull to pray over her and told him to explain to people what prayer was and why there was no point in praying. Hull admitted that he was uncomfortable but agreed to comply with her wishes.

Hull felt that Amelia suffered "vicariously" due to people's ignorance and "killed herself doing her best to rid the country of both ignorance and sin." Remembering that she feared for America's safety and never ceased to warn others of the fragility of democracy, he reported that she often said, "Republics are the best governments in the world, where the people have the intelligence to know what they want; but where the people are either lacking in intelligence or integrity, republics are the worst despotisms the world ever saw." He added that there "never was an administration where she did not see room for improvement, and she never failed to point out the mistakes of those in power."

Hull reminded the crowd that Amelia's denunciations of Christianity and its ministers caused many to "put her down as a raver and ranter at religion itself, but it was not so. She believed in natural law, and when they threatened her with the wrath of a vacillating and capricious deity, she always defied Him." Understanding the church was taking away the power of the people, she "buckled her armor on and went at the herculean task" of restoring their power. Hull stated that Amelia did not like the word "religion." Still, he concluded, "she was one of the most profoundly religious persons I ever met." She emulated Paine's religion "to do good," and believed that pure religion was to attend to fatherless children, widows, and "keep oneself unspotted from the world."

Reminding the audience of Amelia's perseverance and criticism of Lake Pleasant, Hull spoke of her abject denunciation of Anthony Comstock; her support of D.M. Bennett and other freethinkers; and her advocacy of women's rights, abolition, temperance, and the freedoms guaranteed by the Constitution. Before her death, Amelia told Hull, "I do not want to go. There is too much work to be done, but if my work is done, I hope they will soon let me go, for I am so weary. I know I shall resume my work on the other side, but there is so much to be done here, and so few to do it." He reported how a few weeks before Amelia died, she called her caregiver, Mrs. Lydia Marks, to her side and asked her to write down her final words: "I die thus young in the years of my life, that the liberties of my countrymen may live."[273] It is no surprise that she would leave with one last statement about freedom and liberty.

Amelia's friends held memorial services honoring her life and work across the country, including in Norwich, Boston, and Philadelphia. At every service, the words "fearless," "grand," and "noble" described Amelia. The correspondent from Norwich went further and stated that they knew her as a "fearless advocate" who worked "for the uplifting of humanity from the bondage of slavery, in whatever department of human experience found—religious, political, or social." She was also a "loving, warm-hearted woman, sister, and friend, devoted to her children and grandchildren with that strong attachment born of loyalty to truth."[274]

POSTSCRIPT

AMELIA WAS CONTROVERSIAL IN life and remained so in death. Several months after she died, the executor of her estate made an unsettling discovery. At the time of her death, Amelia had signed over thousands of dollars in property and banknotes to Lydia Marks, the caregiver she had lived with for more than a year. Marks had been telling Amelia she was poverty-stricken even though she owned three properties and had money in the bank. Amelia must have believed Marks' assertion that she was financially destitute and passed that information to Moses Hull in October during one of his visits with her, before he attended the National Convention in Washington. The executor filed an appeal in the courts stating that Marks had unduly influenced Amelia, who did not understand the documents she had signed in her debilitated state.

Amelia's daughter, Estella, who had returned from Texas, was outraged when the executor of Amelia's estate shared the story behind the entire affair. The executor and Amelia's granddaughter had pieced the story together following Amelia's death. Weakened after her stroke in 1895, Amelia stayed at the home of her granddaughter, Olive Powell, and her husband. When the young couple decided to go away on a trip, Marks—a Spiritualist whom Amelia had met at Camp Chesterfield and befriended several years before—told Amelia that a spirit control came to her, ordering Amelia to leave her granddaughter's home and move in with her. Amelia, whose mind was debilitated by her stroke, obeyed

Marks' command. Over the next eighteen months, Marks induced Amelia to sign over the deeds to three properties, including her Camp Chesterfield home, and $4,000 in banknotes. Amelia's estate was worth more than $10,000 (around $250,000 in today's money) at the time of her death, and she relinquished all of it to Marks by the time she died.

Jasper North, the administrator of Amelia's estate, filed charges against Marks to have the will set aside since he believed that Amelia was "not in her right mind." As the case wound up, the prosecutor pointed out that Marks was not just a Spiritualist; she was a practicing hypnotist and he charged her with hypnotizing Amelia and exerting undue influence. The case made national headlines. When the judge agreed with the prosecutor's accusation that Marks had hypnotized Amelia (the proceedings did not mention her stroke), all her money and property were returned to the estate for distribution to Amelia's heirs.[275] It was the first time any American court recognized hypnotism as a viable agency to influence another person. Marks appealed the decision to the Indiana Supreme Court, which upheld the lower court's decision.[276] Marks refused to give up and somehow obtained a change of venue from Delaware County (Muncie) to Madison County (Anderson). She appealed again in the new county despite having lost in court twice. Amelia's home at Camp Chesterfield was part of Madison County, whereas her other Muncie properties were in Delaware County. Thus, Marks attempted to gain control of the Chesterfield home with the new lawsuit. The case languished for several years until 1903, when a Madison County judge brought the same verdict and returned the Chesterfield home to Amelia's heirs.[277]

Amelia would have been appalled at this deceit from a friend. Equipped as she was with a fierce intellect and a passion for truth, honesty, and reason, it seems ironic and unfair that her strong mind and intellect failed her in the end. Amelia would have never relinquished her estate to anyone other than her remaining child and grandchildren, so strong was her belief in family.

Amelia was a legendary figure in her time. Vibrant, tireless, and sarcastically witty, she was instrumental in forming two Spiritualist camps and the Morris Pratt Institute, all of which remain in existence today. Her incalculable contribution to Spiritualism and her advocacy of free speech, free thought, and women's rights left a lasting legacy, even though modern history has forgotten her. She was a consummate, revolutionary, Spiritualist woman who deserves a prominent place in history.

ENDNOTES

1   Stuart, Nancy Rubin. *The Reluctant Spiritualist: The Life of Maggie Fox.*
    Orlando: Harcourt Books, 2005; pp. 32–33. For more details on Isaac
    and Amy Post, see Hewitt, Nancy. *Radical Friend: Amy Kirby Post and Her
    Activist Worlds.* Chapel Hill: The University of North Carolina Press, 2018.

2   Goldsmith, Barbara. *Other Powers: The Age of Suffrage, Spiritualism, and the
    Scandalous Victoria Woodhull.* New York: Alfred A. Knopf, 1998; p. 12.

3   Gurko, Miriam. *The Ladies of Seneca Falls: The Birth of the Women's Rights
    Movement.* New York: Schocken Books, 1974; p. 95.

4   Ibid., p. 98.

5   Braude, Ann. *Radical Spirits: Spiritualism and Women's Rights in
    Nineteenth-Century America.* Boston: Beacon Press, 1989; pp. 27–29. For
    Anthony, p. 196; for Woodhull and Claflin, see MacPherson. *The Scarlet
    Sisters: Sex, Suffrage and Scandal in the Gilded Age.* New York: Hatchett
    Book Group, 2014; pp. 40–45.

6   Braude, *Radical Spirits*; pp. 25–26.

7   Kuenning, Larry. "Quaker Theologies in the 19th Century Separations."
    Originally written for a church history course at Westminster
    Theological Seminary. Philadelphia: December 1, 1989. (http://www.
    qhpress.org/essays/separations.html)

8   Boyle, Joseph Lee. "Death Seem'd to Stare: The New Hampshire and
    Rhode Island Regiments at Valley Forge." (Database online) Provo, UT.
    Ancestry.com; Original book published in Baltimore, MD. (no date).

9   Paine, Thomas. "Epistle to Quakers" included in the Appendix of the
    third edition of *Common Sense.* Retrieved online from www.bartleby.
    com/184/116.html

10   Records of the Amesbury and Hampton Monthly Meeting, Society of Friends, Amesbury, Massachusetts, Vital Records to the end of the year 1849; Google Books online; https://books.google.com; p. 390.

11   1870 Federal Census. (Database online); Ancestry.com

12   Illinois Land Purchase Records; Bureau of Land Management, 1840, (Database online); https://apps.ilsos.gov/isa/landSalesSearch.do

13   *The Muncie Daily Times* (Muncie, Indiana), August 27, 1891; p. 4. (Database online); www.newspapers.com

14   *The Friend of Progress* (New York, NY), November 1864; pp. 16–20. Each day of details of the convention were also reported in the *Banner of Light* editions from August 20 to September 10, 1864. (Database online); www.iapsop.com

15   *Religio-Philosophical Journal* (Chicago, Illinois), May 9, 1868. (Database online); www.iapsop.com

16   *The Richmond (Indiana) Telegram*, Friday, September 23, 1870. (Database online); http://iapsop.com/spirithistory/listing_of_19th_century_spiritualists.html

17   *The Indiana Radical* (Richmond, Ind.), Thursday, September 22, 1870. (Database online); http://iapsop.com/spirithistory/listing_of_19th_century_spiritualists.html

18   Buescher, John. *The Other Side of Salvation: Spiritualism and the Nineteenth-Century Religious Experience.* Boston, 2004, p. 158.

19   Ibid., pp. 182–183.

20   *The Indianapolis News* (Indianapolis, IN.); June 19, 1871, p. 3. (Database online); www.newspapers.com.

21   *New York Tribune* (New York, New York), September 16, 1871, p. 8. (Database online); www.newspapers.com.

22   Woodhull, Victoria. "Children – Their Rights and Privileges" given at the Eighth National Convention of the American Association of Spiritualists, September 13, 1871. (Database online); www.victoria-woodhull.com/speech.htm. Reprinted as "The Training of Children – Good Advice to Mothers" in the *Woodhull & Claflin Weekly,* October 7, 1871.

23   Frisken, Amanda. *Victoria Woodhull's Sexual Revolution: Political Theater and Popular Press in Nineteenth Century America.* Philadelphia, 2004; p. 39, ebook.

24   Woodhull, Victoria. *"And the Truth Shall Make You Free,"* pp. 23–24. (Database online). Library of Congress. National American Woman Suffrage Association Collection. www.loc.gov/resource/rbnawsa.n8216/?sp=24

25   Braude, *Radical Spirits*; pp. 117–120.

26   *Banner of Light* (Boston, MA), December 6, 1873. (Database online); www.iapsop.com

27 Allen, Alice. *Addie L. Ballou: Spiritualist Reformer, Poet, and Artist.* South Carolina, 2014; pp. 369–371. (ebook)

28 Buescher, John B. "Who Was Kersey Graves?" (Database online); www.spirithistory.org

29 *Banner of Light,* December 6, 1873. (Database online); www.iapsop.com

30 Ibid., January 17, 1874.

31 *A Portrait and Biographical Record of Delaware and Randolph Counties, Indiana.* (Chicago, 1894); pp. 691–692. (Database online); www.archives.org

32 *Dunn County News* (Menomenie, Wisconsin), June 13, 1874. (Database online); www.newspapers.com

33 Ibid., September 26, 1874.

34 *Banner of Light,* March 1, 1884; p. 69 online. From a lecture given at the Boston Spiritual Temple on February 24, 1884, titled "Mediumship as True – Mediumship as False". (Database online); www.iapsop.com

35 Ibid., January 16, 1875. Letter from Annie Lord Chamberlain.

36 Letter from Annie Lord Chamberlain to *The Spiritualist at Work,* June 19, 1875; p. 8. (Database online); www.iapsop.com

37 *Omaha Daily Bee* (Omaha, Nebraska), March 2, 1875. Mrs. Van Cott was a wildly popular Methodist revivalist who ultimately applied for ordination but was turned down by a Methodist bishop because she was a woman. (Database online); www.newspapers.com

38 *The Spiritualist at Work,* August 14, 1875; p. 7. (Database online); www.iapsop.com

39 Ibid, August 14, 1875; p. 5.

40 Ibid., April 10, 1875; p. 5. The *Chicago Times* cannot be accessed, but the article was referenced in *The Spiritualist at Work* and therefore noted in the text.

41 Ibid., October 9, 1875; p. 5.

42 "Railroads and Westward Expansion 1870s"; www.american-rails.com/1870s.html

43 *Banner of Light,* December 4, 1875. (Database online); www.iapsop.com.

44 Letter from Mrs. Julia Mace. *The Spiritualist at Work,* January 1, 1876. (Database online); www.iapsop.com

45 *The Galveston Daily News* (Galveston, Texas), February 3, 1876; p. 4. (Database online); www.newspapers.com

46 *Tri-Weekly Herald* (Marshall, Texas), February 12, 1876; p. 2. (Database online); www.newspapers.com

47 Letter from Mrs. J.K. Painter to the *Banner of Light* (Boston, Massachusetts), February 3, 1877; p. 34. (Database online); www.iapsop.com

48 Ibid., p. 34.

49   *The Spiritualist at Work*, April 1, 1876; p. 4. The *Religio-Philosophical Journal* was based in Chicago. Its editor, Stephen S. Jones, had a long-standing dispute with E.V. Wilson, who he called "a free lover" and argued that the "social freedom" questions such as marriage reform, women's rights, etc. were not germane to Spiritualism. Jones was later murdered in 1877 by a man who accused Jones of having an adulterous affair with his wife. The murderer was later judged insane.

50   MacDonald, Eugene. *Fifty Years of Free Thought*. New York: The Truth Seeker Company, 1929; p. 193. (www.archive.org)

51   Letter from Mrs. O.K. Smith to Mrs. Juliet Severance. *The Truth Seeker*, January 19, 1884. (Database online); www.iapsop.com

52   *Fort Worth Gazette* (Fort Worth, Texas), April 17, 1884. William Booth was a British Methodist minister who founded The Salvation Army with his wife, Catherine. He was the Army's first "General." (Database online); www.newspapers.com.

53   *The Kansas City Times* (Kansas City, Missouri), May 15, 1877; p. 4. Nettie Pease Fox was a well known medium, lecturer, author, and co-editor of *The Spiritual Offering*, a Spiritualist newspaper in collaboration with her husband Dorus Fox, also an author and lecturer. (Database online); www.newspapers.com

54   Ibid., p. 4.

55   MacPherson, Myra. *The Scarlet Sisters: Sex, Suffrage, and Scandal in the Gilded Age*. New York, New York: Twelve, Hachette Book Group, 2014; pp. 115–116.

56   *Pleasanton Observer-Enterprise* (Pleasanton, Kansas), May 26, 1877. (Database online); www.newspapers.com

57   Ibid., February 2, 1878; p. 3.

58   Ibid., February 9, 1878; p. 3.

59   Ibid., February 9, 1878; p. 3.

60   A correspondent to the *Banner of Light*, August 3, 1878. (Database online); www.iapsop.com

61   *The Truth Seeker*, September 7, 1878. (Database online); www.iapsop.com

62   Bradford, Roderick. *D.M. Bennett: The Truth Seeker*. Amhurst, N.Y.: Prometheus Books, 2006. (ebook)

63   *The Truth Seeker*, September 14, 1878. (Database online); www.iapsop.com

64   Bennett, De Robigne Mortimer. *Open Letter to Jesus Christ*. Originally published by *The Truth Seeker*, November 1875. Reprint from the collection of the University of Michigan Library, 2021; pp. 19–20. Book may also be found in the HathiTrust digitized archives at www.hathitrust.org

65   Bradford, *D.M. Bennett: The Truth Seeker.* See also Jacoby, Susan. *The Freethinkers: A History of American Secularism.* New York: Henry Holt & Co., 2004.

66   *The Truth Seeker,* December 1, 1877. (Database online); www.iapsop.com

67   Ibid., December 1, 1877.

68   Bradford, *D.M. Bennett: The Truth Seeker.*

69   Letter from Jay Chaapel. *The Truth Seeker,* January 5, 1884. (Database online); www.iapsop.com

70   *The Brooklyn Daily Eagle* (Brooklyn, N.Y.), September 22, 1879. (Database online); www.newspapers.com

71   *The Buffalo Sunday Morning News* (Buffalo, N.Y.), October 19, 1879. (Database online); www.newspapers.com

72   Ibid., January 11, 1880. Webster was an editor and author who created the "Blue-backed Speller" books teaching generations of American children how to read and spell. He also wrote *An American Dictionary of the English Language,* which later became the *Merriam-Webster Dictionary.*

73   *Banner of Light,* January 17, 1880. (Database online); www.iapsop.com

74   Farley, Doug. "Erie Canal Discovery: Packet Boats on the Erie". *Lockport Union-Sun & Journal* (Lockport, N.Y.), September 21, 2007. www.lockportjournal.com

75   *Banner of Light,* April 17, 1880 (Database online); www.iapsop.com

76   *Democrat and Chronicle* (Rochester, N.Y.), April 12, 1880. (Database online); www.newspapers.com

77   Ibid., April 19, 1880. Ira Sankey was an immensely popular evangelical vocalist, musician, and hymn-writer who traveled with the evangelist Dwight Moody for years.

78   *Banner of Light,* May 22, 1880. (Database online); www.iapsop.com

79   Jacoby, Susan. *The Freethinkers: A History of American Secularism.* New York: Henry Holt & Co., 2004; pp. 28–33.

80   McAllister, David. *Christian Civil Government in America: The National Reform Movement, Its History and Principles.* Sixth Edition; Pittsburg: The National Reform Association, 1927; p. 23.

81   Ibid., p. 21. See also Jacoby, p. 222 and the National Reform Association website: https://nationalreformassociation.weebly.com

82   *The Truth Seeker,* May 8, 1880. (Database online); www.iapsop.com

83   Jacoby, Susan. *The Great Agnostic: Robert Ingersoll and American Freethought.* New Haven: Yale University Press, 2013; p. 11. (ebook)

84   *Democrat and Chronicle,* May 24, 1880. (Database online); www.newspapers.com

85   Calvin, John. *Institutes of the Christian Religion, Book III, Chapter 21, Part V.* Philadelphia: Princeton Theological Seminary Library, 1909; pp. 144–147.

(Database online); https://archive.org/details/institutesofchr01calv/mode/1up?view=theater

86   Dodds, James. *The Fifty Years' Struggle of the Scottish Covenanters, 1638–1688*. Edinburgh: Edmonston & Douglas, 1860; pp. 325–327.

87   Drummond, William H. *The Life of Michael Servetus, the Spanish Physician, who for the alleged crime of heresy, was Entrapped, Imprisoned and Burned by John Calvin the Reformer in the city of Geneva October 27, 1553*. London: Oxford University Collections, 1848, p. 156. (Database online); https://www.archive.org

88   Holt, Mac P. *The Duke of Anjou and the Politique Struggle During the Wars of Religion*. Cambridge University Press, 2002; p. 20.

89   *Democrat and Chronicle*. May 24, 1880. (Database online); www.newspapers.com

90   *Democrat and Chronicle,* June 7, 1880, and June 26, 1880. (Database online); www.newspapers.com

91   *Banner of Light,* July 17, 1880. (Database online); www.iapsop.com.

92   Ibid., August 14, 1880.

93   Ibid., August 21, 1880, and September 4, 1880.

94   *The Charlotte Observer* (Charlotte, N.C.), September 8, 1880. (Database online); www.newspapers.com

95   Excerpt from lengthy report by George Chainey to *The Truth Seeker*, September 11, 1880. (Database online); www.iapsop.com

96   *Democrat and Chronicle*. October 27, 1880. (Database online); www.newspapers.com

97   Ibid., October 27, 1880.

98   "Long Depression" at www.en.wickipedia.org/wiki/Long_Depression

99   *Democrat and Chronicle,* October 27, 1880. (Database online); www.newspapers.com

100   "Greenback Party"; https://en.wikipedia.org

101   U.S. Mint History: The "Crime of 1873". Office of Corporate Communications, March 22, 2017. U.S. Mint online.

102   *Democrat and Chronicle,* October 27, 1880. (Database online); www.newspapers.com

103   Hewitt, Nancy A. *Radical Friend: Amy Kirby Post and Her Activist Worlds*. Chapel Hill: The University of North Carolina Press, 2018. pp. 277–280.

104   Letter from Grace L. Parkhurst to *The Truth Seeker,* April 23, 1881. (Database online); www.iapsop.com

105   *The New York Times,* May 10, 1881. (Database online); www.newspapers.com.

106   *The Inter Ocean* (Chicago, Illinois), December 2, 1881; p. 1. (Database online); www.newspapers.com

107   *The Truth Seeker,* April 23, 1881. (Database online); www.iapsop.com

108   Ibid., May 21, 1881.

109   Bradford, *D.M. Bennett: The Truth Seeker*, pp. 157–158.

110   Thomas, Allen C. "Congregational or Progressive Friends. A Forgotten Episode in Quaker History." *Bulletin of Friends' Historical Society of Philadelphia,* Eleventh Month, 1920; pp. 21–32. Friends Historical Association. (Online at jstor.org)

111   Fager, Chuck. *Remaking Friends: How Progressive Friends Changed Quakerism & Helped Save America 1822–1940.* Durham, N.C.: Kimo Press, 2014; p. 40. Lucretia Mott, Martha C. Wright, Jane Hunt, Mary McClintock, and Susan B. Anthony were Quakers. Elizabeth Cady Stanton was not, but identified with the social reform policies her Quaker friends promoted.

112   *The Truth Seeker,* June 18, 1881. (Database online); www.iapsop.com

113   *Mind and Matter,* October 1, 1881. (Database online); www.iapsop.com

114   Buescher, John B. *The Other Side of Salvation: Spiritualism and the Nineteenth Century Religious Experience.* Boston: Skinner House Books, 2004; pp. 170–172; 203.

115   Letter from Harry Hoover of Pittsburgh to *The Truth Seeker,* November 12, 1881. (Database online); www.iapsop.com

116   Foner, Philip S., Ed. *Thomas Paine – Collected Writings – Common Sense; The Crisis; Rights of Man; The Age of Reason; Agrarian Justice.* Victoria, BC, Canada: Must Have Books, 2019, pp. 345–346.

117   Ibid., pp. 461–462.

118   Ibid. (*The Age of Reason Being an Investigation of True and Fabulous Theology, Part First*); p. 464.

119   Ibid., 461.

120   Letter from Caroline H. Spear, M.D., *Banner of Light,* December 10, 1881. (Database online); www.iapsop.com

121   *Banner of Light,* December 17, 1881. (Database online); www.iapsop.com

122   Ibid., February 25, 1882.

123   Underhill, A. Leah. *The Missing Link in Modern Spiritualism.* New York: T.R. Knox & Co., 1885; pp. 472–473. (Database online); www.archive.org

124   "The Boston Music Hall: From Then ... To Now: A Timeline History of the Original Home of the 'Great Organ'." (Online at www.mmmh.org)

125   Letter from James Shumway. *Banner of Light,* April 22, 1882. (Database online); www.iapsop.com

126   Letter from "J.A.K." *Banner of Light,* April 29, 1882. (Database online); www.iapsop.com

127   Letter from Jay Chaapel. *Banner of Light,* July 8, 1882. (Database online); www.iapsop.com

128   *Democrat and Chronicle.* Rochester, N.Y., July 28, 1882. (Database online); www.newspapers.com

129   *Banner of Light,* September 9, 1882. (Database online); www.iapsop.com

130   Ibid., October 28, 1882.

131   Ibid., October 28, 1882.

132   Foner, *Thomas Paine – Collected Writings;* "The Age of Reason", pp. 469–470.

133   Ibid., p. 570.

134   *Banner of Light,* February 10, 1883. (Database online); www.iapsop.com

135   Ibid., March 17, 1883.

136   Ibid., April 21, 1883.

137   Ibid., July 21, 1883.

138   Budington, H.A. *History of the New England Spiritualist Campmeeting Association at Lake Pleasant, Mass.* Springfield: Star Publishing Company, 1907; pp. 2–4.

139   Ibid., p. 20.

140   Ibid., p. 64.

141   Letter from J. William Fletcher. *Mind and Matter,* September 29, 1883; p. 3. It is suspicious that the woman who complained was Maude Lord, a materializing medium and board member of the New England Spiritualist Association. (Database online); www.iapsop.com

142   Passet, Joanne E. *Sex Radicals and the Quest for Women's Equality.* Urbana and Chicago: University of Illinois Press, 2003; p. 128.

143   *Quad-City Times* (Davenport, Iowa), August 24, 1883; p. 4 and *The Kansas City Daily Times* (Kansas City, Missouri), August 27, 1883; p. 8. The word "gammon" was used as a political pejorative to mean nonsense. (Database online); www.newspapers.com

144   Colby, Amelia H. *The Colby Bombshell: President Joseph Beals and Speaker Mrs. A.H. Colby, at Lake Pleasant, August 1883.* Springfield, MA: Star Publishing Company, 1883.

145   Ibid., p. 4.

146   Ibid., p. 5.

147   Ibid., p. 6.

148   Democrat and Chronicle, Rochester, N.Y., September 1, 1883. (Database online); www.newspapers.com

149   Ibid., September 1, 1883.

150   *The Truth Seeker,* September 15, 1883. (Database online); www.iapsop.com

151   Ibid., September 15, 1883.

152   Severance, Juliet H., M.D. *A Lecture on Religious, Political and Social Freedom.* Milwaukee: Godfrey & Crandall Printers, 1881; p. 7.

153   Correspondent letter to *The Truth Seeker,* October 20, 1883. (Database online); www.iapsop.com

154   Letter from J. William Fletcher. *Mind and Matter,* September 29, 1883; p. 3. (Database online); www.iapsop.com

155 *Banner of Light,* November 17, 1883; p. 1. (Database online); www.iapsop.com

156 Funeral oration of J. William Fletcher for Edward Wheeler. "Obsequies of Edward S. Wheeler", *Banner of Light,* November 24, 1883; p. 8. (Database online); www.iapsop.com

157 *The Evening Telegraph,* Buffalo, N.Y., November 20, 1883; p. 2. (Database online); www.newspapers.com

158 Colby, *The Colby Bombshell: President Joseph Beals and Speaker Mrs. A.H. Colby, at Lake Pleasant, August 1883*; pp. 6–8.

159 Letter from Moses Hull. *The Truth Seeker,* December 29, 1883; p. 822. (Database online); www.iapsop.com

160 Letter from J. William Fletcher. *The Truth Seeker,* January 19, 1884; p. 39. (Database online); www.iapsop.com

161 Lecture in trance to the Boston Spiritual Temple on December 2, 1883, and reported in the *Banner of Light,* December 8, 1883. (Database online); www.iapsop.com

162 Ibid., December 8, 1883.

163 Lecture in trance to the Boston Spiritual Temple on December 8, 1883, and reported in the *Banner of Light,* December 15, 1883. (Database online); www.iapsop.com

164 Ibid., December 22, 1883; p. 8.

165 Ibid., December 22, 1883; p. 8.

166 Lecture in trance to the Boston Spiritual Temple reported in the *Banner of Light,* December 29, 1883; p. 8. This appears to be a simplified version of natural selection. (Database online); www.iapsop.com

167 See Cox, Robert S. *Body and Soul: A Sympathetic History of American Spiritualism.* Charlottesville: University of Virginia Press, 2003; pp. 211–232 for a summary of each man's ideas on the origin of race.

168 Ginzberg, Lori D. *Elizabeth Cady Stanton: An American Life.* New York: Hill and Wang, 2009; pp. 124–130.

169 *Banner of Light,* December 29, 1883; p. 8. (Database online); www.iapsop.com

170 Ibid, January 5, 1884; p. 8.

171 Stuart, Nancy Rubin. *The Reluctant Spiritualist: The Life of Maggie Fox.* Orlando: Harcourt, Inc, 2005; pp. 272–275.

172 *Banner of Light*, April 29, 1884. (Database online); www.iapsop.com

173 *The Morning Journal-Courier,* New Haven, CT., August 28, 1884. (Database online); www.newspapers.com. See also *Banner of Light,* June 28, 1884. (Database online); www.iapsop.com

174 MacDonald, *Fifty Years of Freethought*; pp. 360–361.

175 *Banner of Light,* October 18, 1884. (Database online); www.iapsop.com

176 Ibid., October 25, 1884.

177 Ibid., November 1, 1884.

178 Ibid., November 1, 1884.

179 Ibid., December 13, 1884.

180 Ibid., December 13, 1884.

181 Ibid., December 20, 1884.

182 Ibid., December 27, 1884.

183 Ibid., December 27, 1884.

184 Ibid., January 8, 1885.

185 Ibid., January 8, 1885.

186 Ibid., March 7, 1885.

187 Braude, *Radical Spirits*; p. 143. Braude has an excellent chapter on this issue and is covered in depth.

188 *Banner of Light*, March 14, 1885. (Database online); www.iapsop.com

189 Ibid., March 21, 1885.

190 Ibid., March 21, 1885; p. 8.

191 Ibid., March 28, 1885.

192 Ibid., March 28, 1885; p. 8.

193 Ibid., April 4, 1885; p. 8.

194 Shepard, Leslie, Ed. *Encyclopedia of Occultism and Parapsychology, Vol. I.* Detroit: Gale Research, Inc., 1991; p. 597.

195 *Banner of Light;* April 18, 1885. (Database online); www.iapsop.com

196 *St. Louis Globe-Democrat* (St. Louis, Missouri), April 30, 1885. (Database online); www.newspapers.com

197 *The Truth Seeker,* May 23, 1885. (Database online); www.iapsop.com

198 Letter from Eliza O. Gates to the *Banner of Light,* July 18, 1885. (Database online); www.iapsop.com

199 Letter from Dr. Abbie Cutter to the *Banner of Light,* May 31, 1884. (Database online); www.iapsop.com

200 Letter from Annie D. Fisher to the *Banner of Light,* November 7, 1885. (Database online); www.iapsop.com

201 *Banner of Light,* November 7, 1885. (Database online); www.iapsop.com

202 Ibid., November 21, 1885.

203 Moore, R. Laurence. *In Search of White Crows: Spiritualism, Parapsychology, and American Culture.* New York: Oxford University Press, 1977; pp. 80–81.

204 Letter from Thomas W. Sutton to the *Banner of Light,* March 6, 1886. (Database online); www.iapsop.com

205 Moore, *In Search of White Crows,* pp. 115–116.

206 *Banner of Light,* March 13, 1886. (Database online); www.iapsop.com

207 Novak, Ralph Martin. *Christianity and the Roman Empire: Background Texts.* Harrisburg, PA: Bloomsbury Publishing, 2010, pp. 239–241.

208 *Banner of Light,* March 27, 1886. (Database online); www.iapsop.com

209 Hewitt, *Radical Friend: Amy Kirby Post and Her Activist Worlds*; pp.202–204.

210 *Banner of Light,* December 11, 1886. (Database online); www.iapsop.com

211 Ibid., December 18, 1886.

212 Foner, *Thomas Paine – Collected Writings;* pp. 413–414.

213 This entire lecture is found in the *Banner of Light,* January 1, 1887. (Database online); www.iapsop.com

214 *Banner of Light,* January 15, 1887. (Database online); www.iapsop.com

215 *Banner of Light,* March 15, 1884. (Database online); www.iapsop.com

216 Ibid., April 2, 1887.

217 *Indiana Association of Spiritualists Meeting Minutes,* November 5, 1887.

218 Illinois Labor History Society, "The Haymarket Affair"; www.illinoislaborhistory.org

219 *Banner of Light,* November 12, 1887. (Database online); www.iapsop.com

220 Ibid., April 7, 1888.

221 *The Boston Globe,* April 30, 1888. (Database online); www.newspapers.com

222 *Banner of Light,* May 5, 1888. (Database online); www.iapsop.com

223 *Banner of Light,* January 5, 1889. (Database online); www.iapsop.com

224 Letter from M.S. Townsend-Wood to the *Banner of Light,* January 26, 1889. (Database online); www.iapsop.com

225 Her remarks were taken from *The Providence Evening Dispatch* (date unknown) and reprinted in the *Banner of Light,* February 16, 1889. (Database online); www.iapsop.com

226 Letter from Julia R. Galloway to the *Banner of Light,* March 23, 1889. (Database online); www.iapsop.com

227 *The Philadelphia Inquirer* (Philadelphia, Pennsylvania), April 1, 1889; p. 3. (Database online); www.newspapers.com

228 Letter from J.S. Loveland to the *Banner of Light,* May 11, 1889. Loveland was a seminary-trained ex-Methodist preacher who ultimately moved through Spiritualism to Theosophy, and Lockwood, a photographer who became a prolific author of scientific tracts related to Spiritualism. Both were liberal freethinkers. A biography of Loveland, written in his own hand, can be found in "The Loveland-More Journal, 1852–53" at http://iapsop.com/spirithistory/fading_records_of_19th_century_american_spiritualism.html

229 "Morris Pratt: The Visionary" Retrieved from www.morrispratt.org/history/

230 *The Indianapolis Journal* (Indiana), September 30, 1889. (Database online); www.newspapers.com

231 *The Republic* (Columbus, Indiana); September 30, 1889. (Database online); www.newspapers.com

232 "Minutes of the Third Annual Convention of the Indiana Association of Spiritualists, Second Day", Anderson, Indiana, Westerfield Hall, September 27, 1889.

233 *Quamquam Pluries: Encyclical of Pope Leo XIII on Devotion to St. Joseph.* August 15, 1889. Retrieved from www.vatican.va

234 *Exeunte Iam Anno: Encyclical of Pope Leo XIII on the Right Ordering of Christian Life.* December 25, 1888. Retrieved from www.vatican.va

235 *The Representative* (Fox Lake, Wisconsin); October 25, 1889; p. 4. (Database online); www.newspapers.com

236 "Quarterly Meeting Minutes of the Indiana State Association of Spiritualists", June 13, 1890.

237 *Banner of Light,* August 16, 1890. (Database online); www.iapsop.com

238 Ibid., August 30, 1890.

239 *Pittsburgh Daily Post* (Pittsburgh, PA), December 1, 1890; p. 3. (Database online); www.newspapers.com

240 Gaylor, Annie Laurie, Ed. *Women Without Superstition "No Gods – No Masters": The Collected Writings of Women Freethinkers of the Nineteenth and Twentieth Centuries.* Madison, WI: Freedom from Religion Foundation, 1997; pp.229–231.

241 "Meeting Minutes of the Fourth Annual Convention of the Indiana State Association of Spiritualists", Indianapolis, Indiana. October 9–12, 1890.

242 *The Cincinnati Enquirer* (Cincinnati, Ohio), March 30, 1892; p. 4. (Database online); www.newspapers.com

243 *The Muncie Daily Times* (Muncie, Indiana), August 4, 1891; p. 1. (Database online); www.newspapers.com

244 Ibid., August 27, 1891; p. 4.

245 *The Indianapolis News*, May 14, 1892; p. 6. (Database online); www.newspapers.com. Attempting to gain an inheritance early by accusing a Spiritualist family member of being insane was not a new tactic. James was certainly aware of the trick and had the good sense to take legal steps against it. He would have had to have been judged sane in order to appoint an administrator, so he had taken matters into his own hands. The surprising thing is that the whole affair was reported by the newspaper.

246 "Meeting Minutes of the Sixth Annual Convention of the Indiana Association of Spiritualists", Chesterfield, Indiana, July 29, 1892.

247 Ward, Willis, et. al. *Chesterfield Lives: 1886–1986 "Our First Hundred Years".* Chesterfield, Indiana, June 1986; p. 19.

248 *The Rushville Republican* (Rushville, Indiana), August 4, 1893; p. 2. (Database online); www.newspapers.com

249 *Proceedings of the National Delegate Convention of Spiritualists",* Chicago, Illinois, September 27, 28, 29, 1893; pp. 90–91.

250 Ibid., pp. 85–86.

251 Ibid., 122.

252 Ibid., p. 149.

253 Letter from Lyman C. Howe to the *Banner of Light,* January 26, 1895. (Database online); www.iapsop.com

254 Simon, Matthew. "The Morgan-Belmont Syndicate of 1895 and Intervention in the Foreign Exchange Market". *The Business History Review,* Winter 1968; pp. 385–417. Retrieved from www.jstor.org. A full article outlining the condition of the Treasury and the consequences both at home and abroad of the government subcontract to business. The brief summary of Amelia's lecture was reported in the *Banner of Light,* February 16, 1895.

255 *Banner of Light,* March 2, 1895. (Database online); www.iapsop.com

256 Ibid., April 13, 1895. The building where the NSA met was the property of Theodore J. Mayer, one of the members of the committee who started the movement of the national association. A few years subsequent to moving there, Mr. Mayer promised to deed over the building provided the organization raised a certain sum of money for the treasury. This amount was raised, and the building became the property of the association in 1900. By 1910, the association owned the building adjoining the one occupied and also two frame houses at the rear, all of which came from Mr. Mayer. (NSA Headquarters was at 600 Pennsylvania Avenue, S.E. in Washington) *The Washington Post,* April 3, 1910.

257 *Banner of Light,* April 13, 1895; p. 7 (Database online); www.iapsop.com

258 Ibid., April 20, 1895.

259 Ibid., April 20, 1895.

260 Ibid., April 27, 1895.

261 Ibid., May 4, 1895.

262 Ibid., June 1, 1895.

263 "Meeting Minutes of the Ninth Annual Convention of the Indiana Association of Spiritualists", August 2–3, 1895.

264 *Banner of Light,* November 2, 1897. (Database online); www.iapsop.com

265 *The Muncie Morning News,* December 4, 1895; p. 1. (Database online); www.newspapers.com

266 *The Indianapolis News,* July 29, 1896; p. 7. (Database online); www.newspapers.com

267 *The Cincinnati Enquirer,* March 8, 1896; p. 5. (Database online); www.newspapers.com

268 *The Muncie Daily Times,* May 19, 1897; p. 4. (Database online); www.newspapers.com

269 *The Muncie Morning News,* June 17, 1897; p. 5. (Database online); www.newspapers.com

270 *The Muncie Daily Herald*, July 24, 1897; p. 8. (Database online); www.newspapers.com

271 "Proceedings of the Fifth Annual Convention of the National Spiritualist Association", Washington, D.C., October 19, 20, 21, 1897; pp. 90–91.

272 Ibid., pp. 130–131.

273 *Banner of Light*, January 8, 1898. (Database online); www.iapsop.com

274 Letter from Mrs. J.A. Chapman, Secretary First Spiritual Union of Norwich, CT to the *Banner of Light*, January 22, 1898. (Database online); www.iapsop.com

275 *The Pittsburgh Press* (Pittsburgh, Pennsylvania), October 28, 1898; p. 14. See also *Buffalo Evening News* (Buffalo, New York), October 29, 1898; p. 9 and *The Muncie Morning News*, October 28, 1898; p. 5. All newspapers can be found at www.newspapers.com

276 *The Muncie Daily Times*, June 30, 1900; p. 1. (Database online); www.newspapers.com

277 *The Richmond Item* (Richmond, Indiana), May 11, 1903; p. 6. (Database online); www.newspapers.com

REFERENCES

PRIMARY SOURCES

1860, 1870 Federal Census (database online at Ancestry.com)

A Portrait and Biographical Record of Delaware and Randolph Counties, Indiana. Chicago: A.W. Bowen & Company, 1894. (Database online) www.archives.org

Exeunte Iam Anno: Encyclical of Pope Leo XIII on the Right Ordering of Christian Life. December 25, 1888. Retrieved from www.vatican.va

Indiana Association of Spiritualists Meeting Minutes, November 5, 1887. Chesterfield, Indiana.

Illinois Land Purchase Records, 1840. Bureau of Land Management. https://apps.ilsos.gov/isa/landSalesSearch.do

"Meeting Minutes of the Fourth Annual Convention of the Indiana State Association of Spiritualists", October 9–12, 1890. Indianapolis, Indiana.

"Meeting Minutes of the Ninth Annual Convention of the Indiana Association of Spiritualists", August 2–3, 1895. Chesterfield, Indiana.

"Meeting Minutes of the Sixth Annual Convention of the Indiana Association of Spiritualists", July 29, 1892. Chesterfield, Indiana.

"Minutes of the Third Annual Convention of the Indiana Association of Spiritualists, Second Day", September 27, 1889, Anderson, Indiana.

Proceedings of the Fifth Annual Convention of the National Spiritualist Association, October 19, 20, 21, 1897; Washington: National Spiritualist Association.

Proceedings of the National Delegate Convention of Spiritualists, September 27, 28, 29, 1893. Chicago: National Spiritualist Association.

Quamquam Pluries: Encyclical of Pope Leo XIII on Devotion to St. Joseph. August 15, 1889. Retrieved from www.vatican.va

"Quarterly Meeting Minutes of the Indiana State Association of Spiritualists", June 13, 1890. Chesterfield, Indiana.

Records of the Amesbury and Hampton Monthly Meeting, Society of Friends. (Vital Records to the end of 1849). Amesbury, Massachusetts. Retrieved from https://books.google.com

Woodhull, Victoria. "Children – Their Rights and Privileges". Eighth National Convention of the American Association of Spiritualists, September 13, 1871; online database: www.victoria-woodhull.com/speech.htm

Woodhull, Victoria. "And the Truth Shall Make You Free: A Speech on The Principles of Social Freedom" (Database online). Library of Congress. National American Woman Suffrage Association Collection. www.loc.gov/resource/rbnawsa.n8216/?sp=24

NEWSPAPERS AND PERIODICALS

Banner of Light. Boston, Massachusetts

Boston Globe. Boston, Massachusetts

Brooklyn Daily Eagle. Brooklyn, New York

Buffalo Evening News. Buffalo, New York

Buffalo Sunday Morning News. Buffalo, New York

Charlotte Observer. Charlotte, North Carolina

Cincinnati Enquirer. Cincinnati, Ohio

Democrat and Chronicle. Rochester, New York

Dunn County News. Menomenie, Wisconsin

Evening Telegraph. Buffalo, New York

Fort Worth Gazette. Fort Worth, Texas

Friend of Progress. New York, New York

Galveston Daily News. Galveston, Texas

Indiana Radical. Richmond, Indiana

The Indianapolis Journal. Indianapolis, Indiana

Indianapolis News. Indianapolis, Indiana

Inter Ocean. Chicago, Illinois

Kansas City Times. Kansas City, Missouri

Kansas City Daily Times. Kansas City, Missouri

Mind and Matter. Philadelphia, Pennsylvania

Morning Journal-Courier. New Haven, Connecticut

The Muncie Daily Herald. Muncie, Indiana

Muncie Daily Times. Muncie, Indiana.

The Muncie Morning News. Muncie, Indiana

New York Times. New York, New York

New York Tribune. New York, New York

Omaha Daily Bee. Omaha, Nebraska

Philadelphia Inquirer. Philadelphia, Pennsylvania

Pittsburgh Daily Post. Pittsburgh, Pennsylvania

The Pittsburgh Press. Pittsburgh, Pennsylvania

Pleasanton Observer-Enterprise. Pleasanton, Kansas

Quad-City Times. Davenport, Iowa

Religio-Philosophical Journal. Chicago, Illinois.

St. Louis Globe-Democrat. St. Louis, Missouri

The Representative. Fox Lake, Wisconsin

The Republic. Columbus, Indiana

The Rushville Republican. Rushville, Indiana

The Richmond Item. Richmond, Indiana

The Richmond Telegram. Richmond, Indiana

The Spiritualist At Work. New York, New York

The Truth Seeker. New York, New York

Tri-Weekly Herald. Marshall, Texas

The Washington Post. Washington, D.C.

Woodhull & Claflin's Weekly. New York, New York

SECONDARY SOURCES

Allen, A. (2014). *Addie L. Ballou: Spiritualist Reformer, Poet, and Artist.* North Charleston: CreateSpace Independent Publishing.

Bennett, D. R. (1875). *Open Letter to Jesus Christ.* New York: The Truth Seeker Company.

Boyle, J. L. (2005). *Death Seem'd to Stare: The New Hampshire and Rhode Island Regiments at Valley Forge.* Baltimore: MyFamily.com, Inc.

Bradford, R. (2006). *D.M. Bennett: The Truth Seeker.* Amhurst: Prometheus Books.

Braude, A. (1989). *Radical Spirits: Spiritualism and Women's Rights in Nineteenth-Century America.* Boston: Beacon Press.

Budington, H. (1907). *History of the New England Spiritualist Campmeeting Association at Lake Pleasant, Mass.* Springfield: Star Publishing Company.

Buescher, J. (2004). *The Other Side of Salvation: Spiritualism and the Nineteenth-Century Religious Experience.* Boston: Skinner House Books.

Calvin, J. (1909). *Institutes of the Christian Religion, Book III.* Philadelphia: Princeton Theological Seminary Library.

Colby, A. H. (1883). *The Colby Bombshell: President Joseph Beals and Speaker Mrs. A.H. Colby, at Lake Pleasant, August 1883.* Springfield: Star Publishing Company.

Cox, R. S. (2003). *Body and Soul: A Sympathetic History of American Spiritualism.* Charlottesville: University of Virginia Press.

Dodds, J. (1860). *The Fifty Years' Struggle of the Scottish Covenanters, 1638–88.* Edinburgh: Edmonston & Douglas.

Drummond, W. (1848). *The Life of Michael Servetus, the Spanish Physician, who for the alleged crime of heresy, was Entrapped, Imprisoned and Burned by John Calvin the Reformer in the city of Geneva October 27, 1553.* London: Oxford University Collections.

Fager, C. (2014). *Remaking Friends: How Progressive Friends Changed Quakerism & Helped Save America 1822–1940.* Durham: Kimo Press.

Farley, D. (September 2007). "Erie Canal Discovery: Packet Boats on the Erie". *Lockport Union-Sun & Journal.* Retrieved from www.lockportjournal.com.

Foner, P. S. (2019). *Thomas Paine – Collected Writings – Common Sense; The Crisis; Rights of Man; The Age of Reason; Agrarian Justice.* Victoria, B.C.: Must Have Books.

Gaylor, A. L. (1997). *Women Without Superstition "No Gods – No Masters":* *The Collected Writings of Women Freethinkers of the Nineteenth and Twentieth Centuries.* Madison: Freedom From Religion Foundation.

Ginzberg, L. D. (2009). *Elizabeth Cady Stanton: An American Life.* New York: Hill and Wang.

Hewitt, N. A. (2018). *Radical Friend: Amy Kirby Post and Her Activist Worlds.* Chapel Hill: The University of North Carolina Press.

Holt, M. P. (2002). *The Duke of Anjou and the Politique Struggle During the Wars of Religion.* New York: Cambridge University Press.

Jacoby, S. (2004). *The Freethinkers: A History of American Secularism.* New York: Henry Holt & Company.

Jacoby, S. (2013). *The Great Agnostic: Robert Ingersoll and American Freethought.* New Haven: Yale University Press.

Kuenning, L. (1989). "Quaker Theologies in the 19th Century Separations". Philadelphia. Retrieved from www.qhpress.org/essays/separations.html

MacDonald, E. (1929). *Fifty Years of Free Thought.* New York: The Truth Seeker Company.

McAllister, D. (1927). *Christian Civil Government in America: The National Reform Movement, Its History and Principles; Sixth Edition.* Pittsburgh: The National Reform Association.

Moore, R. L. (1977). *In Search of White Crows: Spiritualism, Parapsychology, and American Culture.* New York: Oxford University Press.

Novak, R. M. (n.d.). *Christianity and the Roman Empire: Background Texts.* Harrisburg: Bloomsbury Publishing.

Paine, T. (n.d.). *Epistle to the Quakers.* Philadelphia. Retrieved from www.bartleby.com/184/116.html

Passet, J. E. (2003). *Sex Radicals and the Quest for Women's Equality.* Chicago: University of Illinois Press.

Severance, J. H. (1881). *A Lecture on Religious, Political and Social Freedom.* Milwaukee: Godfrey & Crandall Printers.

Shepard, L. E. (1991). *Encyclopedia of Occultism and Parapsychology, Vol. I.* Detroit: Gale Research, Inc.

Simon, M. (1968, Winter). "The Morgan-Belmont Syndicate of 1895". *The Business History Review*, pp. 385–417.

Stuart, N. R. (2005). *The Reluctant Spiritualist: The Life of Maggie Fox.* Orlando: Harcourt, Inc.

Thomas, A. C. (1920, November). "Congregational or Progressive Friends: A Forgotten Episode in Quaker History". *Bulletin of Friends' Historical Society of Philadelphia.*

Underhill, A. L. (1885). *The Missing Link in Modern Spiritualism.* New York: T.R. Knox & Company.

Weisberg, B. (2004). *Talking to the Dead: Kate and Maggie Fox and the Rise of Spiritualism.* HarperCollins ebooks.

WEBSITES

Railroads and Westward Expansion 1870s. https://www.american-rails.com/1870s.html

For additional information on adding God and Jesus to the Constitution https://nationalreformassociation.weebly.com

The Long Depression. https://www.en.wickipedia.org/wiki/Long_Depression

"Greenback Party". https://en.wikipedia.org/wiki/Greenback_Party

U.S. Mint History: The "Crime of 1873". https://usmint.gov/news/inside-the-mint/mint-history-crime-of-1873

"The Boston Music Hall: From Then to Now: A Timeline History of the Original Home of the 'Great Organ'." Methuen Memorial Music Hall. www.mmmh.org/ wp-content/uploads/2017/02/THE-BOSTON-MUSIC-HALL_-FROM-THEN-1.pdf

https://www.morrispratt.org – for information on the educational arm of the National Spiritualist Association of Churches

International Association for the Preservation of Spiritualist and Occult Periodicals; www.iapsop.com.

Newspapers.com by Ancestry; www.newspapers.com.

ABOUT THE AUTHOR

Vicki Grose Corkell received her undergraduate degree from
Indiana University and M.Div. from Earlham School of Religion,
a Quaker seminary.

She is an ordained Spiritualist minister and lives on the grounds of
Camp Chesterfield, a Spiritualist community.

INDEX

ACL indicates Amelia Colby Luther.

Made in the USA
Monee, IL
27 July 2023

39957495R00154